WI

✓ KT-583-536

UNIVERSITY OF
WINCHESTER

Mar

:

KA 0392125 5

Philosophy and Modern Liberal Arts Education

Philosophy and Modern Liberal Arts Education

Freedom is to Learn

Nigel Tubbs
University of Winchester, UK

UNIVERSITY OF WINCHESTER LIBRARY

palgrave
macmillan

© Nigel Tubbs 2015

All rights reserved. No reproduction, copy or transmission of this publication may be made without written permission.

No portion of this publication may be reproduced, copied or transmitted save with written permission or in accordance with the provisions of the Copyright, Designs and Patents Act 1988, or under the terms of any licence permitting limited copying issued by the Copyright Licensing Agency, Saffron House, 6–10 Kirby Street, London EC1N 8TS.

Any person who does any unauthorized act in relation to this publication may be liable to criminal prosecution and civil claims for damages.

The author has asserted his right to be identified as the author of this work in accordance with the Copyright, Designs and Patents Act 1988.

First published 2015 by
PALGRAVE MACMILLAN

Palgrave Macmillan in the UK is an imprint of Macmillan Publishers Limited, registered in England, company number 785998, of Houndmills, Basingstoke, Hampshire RG21 6XS.

Palgrave Macmillan in the US is a division of St Martin's Press LLC, 175 Fifth Avenue, New York, NY 10010.

Palgrave Macmillan is the global academic imprint of the above companies and has companies and representatives throughout the world.

Palgrave® and Macmillan® are registered trademarks in the United States, the United Kingdom, Europe and other countries.

ISBN 978–1–137–35891–2

This book is printed on paper suitable for recycling and made from fully managed and sustained forest sources. Logging, pulping and manufacturing processes are expected to conform to the environmental regulations of the country of origin.

A catalogue record for this book is available from the British Library.

Library of Congress Cataloging-in-Publication Data
Tubbs, Nigel.
    Philosophy and modern liberal arts education : freedom is to learn / Nigel Tubbs.
        pages   cm
    Summary: "In the age that announces the death of metaphysics, that is alive to the existence of the 'other', and defends democratic citizenship against the privilege of masters, what future can there be for a liberal arts education grounded in the pursuit of first principles? This book explores the tradition of first principles within liberal arts education, retracing the themes of discipline and freedom within its history from antiquity to RM Hutchins. It then offers a challenge to the logic of that tradition as it appears within metaphysical, natural and social relations, arguing that this ancient logic is no longer fit for purpose. Philosophy and Modern Liberal Arts argues for a modern version of liberal arts education, exploring first principles within the divine comedy of a modern educational logic, reforming the three philosophies of metaphysics, nature and ethics upon which liberal arts education is based. At a time when there is something of a resurgence of liberal arts education in Europe, and a crisis around liberal arts education in the USA, this book offers a profound transatlantic philosophical and educational challenge to its students and practitioners" — Provided by publisher.
    Includes bibliographical references.
    ISBN 978–1–137–35891–2 (hardback)
    1. Education, Humanistic—Philosophy.
    2. Education, Higher—Philosophy.   I. Title.
    LC1011.T84 2014
    378.001—dc23   2014028181

Transferred to Digital Printing in 2015

Socrates of our age!, you can no longer have effect like Socrates

– Herder, This Too a Philosophy

If there were nothing but dichotomies, doubt would not exist, for the possibility of doubt resides precisely in the third, which places two in relation to each other

– Kierkegaard, Philosophical Fragments/Johannes Climacus

UNIVERSITY OF WINCHESTER

378.
001
TUB   039 212 53

Contents

Preface   viii

Acknowledgements   xi

Introduction   1

Part I
Introduction   7

1   Antiquity: Finding Virtue in Necessity   11

2   The Seven Liberal Arts: Varro's Secret Path   25

3   Renaissance Humanism   37

4   *Bildung* and the New Age   50

Conclusion to Part I   63

Part II
Introduction   73

5   Metaphysical Education   83

6   Natural Education   98

7   Social Education   112

Part III
The Song That Dialectic Sings   127

8   Divine Comedy of Barbarian Virtue   133

9   The Work of Education   146

Notes   160

Bibliography   189

Index   196

Preface

Robert Maynard Hutchins, while at the University of Chicago, US, reminded his audience that the three relations of man and God, man and man, and man and nature no longer had a 'principle of unity'[1] within them or between them. Theology used to fulfil this role. It no longer did so. As such, Hutchins said that American higher education lacked any rational or practical coherence for its purpose or curriculum or organisation. The need was to return to the study of first principles, or to metaphysics, for an ordering *logos*, something which, if achieved, would be 'nothing less than a miracle.'[2] I think we can find this miracle in the *divine comedy* of Western philosophical education. But it is not really such a miracle. Discovering this education to be a first principle within the difficulties and tensions of liberal arts education is rather like the person who has been searching for his glasses, all the time wearing them and failing to see what is in fact right under his nose.[3] Such is the continuing comedy of the Western tradition.

I want very briefly to summarise in advance the case this book attempts to make. Liberal arts education explores first principles. For 2500 years, it has defined first principles, and the search for first principles, according to an ancient logic of harmony. I retrieve from within this ancient logic a different, modern, educational logic and a different understanding of first principles: a *modern metaphysics*. The difference here is that this is a modern logic of the difficulty that the idea of harmony creates, or more accurately, the difficulty of the logic of relation that it falls into. This logic does not overcome ancient logic. It sits within ancient logic. It emerges within three areas of liberal arts education: the three philosophies of metaphysics, physics and ethics. It makes itself known to us as difficulty, specifically the difficulty caused by curiosity, by asking questions and by wrestling with the doubts that the 'big questions' generate. For many, this doubt is not just troubling, not just difficult; it is pernicious and destructive. Against this I will argue that in a modern liberal arts education, this doubt and this difficulty have their own educational truth, the elusive idea of education in-itself. This educational truth lies suppressed, however, in the appearance of difficulty within the three philosophies as mere dualism or opposition. It is this appearance that is to be blamed for the reputation of the work of doubt and difficulty as deleterious, malign and, indeed, useless.

In liberal arts, the foremost dualism is between philosophy and rhetoric. Part I relates the history of liberal arts seen as this dualism. Part II relates this history differently according to the educational logic of the three philosophical relations: metaphysical, natural and social. Each of these gives actuality to a fourth relation, that of property. Part III emerges from the logic of the three philosophical educations capable of exploring the idea of difficult, even barbarian, education in Plato, Dante and Nietzsche. The final chapter asks what this educational logic means for the teachers, students and the curriculum of a modern liberal arts education.

This summary may appear somewhat abstract and a long way from the quotidian problems faced by teachers of the liberal arts. But the difficulty of educational logic (for me, at least) is difficult to write and equally difficult to read. It is unfamiliar and demands a different – and difficult – notion of what is to count as understanding something. But it is unrelenting in the logical demands it makes upon our thinking. Perhaps it is too difficult. However, I pay tribute to our own students on the Modern Liberal Arts degree at Winchester who are giving to this difficulty their own subjectivity and substance. In any case, this logic is the same logic that is experienced in the difficulty of teaching and defending liberal arts, whether that be in drawing students into the worlds of Plato, Dante and Nietzsche or into the world beyond the canon. It is the same logic experienced in exploring truth or first principles in a world of relativism and pluralism, or experienced when faith is unsettled by doubt, or experienced in the controversy of liberal arts as elitist, or in the defence of *sophia* against *techne*. It also stands at the heart of the idea of liberal arts as the pursuit of the good life, demanding that we question what has counted as virtuous and good in liberal arts to date. At a recent conference, I was told by a colleague that 'difficulty is not a virtue.' I hope by the end of this book to have encouraged the reader to think otherwise.

Finally, I am aware that liberal arts colleagues, particularly in the United States, are often suspicious of some modern European philosophies, believing them to be idle speculation, sometimes of the most obtuse kind, compared to rhetoric which is the virtuous education of imaginative and moral nation-building. I have no doubt that for some educators my philosophical approach will only increase the divide. Perhaps the best I can hope is for European and American education to meet somewhere over the Atlantic Ocean in a shared confusion about whether the invitation offered is to travel east or west. The ambition of the invitation may well be left by both parties to sink under its own weight: so be it. We set sail nonetheless.

Acknowledgements

I want to express my thanks to Joy Carter, Liz Stuart and Karen Pendlebury who have offered unstinting support to the Modern Liberal Arts project at the University of Winchester from its inception.

I pay tribute to our very first group of Modern Liberal Arts (MLA) students who were curious enough and brave enough to risk their higher education with us: Rosie, Cha Cha, Danielle, Kerry, Madeleine, Pauline, Sherry, Bruce, Jess, Emily, Lexie, Lucy and Sooz.

I acknowledge too the contribution of the class of 2014. They pushed the degree and its tutors beyond our expectations, but did so by staking their own subjective substance. By name, they are Ami, Akil, Abi, Becky, Amelia, Faye, Harry, Helen, Jamie, Katrina, Laura, Ned and Seamus. But as 'freedom is to learn' they are, in no particular order – the poet, the actor, the sceptic, the faithful, the teacher, the singer, the harmonic, the polymath, the devoted, the will-to-love, the resistor, the magister and the biophile. As they leave, the programme is already being reshaped again by the work of the students who follow them. Without each of these groups of people, there would be no modern liberal arts project. I thank each of you.

I thank Howard, as always, for reminding me of the dangers of succeeding in education from 'a philosophically secured position' (this book, I hope and expect, will both attenuate and exemplify his concerns), and Rowan for agreeing to be our external examiner, and for welcoming the class of 2014 into his home.

Finally, my thanks to Catherine, Tony, Becky and Derek who in different ways have nurtured the infant with love and care. As I write, we look forward to Jess and Elina joining us and bringing with them their wisdom and their deep respect for human learning.

Above all, I trust and dedicate this book, its work, and its love, to my reader, the re-writer of my circle...

Introduction

Dante, in *Convivio*, notes that 'the supreme desire of all things, and the one first given to them by nature, is to return to the first cause.'[1] Liberal arts education expresses this desire for a *universal* understanding, beginning in the experience of awe and wonder at the natural universe and of life within it. This experience expresses itself in the doubt that accompanies curiosity, the same doubt that leads the great minds of Western antiquity to ask how and why the universe was formed, to seek its first principles – those universal principles which are the condition of the possibility of the existence of anything and everything. For Aristotle, the sensation of awe and wonder leads thought to enquire 'about the phenomena of the moon and those of the sun and the stars, and about the genesis of the universe.'[2] Experience then leads thought to associate different ideas, leading in turn to wisdom regarding universals. As such, says Aristotle, wisdom deals with 'the first causes and the principles of things.'[3]

Perhaps the most famous first principle in liberal arts education is Aristotle's Prime Mover. But it is more than just an abstract idea. It is something like an archaeological artefact imprinted with ancient thinking regarding truth, nature, politics and property. The Prime Mover is deemed true because it is a self-completing whole, a One, something in-itself; it is nature because its necessity is self-animation; and it is independent because it is free from any prior or heteronomous cause. It is its own condition of possibility. Everything else is derivative or composite, that is, not in-itself but for-another; not self-animation but moved by another; and not independent but dependent upon another. This self-animating One, therefore, is truth not error, freedom not slavery, harmony not disorder, liberal not barbarian, life not death, tranquillity not unrest, certainty not uncertainty, knowledge not doubt, immanent

1

not contingent, God not man, single not composite, substance not subject, harmony not difficulty and absolute not relative. Liberal arts education has always set itself to work for the former and against the latter in each pairing.

The nemesis of this first principle is *infinite regression*. If there is infinite regression, there can be no first cause and therefore no existence, because the regression never ends. Since we exist, and does the universe, Aristotle reasons logically that there cannot be infinite regression; 'the series cannot go on to infinity, [therefore] there must be some first mover'[4] – a logic that survives for 2,000 years to Descartes, who confirms that 'although one idea may perhaps originate from another, there cannot be infinite regress here; eventually one must reach a primary idea.'[5] What must be logically presupposed as preventing infinite regression is a first cause which must itself be eternal and its own condition of possibility so that it is not dependent on a prior stimulus for its beginning. The first cause must be the most simple, single, complete thing possible, for if it were composite it could be reduced to something simpler and would not therefore be its own self-determining, self-animating principle.

The logic that judges the One superior to the composite, the natural superior to the artificial and the master superior to the slave expresses itself as the logic of possession and property. Individuals can immunise themselves against the chaos of infinite regression, against that which does not have its own principle in-itself, by having it as *property* owned by (and therefore kept separate from) the owner. The object that is owned becomes the site of pure infinite regression and pure dependency, never being in-itself, and only ever having its principle in something else – in the owner. Liberal arts education was forged in this structure of a first principle. To the self-completing identity of truth, of the owner and of the first principle is assigned a life of leisure. To the barbarian who had no such principle in-itself, and to the object, is assigned a life of work.

Ancient liberal arts, working with this dualism of free man and barbarian, owner and owned, single and composite, reveals how the ambivalence of such dualisms pertains both to *property* and to *thinking*. Property and thinking are always unavoidably in relation to their objects. Ownership is the *work* of property, compounding individuals and their possessions, yet property is the *independence* of the master lived as his own first principle. Similarly, thought is the *work* of philosophy, compounding thoughts and objects; however, philosophy is the *leisure* of thought lived as a first principle and free from composition. The ambivalence of property and thought here has defined liberal arts education, and the logic of first principles, to the present day. It is an ambivalence within which I will retrieve a modern liberal arts education and a modern educational logic of first principles.

In this ambivalence of thought as composition, or in bringing one thought to another – including bringing the thought of itself to itself – thought could only judge itself to be the work of infinite regression. Since infinite regression could never arrive at truth, logically, thought could never arrive at truth either. The unity that escaped thought – the unity of the One – became defined by thought here as ineffable, requiring ecstatic or other immediate states of consciousness to overcome thinking seen here as merely a tool. Two things followed which are still with us today. Truth became unknowable to thinking, that is, truth cannot be known by us; and thinking became associated with the work of infinite regression and with relativism. Liberal arts education has never escaped the ambivalence that thought is needed to be the work of truth, and that in being the work it cannot also be the leisure, the principle in-itself, of truth. We will see in Parts I and II some of the attempts made to claim tranquillity for the work of thinking. The modern controversies that currently haunt liberal arts education have their origin and their logic precisely in this continuing ambivalence. If Allan Bloom perhaps argues for leisure over work, and Martha Nussbaum perhaps argues for work over leisure, neither is able to find the truth that is re-educating us about how this ambivalence can be a modern educational first principle.

I will suggest that the logic and the character of ancient first principles are no longer fit for purpose in the Western world. Theirs is the logic of harmony. But this harmony now exists – or, rather, its universality has ceased to exist – within modern negation, deconstruction, fragmentation and alienation. More generally, harmony in the modern world is now seen for what it is: a vision of universal truth forged in the image of the leisured West over the rest of the working world. What liberal arts now requires is a new logic of first principles forged in the image of the West working within the imperialism, sexism, racism and colonialism of its leisured, propertied and masterful existence. I will argue that in the explosive challenges of relativism and imperialism, there is a modern logic and a modern shape of first principles waiting to be retrieved.

This logic has its own educational necessity (and its own form of harmony) in *difficulty*. This difficulty is experienced in the way ancient first principles and the ancient logic of harmony are opposed by the modern shape of relativism and the critique of imperialism. The experience of this difficulty is our education and can be understood as a modern liberal arts education regarding first principles. This difficulty, this education, will involve learning to retrieve the barbarian in the virtuous, the relative in the true and infinite regression in first principles. It will commend that we retrieve difficulty as its own educational logic and necessity or as *learning*. It will also ask that we re-educate ourselves to understand oppositions no longer as dualisms but as experienced in an educational logic of *relation*. Relation here does not mean the middle ground between two elements. As Galileo and Newton observe, all observers are in motion, lacking a fixed point of reference in the universe by which motion and non-motion could be differentiated. This changes fundamentally the idea of what a relation is. A relation can only be a middle ground between two elements if one assumes the fixed position of the two elements by also assuming that the observer of the relation – the third party – is also fixed in relation to the relation. But both philosophy and science agree that this is not the case. The two elements are not in a definitive relation because they are in relation to a third party who is also in relation to others, ad infinitum. This is the crisis of relativity opened up by Galileo and Newton in science, and by Kant and Hegel in philosophy. Everything is in relation to everything else, with no fixed point available by which anything can be fixed or stabilised. In the natural universe, as in metaphysics, all is in flux, nothing is fixed, and the idea of truth or tranquillity dissolves into movement in all directions all the time(s). This is now the modern world of science and philosophy: relativity.

In the three relations that the West has defined itself within – metaphysical, natural and social – relation has become infinite regression, being relation in relation in relation ad infinitum. The most important consequences are the loss of truth in metaphysics, of objectivity in science and of shared humanity in social theory. I will argue for a modern understanding of these three relations that finds a different significance to this infinite regression of mediation and retrieves from within this regression to nihilism an educational truth. I must add here, against an all-too-common misconception, by relation I do not mean inter-subjectivity, mutuality or any magical position that can calm the difficulty of relation. The only truth that relation has which is true to itself is learning *of* relation *as* relation. But the temptation to turn it into something else, something that guarantees the resolution of relation of relation of relation ad infinitum, is very strong, including the guarantee of action in the world which can be described as ethical or virtuous. The power of relation demands that we re-consider the educational significance of the failure of such guarantees, asking us to be more sensitive to riding roughshod over the educational difficulty of relation.

This re-education regarding the logic of learning involves, in part, returning to a set of specialist philosophical terms. These are in-itself, for-another, for-itself and of-itself (I will sometimes abbreviate them collectively as 'the work' of education). I will explain these terms below, but in addition I will find within them three stages in the history of education regarding the Western notion of freedom. The in-itself is *freedom is to think*; the in-itself that is for-itself is *freedom is to think for itself*; and the in-of-and-for-itself in relation to otherness is *freedom is to learn*. I will argue that this latter is the basis of modern metaphysics and of a modern liberal arts education. There is an additional complexity here. I will also argue that these three shapes of freedom are not just stages in the history of Western freedom, but are actual shapes of *subjectivity*; they are real people, you and me. It is these shapes of subjectivity which then relate to truth, nature and humanity as, respectively, the metaphysical, natural and social relations. The relation to otherness employed in liberal arts education over the last 40 years or so has enabled the tradition to critique its own mastery. However, my argument for subjectivity will not be trusted, I suggest, by the post-men and post-women for whom subjectivity is just another Western logocentric mastery. I ask their patience. The notion of subjectivity I am working with is neither an abstract mastery nor an avoidance of mastery. It is subjectivity as the complicity of mastery, one which opens up the opportunity for a modern liberal arts education to do justice to the inequalities and prejudices of its own history. It is precisely this *learning subjectivity* which gives modern liberal arts education the chance to be a significant culture of the present and of its own time apprehended in thought.

Finally, I will be describing the modern educational logic of difficult education in general, and of the relation between discipline and freedom in particular, as a divine comedy of errors. Divine comedy concerns actions in the world. Tragedy characterises the way ethical forces – of the gods or of the community – oppose themselves in the actions of individuals. Tragedy expresses one's vulnerability to the hostility between these powers. Comedy characterises the absurdity of individual actions which lack universal significance and are folly and self-defeating. Together, tragedy and comedy are 'pathos' or the 'moving power in human decisions.'[6] But they are also the divine comedy of our *education* regarding human actions in the world. Liberal arts has its own divine comedy in the collision and opposition of discipline and freedom. This is the divine comedy of first principles, that is, the tragic and comic experience of their collision with other powers, their thwarted actions and their unanticipated consequences.

In liberal arts, this divine comedy has been the sublime experience of leadership, specifically the magnanimous, noble and virtuous practice of the liberally educated gentleman (*ars liberalis*). Plato's educated man and woman have a moderation in all things which creates a harmony of all the parts. Under this leadership, all in the city 'sing the same song together.'[7] Aristotle's great-souled man (*megalopsychos*) is also the man of moderation, 'intermediate between excess and defect,'[8] neither 'over-joyed by fortune nor over-pained by evil.'[9] Newman's liberal, philosophical and educated gentleman has a universal knowledge which 'puts the mind above the influences of chance and necessity, above anxiety, suspense, unsettlement'[10] and whose attributes are 'equitableness, calmness, moderation and wisdom.'[11] But this understanding of first principles grounded in the ancient logic of masterful freedom, collides with democratic ideals. I will argue that first principles are now to be found in difficulty, and difficulty belongs to everyone. No longer can liberal arts education excuse its elitism on the grounds that the difficulty of first principles is relevant to and comprehensible only by the few. Difficulty is essentially democratic, and in this difficult universality all find themselves within the comedy of God trying to be man and of man trying to be God. Neither of these 'work' – in the sense of being successfully accomplished – and this repeated incompletion is the 'work' – the comedic work – in which they are engaged. Dante's pilgrim lives and dies in this comedy. It is Dante's genius that he can hold together impossible and contradictory elements knowing that this comedy has its truth as education. It is with this in mind that I now invite the reader to pursue a modern liberal arts education in the divine comedy of the freedom and discipline that defines liberal arts education.

Part I
Introduction

Philosophers and orators: Discipline and freedom

The dualism in liberal arts between philosophy and rhetoric carries its own educational significance. Here I take as my guide Bruce Kimball's book *Orators and Philosophers*. He presents the history of the *artes liberales* as the 'story of a debate between orators and philosophers,'[1] which he says is carried by attitudes towards dialectic and rhetoric. In general terms, for the philosophers who are steeped in the rigour of dialectical reasoning, rhetoric is merely an appeal to 'emotion, sensitivity, and predisposition in order to effect persuasion.'[2] The philosophers see rhetoric attending 'more to devising persuasive techniques than to finding true arguments'[3] while the orators see in philosophy an endless search for 'that highest truth [which] is never attained.'[4] To the orators, rhetoric is 'the supreme art'[5] that relies on dialectic for the logic of an argument, but has for itself the art of settling the 'great and important questions'[6] of public concern and significance. From Zeno this debate has achieved its own rhetorical flourish, characterised as between the open palm of interpretation and the closed fist of absolute or scientific knowledge. One of the aims of Kimball's book is to show that some of the confusions which plague the recent history of American higher education are due to liberal education having Socrates, rather than Cicero, 'as its paragon.'[7]

I will rehearse Kimball's thesis in Part I now, by reading the history of liberal arts education according to the opposition between philosophy and rhetoric. With Zeno, I characterise philosophy as the closed fist because it deals with eternal and unchangeable truths, and rhetoric as the open palm of the changeable, of interpretation and of creativity. The closed fist of necessity is, at different times, the method of philosophy, the logic of the in-itself including truth and God, the first principle of the natural universe, the empiricism of science, the dialectic of scholasticism, the core curriculum, generalist education, teaching and the tradition of the Great Books. The open palm of freedom is, again at different times, the virtue of the liberally educated person, the logic of the for-itself including reflection and self-critique, the freedom of human culture, the creativity of oratory, the humanism of classical literature including reading, writing and emulating great characters from antiquity, the system of electives and specialist research and expertise.

In advance of the arguments made in Part II, I re-read this history as characterising the ambiguous relation between the disciplined and predetermined nature of a skill or principled practice – *ars* – and the freedom conveyed by *liberalis*: in sum, the contradiction carried in *artes liberales*. One can then re-read the relation between philosophy and rhetoric as a difficult relation which has its own kind of educational truth. I argue that the dualism of philosophy and rhetoric, of the closed fist of discipline and the open palm of freedom, is not just a dialectic between two elements. It is also the relation of two elements whose struggle against each other is its own educational logic. I concur with Kimball's analysis that interpreters deny the ambiguities expressed in this work in the search for clarity and certainty. But I go further, and argue for preserving these ambiguities as having meaning in their own right and with having profound educational significance. I argue that it is the difficulties posed for a liberal arts education in the relation or work between philosophy and rhetoric that can be said to define liberal arts. If philosophy is the art or method of arriving at true knowledge, and rhetoric requires its imaginative and creative use for the good of society, seen in this way, liberal arts education exists in the contradiction between discipline and freedom.

It is with this in mind that in Part I, I survey a history of liberal arts education played out as the dualism between discipline (philosophy) and freedom (rhetoric), and in Part II, I retrieve a philosophy of education from within their relation. More specifically, in Part I the heavy hand of philosophical necessity appears as philosophy, harmony, the Prime Mover and logic (Chapter 1); doctrine, the encyclopaedic seven liberal arts, *humanitas*, theology, philosophy and discipline (Chapter 2); Aristotelian logic, dialectical scholastic method including in teaching, philosophy, the church, history and the university (Chapter 3); the state, philosophy, law, humanity, duty and the US-style faculty-led generalist classical curriculum (Chapter 4). Ranged against such necessity are various shapes of the open palm of freedom: rhetoric, virtue, sophism and language (Chapter 1); humanism, *humanitas* and faith informed by education (Chapter 2); humanism, the *studia humanitatis*, classical emulation of Latin and Greek, subjectivity, civics, freedom and education (Chapter 3); individuality, inwardness, aesthetics, humanism, growth, development, freedom, culture and the electives of a specialist type research-based higher education (Chapter 4). It is an obvious point that these divisions look forced in that they cross each other all the time. But that is the point. I want to illustrate how frail such separations are, and to illustrate how the educational concepts of liberal arts, *paideia*, humanism, rhetoric, *Bildung* and philosophy try to express just such difficult relations. From this survey of difficulty, focussed around the relation of the universal as the iron fist of speculative and scholastic necessity and freedom as the open palm of practical, humanistic rhetorical creativity, we find not the victory of the one over the other, but their sustained relation to each other. What emerges here are the conditions for a modern conception of liberal arts education and for a modern educational first principle.

1
Antiquity: Finding Virtue in Necessity

The virtue of harmony

In antiquity a first principle rests on both the logic of its own necessity and the necessity of its own logic. Together these are its *logos*. Aristotle's Prime Mover is its own necessity because it has no condition of its own possibility beyond or outside itself. This necessity is the logic of its existence as a first principle. It is moved by itself, caused by itself, and therefore is a truth in-itself. It is entirely independent. In addition, being the first principle of itself, it is also the condition of the possibility of everything else – the universe and everything in it. All things can trace their own necessity back to the necessity of the self-sufficient first principle. Liberal arts education has its origin in the attempt to discover such first principles and does so by relating first principles to the intellectual, natural and social worlds.

The ancients define this logic of necessity as harmony and proportion.[1] In metaphysics this is truth, in physics this is nature and in the social world this is freedom. In each case the ancients make a virtue out of necessity. Harmony describes that which is at peace with itself because all the parts find their perfect place within the perfect whole. The ambivalence carried by this idea of harmony as a perfect totality will be felt in the tension between philosophy and rhetoric, in particular, and between discipline and freedom in general. We will follow this ambivalence through to Hutchins' call in the 1930s for the miraculous metaphysical reconciliation of these tensions.

The logic of harmony was becoming evident to the ancients in the mathematical harmonies and proportions of the natural universe. They sought to apprehend every object, and every individual, as integral to an overall pattern, and to educate in ways which would reveal where

11

in the totality one truly belonged. 'The Greeks were perhaps the first to recognise that education means deliberately moulding human character in accordance with an ideal.'[2] To learn of one's place in the totality of the intellectual, natural and social worlds is thereafter to lead a life of the highest virtue (*areté*). It is to be at one with the harmony of the universe, and therefore to be at one with its first principles.

That such an education and such a life are a struggle is highlighted by Aristotle in his *Hymn to Hermias* in praise of worth or virtue.

> O worth! Stern taskmistress of humankind,
> Life's noblest prize:
> O Virgin! For thy beauty's sake
> It is an envied lot in Hellas even to die
> And suffer toils devouring, unassuaged... [3]

The Athenian idea of harmony is summed up by the philosophical proverb, credited to Solon (c. 638–558 BCE), 'nothing in excess.'[4] Excess is an imperfection compared to moderation and to the perfect harmony of the totality, which are, in turn, central to the education for virtue expressed by Thales dictum, *know thyself.*[5]

Pythagoras (c. 570–500 BCE)

Pythagoras is perhaps the first in the Western tradition explicitly to seek the first principle of harmony and perfection in educating mind, body and soul to the one end, or according to the one logic of necessity. His group of followers apparently followed a strict regime of diet and behaviour. He selected them 'with great care, and subjected them to a long novitiate, in which silence, self-examination, and absolute obedience played a prominent part... Food, clothing, and exercise were all carefully regulated on hygienic and moral principles.'[6]

What Pythagoras gives to the West is the idea of a universe whose order and proportion were essentially mathematical. Aristotle says that the Pythagoreans (he often, rather dismissively, calls them 'so-called' Pythagoreans) were devoted to mathematics and saw number as the first principle of anything; 'they supposed the elements of numbers to be the elements of all things, and the whole heaven to be a musical scale or a number.'[7] 'It was this tendency, too, to construct universal patterns, which distinguished Greek music and mathematics from those earlier nations, so far as they are known to-day.'[8] Music at this time is a broad concept and includes poetry. It is the form in which the tensions of man and gods are unfolded. If writing or the art of letters began with the attempt to record the oral tradition, then music could be deemed to be the source of all the liberal arts.[9] Pythagoras may have related mathematical cosmology to his own disciplined life and that of his followers, but neither Plato nor Aristotle give him much credit as a philosopher. They refer to him as the founder of a disciplined way of life and as being knowledgeable of what happens to the soul after death.[10]

The most well-known story of Pythagoras is of him passing a blacksmith and deducing the octave from hearing hammers striking the handle.[11] The Tetraktys, seen as one of the founding metaphysical principles of the universe, reveals how the first four numbers not only add up to the perfect number ten but also contain within them the musical ratios of the octave, the fourth and the fifth. Regardless of what can or cannot be attributed to Pythagoras himself, in terms of the development thereafter of liberal arts education, he can be seen to be the person in whom the *logos* expresses itself as the desire to understand the first principles of the universe and to live in harmony with them.

After Pythagoras the idea of harmony, or of first principles, comes to be expressed in the experiences of metaphysics, physics and ethics. The Greek world after Pythagoras becomes reflective and calls upon the world traditionally understood to give an account of itself. Answering the call one finds the Sophists, the philosophers and the orators, each taking a different approach to the education deemed appropriate for the perfect emulation of the harmony and necessity of first principles, but each, too, understanding the need to make the emerging idea of political culture conform to first principles. Each seeks to educate for harmony and moderation in the political culture of the *polis*.

The Sophists

Jaeger credits the Sophists with being the first to conceive of *paideia* as 'educating man into his true form, the real and genuine nature.'[12] He sees this as the genesis of the notion of *humanitas* which appears as 'the universally valid model of humanity which all individuals are bound to imitate,'[13] 'bound' by the logic of necessity that is at work in discerning the truth of humankind, or its first principles. It is here, with the Sophists, that there emerges the idea of human perfection, of human beings in harmony with the totality of the *polis*, and of a logic of necessity called virtue.

The Sophists' political awareness arises in the transition in ancient Greece from the aristocratic ideal of *areté* to the political notion of *areté*.

The new democratic city-state requires a new kind of education for the newly invented concept of the political citizen. The aristocratic ideal of Homer is based on the nobility of bloodlines. A new *areté* is required, which could extend such kinship beyond blood and into a political community, a requirement which is fundamentally educational in nature. The aim of the Sophists here is to 'transcend the aristocratic principle of privileged education ... by the application of logical reasoning,'[14] or by educating the mind and therein forming human character. This is intellectual virtue, designed to prepare the citizen for the democratic *polis*. But if the new law is to avoid reproducing old aristocratic iniquities, it would need 'a universal insight into the true nature of human life,'[15] one which could not just understand political and intellectual virtues but, equally important, could educate for it. 'Protagoras' claim that cultural education is the centre of all human life indicates that his education was frankly aimed at humanism,'[16] since it sought to subordinate technical knowledge (including that taught by other Sophists) to universal political culture. This original notion of humanism is the true *paideia* of 'ethics and politics, taken together.'[17] As such, 'humanism is essentially a creation of the Greeks.'[18]

If this is so, then humanism is born as the cultural education befitting human beings who, in distinguishing the political from the natural (including 'natural' aristocracy and/or religion), sought the first principles of human life. It is in essence the moment when natural religion and culture are understood to be separate and, even more significantly, when this separation is understood as human education. This has three elements: it is where tradition becomes self-conscious and has itself as an object; it is where this relation is understood to be what is essentially human; and it is where it is understood that what is essentially human here is education. This is the birth of a new standard for education, a standard of being human. To the *mathematica* of Pythagoras the Sophists add the *techne* of this culture as grammar, rhetoric and dialectic, or education in language, oratory and thought. Since nothing is heard of them prior to the Sophists, 'they must have invented them.'[19] As such,

> The new *techne* is clearly the systematic expression of the principle shaping the intellect, because it begins by instruction in the form of thought. This educational technique is one of the greatest discoveries which the mind of man has ever made: it was not until it explored these three of its activities that the mind apprehended the hidden law of its own structure.[20]

This is the origin of the *trivium*, of the idea of human culture and of humanism. Harmony and rhythm are retained in the notion of *areté* which now becomes political *areté* – the beauty and harmony of living in balance with the laws which express human nature. Protagoras demonstrates the relationship between humanist education and harmony as a first principle. 'The idea of shaping the soul is implicit in Protagoras's assertion that harmony and the rhythm of poetry and music must be impressed on the soul to make it rhythmical and harmonious.'[21] This is an expression of *paideia* as humanism in its earliest form. Sophism, here, is the culture of humanism, because the new standard that is chosen is the ideal form of human being, 'the *form* of man.'[22] The Sophists are 'the first to conceive of the conscious idea of culture,'[23] not just as a training for the young, but to include the ideal of being educated, the higher education of the human being in regard to the whole spiritual, political and intellectual ideal of what it was to be a human being. Alongside this came the realisation that the individual and the state could be improved by reason and the will. Hence, in the West, the idea of culture is for the first time consciously formulated as education.[24]

An important part of this culture is that it changes the relation between nature and the formation of character. Technical education builds upon nature, upon natural talents, but culture creates a second nature. This is a conflict between 'aristocratic *paideia* and rationalism: it abandons the aristocratic idea that character and morality can be inherited by blood, but not acquired.'[25] This second nature is human cultural nature. Its universalism is expressed by 'human' nature, its contingency is expressed by culture and, as I will argue below, their opposition has its own truth expressed in metaphysical, natural and social relations. For Jaeger, culture, or education, is not just political self-consciousness, it is also the understanding of the nature of political self-consciousness as education. This is an example of the relation – here between nature and culture – relating to itself as learning, or as the relation of the relation. This is expressed in antiquity in the ambiguities of recollection, that is as that which can recollect itself, or know thyself. This culture of recollection looks backwards to the loss of the golden age of tradition, and forwards to its own cultural development, its own ideal. It is 'the climax of autumn, not of summer.'[26] Minerva's owl flies only at dusk, in the remains of the day. 'The domination which the Greek spirit was to win, and which was first practised by the Sophists, was got by Greece at the expense of her youth.'[27] But that is the cost of wisdom. Culture, then as now, means 'an inevitable loss, and yet we cannot resign ourselves to sacrifice the powers achieved by that development. We know that it is only through these powers that we are enabled to admire the earlier irrational stage so freely and so fully.'[28] Today we know the ambiguities of such recollection as the philosophy of history.

There is one aspect of *paideia*, or of the culture of humanism, that is as unavoidable as it is difficult. As Aristotle demonstrates in the *Politics*, the Greeks saw a natural hierarchy in the nature of ruler and ruled. But the emergence of human culture adds to this the idea that the rulers are somehow ahead of the ruled, that their education has progressed beyond the ruled. The reflective is seen as an advance of humanity over nature. For the Sophists, and for Plato and Aristotle in particular, this became the urgent question of political leadership. How could this new reflective culture reproduce itself truthfully unless it now accepted as a natural and cultural necessity the hierarchy of teacher and student, or of the reflective over the unreflective, or the political over the traditional, or, of philosophy over nature? The educated could work to provide the means for the education of all citizens. But to do so by eschewing the accompanying hierarchy would be bad faith and unnatural. If *paideia* is the root of humanism, then humanism, from the moment of its inception, has carried the weight of hierarchy, the divide between the learned and the unlearned.

The philosophers – Plato (427–346 BCE)

Plato's approach to the questions raised by human culture and the search for first principles is to advocate philosophical education. Where philosophy organises itself systematically then 'this content, according to Plato, begins to fall into three parts which we can distinguish as the logical, natural and mental philosophy (*spekulative, Natur – und Geistesphilosophie*). The [speculative or] logical philosophy the ancients called dialectic.'[29] For Hegel, Plato's *Parmenides*, *Timaeus* and *Republic* are the whole system in its three parts.[30]

Plato is perhaps the first to draw the harmonic mathematical universe of the Pythagoreans into a model of higher education, and particularly into a model of philosophical education regarding the first principles of proportion in the universe. Humanism is based on a distinction between man the individual as given by nature and man the higher self. It is Plato who makes it possible for humanism to have this philosophical foundation. In the *Republic* the philosopher is 'a new ideal of humanity.'[31] 'For humanism means education which is deliberately moulded on a certain ideal conception of human nature.'[32] It is 'impossible to mould men without an ideal of humanity,'[33] or without the movement from nature to culture. In the *Republic*, the cave analogy shows the beginning of an education beyond that required for everyday life. Early education is to consist of gymnastics, music and poetry. But Plato designs a higher education for those who leave the cave and are prepared to toil and struggle for balance and harmony in the individual soul, in the city and in the relation between them. 'The just man,' he says, 'won't differ at all from a just city in respect to the form of justice.'[34] The individual soul consists of (irrational) appetite, the calculation of balance in regard to desire, that is, reason; and the tensions felt between them, spirit (*thumos*). Reason needs spirit to side with it if the appetites are to be kept proportionate, with nothing in excess. In the *Phaedrus*, this notion of self-control is described as the struggle between self-restraint and excess.[35] They are likened to two horses driving a chariot – one good, one bad, and requiring the charioteer to try to hold to the desired direction.[36] If *logos* is the struggle for proportion and harmony, then here it is reason and spirit working together to limit personal greed. The city is made up of the same elements of the soul. Appetite defines those in the market-place, spirit defines those who are courageous in the face of the enemy and reason defines the wise who, in combination with spirit, will seek their own worth in the government of the just and worthy society.

There is, therefore, a need for a specialised education for the men and women who will serve the *logos* or the first principles of the soul and the city. The early education of physical training, crafts, music and poetry will have been an education in harmony through habit rather than through knowledge. The higher education needs to abstract itself from the material world and become an intellectual training. First is arithmetic, then geometry (both needed for successful warfare, but also for truths which do not 'attach to visible or tangible bodies'[37]) and astronomy, in which Pythagorean harmonics might be included.[38] These areas of study will form the disciplines of the mediaeval *quadrivium*, but Plato has no such term in mind. The goal of all this learning put together is to learn of the truth which is to be found in 'the song that dialectic sings.'[39]

The orators – Isocrates (436–338 BCE)

The third response to the call for first principles to be grounded in political culture comes from the orators. Zeno describes the relationship between the openness of persuasion and the rigidity of knowledge as follows: the open palm is perception (*phantasia*); a closing hand is assent; the closed fist is comprehension (*katalepsis*) or that which is fit to be grasped; while this fist enclosed by the other fist is knowledge of what is comprehended.[40] Diogenes Laertius notes that the Stoics held dialectic to be the logic of question and answer, while rhetoric was the form of speaking well in plain narrative.[41] Cassiodorus says that Varro (116–27 BCE) perhaps reduced Zeno's four elements to two: 'dialectic and rhetoric are like man's closed fist and open palm,'[42] which sees the one 'compressing its arguments into a narrow compass, the other running about the fields of eloquence with copious speech.'[43] The closed fist represents the ' "compactness" and "brevity" of dialectic, while the open hand with the fingers spread out was intended to simulate the "breadth" of rhetoric.'[44] The reduction from four stages of perception, assent, comprehension and knowledge to a duality of open and closed loses the subtleties of a process of persuasion, comprehension and knowledge. But it gains a sharpness of character in opposing dialectic and rhetoric as, respectively, closed and open.

Kimball carefully demonstrates how it is unreliable to assign the origin of the seven liberal arts, and especially perhaps the idea of liberal education, to any one distinct or stable line of inheritance, be it of theory, etymology or curriculum, harvested from 'the "pedagogical century" extending from about 450–350 BCE.'[45] Instead, Kimball notes that this pedagogical century is a response to the decline of the tradition where virtue was passed on through the recitation of (often) Homeric poetry. The Sophists respond with an art of persuasive speech-making; the philosophers respond with a quest for truth; and Isocrates seeks *areté* and character formation in the orator. The case often made for the origin of liberal education in the philosophers requires, says Kimball, judging against the oratorical tradition which has an equally strong claim to being the source of liberal education.

My argument expressed below is that the origin of the tradition is in the tension between philosophy and oratory, and between discipline and freedom, an ambivalence expressed in the ambiguous relation of *ars* and *liberalis*. These tensions and ambivalences are represented by Isocrates and Plato. Plato distrusts rhetoric, seeing it as an art of convincing crowds by means of stylistic techniques whatever the content happens to be. It is itself incapable of providing rational explanations either for ideals or for the principles of putting them into practice. Eloquence alone is morally indifferent. In *Gorgias* Plato tells us the orators do not 'set their sights on making the citizens as good as possible [because they are] bent upon the gratification of the citizens and [in] slighting the common good for the sake of their own private good.'[46] His target here is the Sophists. Isocrates too sees the Sophists having no interest in truth and seeking only large crowds, practising without knowledge or understanding of the virtue or first principles of rhetoric. However, Isocrates also criticises the philosophers who 'pretend to wisdom and assume the right to instruct the rest of the world.'[47] They give the impression that 'those who choose a life of careless indolence are better advised than those who devote themselves to serious study.'[48] Platonic philosophy here is seen as mere disputation over absolutes that can never be known and therefore never put into practice in real life. Indeed, he ridicules those philosophers 'who think that their moral paradoxes really contribute something to the spiritual upbuilding of the state.'[49]

Isocrates claims for rhetoric, as he understands it and teaches it, a respect for study and virtue together that is missing in the Sophists and the philosophers. He sees it as a cultural education embodying the older Greek tradition of education by poetry and imitation, and as the truth of form and content which is virtuous in-itself. It is an education that has relevance to the ordinary citizen, offering recognisable aims and goals, unlike philosophy. Its political vocation is to inspire nation-building and to bring peace to the constant state of war between Greek states. Isocrates is not himself an orator, suffering from agoraphobia, but he makes it his life's work to shape rhetoric into an education of high moral intent. 'He wished to educate the statesman who could give new direction to the efforts of the misguided masses and to the politics of the Greek states,'[50] and he set about 'to inspire every pupil with a passion for the new aims,'[51] and to instil in him duty and moral responsibility. This sense of citizenship, of an elite trained in the moral responsibility of governing, underpins one particular vision of liberal arts education as the birth-right of a class who see themselves born to govern.

For Isocrates, and as in medicine,[52] the educational task is 'to analyse the individual case into its general aspects,'[53] so that meaning can be acquired. This he shares with the philosophers. But in addition, the orator has to assess the perfect expression of each singular and unique moment in social and political life. This is the 'highest law'[54] of oratory, expressed by Isocrates in *Antidosis*. It is speech that has always laid down the best in human society. As such, 'the power to speak well is taken as the surest index of a sound understanding, and discourse which is true and lawful and just is the outward image of a good and faithful soul.'[55] The virtue of the orator is in having disputes internally on matters in thinking, and externally as public debates. Speech is best employed 'by those who have the most wisdom.'[56] Here a humanist interest emerges which will become a principal feature of liberal arts education thereafter.

The wisdom of knowing the general in the particular and the skill of its perfect public expression suggest that Isocratean oratory is 'imaginative literary creation,'[57] a unity of the aesthetic, the rational and the practical.

It is important to note that the notion of moral perfection in the orator is also related to the idea of harmony expressed by first principles. The graceful speech will know the music of a speech, will encompass the higher moral virtue of the whole over the parts and will comprehend the patterns and forms of speech that are most in harmony with singular events or topics. This is why Isocrates considers his orators to be philosophers. The orator will imitate these harmonies and virtues, else he will not be a good man or an effective speaker. He will be a model for his students who will become virtuous by imitating him. The key to its creativity, its open palm, lies in its having its practice in opinion rather than in immutable absolute truths, but this does not rule out the orator choosing the correct means for the correct political end. If the absolutes of the philosophers are permanently and necessarily out of reach, then the practical truth, or the first principles of oratory, makes a virtue out of this necessity. Based on the strength of this case for retrieving Isocratean rhetoric in the origins of liberal arts education, Kimball discerns seven characteristics of an ideal liberal arts education. These are: training the virtuous citizen to lead society; prescribed standards for character and conduct; respect for those standards; knowing the classical texts which contain the virtues; selecting an elite who have these virtues; holding this to be true; and to be an end in itself. Seen in this way Isocrates can be seen to be 'the father of modern liberal education.'[58] In the struggle between philosophy and rhetoric in antiquity what emerges for Kimball regarding the history of liberal education is that the philosophical tradition does not have exclusive claims to the heritage.

Kimball also notes the rhetorical tradition claimed to be the true pattern of culture. Isocrates, for example, saw culture carried in speech, the name of which was *logos*, the creator of culture. Speech lets man rise above the animals, invent the arts, establish laws, create the possibility of collective life and enact justice. The ability to speak correctly underpins each of these essential aspects of human life. Jaeger says, 'If we sum up the character of this power, we shall find that no reasonable thing is done anywhere in the world without *logos*, that *logos* is the leader of all actions and thoughts, and that those who make most use of it are the wisest of mankind.'[59] The *logos*, as defined by Isocrates, is therefore 'the embodiment of Isocrates' ideal of *paideia*.'[60]

Isocrates may be 'the father of "humanistic" culture'[61] because a line of heritage can be drawn back to him, but for Jaeger this is not the whole story. Isocrates is the 'chief representative of rhetoric, [and] personifies the classical opposition to Plato and his school.'[62] From this opposition stems 'the rivalry of philosophy and rhetoric, each claiming to be the better form of culture.'[63] This rivalry then runs 'like a leitmotif through-out the history of ancient civilisation'[64] and, if Kimball is right, through to the present day. But Jaeger is keen to restore the role of philosophy in the rhetorical and humanistic tradition which 'academic humanism'[65] has overlooked. The history of humanism is 'far broader and richer'[66] than being merely 'a continuation of the rhetorical strain.'[67] It contains 'all the manifold survivals of Greek paideia – including the world-wide influence exercised by Greek philosophy and science.'[68] Jaeger says that philosophy, and especially Greek philosophy, 'has played a decisive role in the development of modern humanism, which would have no impe-tus without it, and would not even have been able to expound its own aims.'[69]

Aristotle (384–322 BCE)

In Plato the logic of first principles is applied consistently across the three philosophies, aiming to integrate truth, nature and justice into the one harmony of the Republic. This is not quite the case with Aristotle who deals with the tension between discipline and freedom differently. Here, the open and creative notion of political wisdom and virtue is dif-ferentiated from the closed and systematic truths of speculation. In time this unfolds more fully into the division between practice and theory. In this sense, it is Aristotelian and not Platonic logic which creates the template for the dualism in liberal arts education between the iron fist of theory and discipline and the open palm of practice and freedom.

In the *Topics* Aristotle divides philosophy into speculative, practical and productive.[70] Each defines a specific type of relation to an object: speculation to knowledge, the will to actions and production to things. Each has different types of virtue associated with it. Of the five intel-lectual virtues, *episteme* (knowledge), *nus* (comprehension) and *sophia* (wisdom) define the virtues of speculation, while *phronesis* defines the virtue of practical wisdom, and *techne* defines the virtue of produc-tion. Here Aristotle introduces a division of labour into the notion of virtue, and the effect is to define three different kinds of harmony, and three different kinds of principles, for thinking, doing and making. Each virtue is a logic of the necessity by which something is its own truth. But whereas Plato retains the dialectical logic of necessity as the truth of the experience of the relation between nature and culture (and this is dealt with more fully in Part III), Aristotle separates nature and culture from each other and assigns different notions of truth to each. To nature, that is to the 'nature' of something, he gives the virtue of certain and unchangeable knowledge discovered in and by the sciences. The logic of necessity here dominates Western thinking for the next two thousand years 'for it alone exists for itself.'[71] It is the logic of non-contradiction, wherein the truth of an object, its logic of necessity, its totality, is that it cannot be other than it is, is unchangeable and defies any further regression into a prior cause or identity. Philosophy or metaphysics here is the science of first principles.[72]

But where the will is concerned, wisdom is changeable, because it has to reflect different circumstances and experiences. As such, practical work occupies a difficult place, where logic has to be related to experience, and forms a different kind of truth. Culture here is defined as other to nature, as other to the logic of non-contradiction, and as other to the unchangeable truth of a first principle. Harmony is to be found in the moral development of virtuous character which is grounded in the first principle of *phronesis*. The practical art of rhetoric, for example, has its scientific and logical principles made into artistic practice, suggesting to some interpreters that *phronesis* or practical wisdom avoids both the rigidity of conformity to science and the mindless repetition of skills.[73] This flexibility and creativity makes *phronesis* a popular choice for those who are critical of the fixed nature of scientific knowledge. The third kind of harmony is, in a sense, the best of both worlds. The natural element of production is the rules (discipline) of procedure required for making an object while the changeable allows the craftsman to react (freely) to difficulties he might encounter.[74] This ambiguity describes the dualism of philosophy and rhetoric that comes to be understood not as the educational logic of their relation, but as the Aristotelian logic of their opposition to each other. *Techne* here lacks the philosophical resources needed to make a virtue out of its own ambivalent necessity and freedom or needed to understand work as the difficulty which expresses the logic of an educational first principle.

The Aristotelian logic of necessity taken up as the first principle of a liberal arts education is therefore a logic of non-contradiction, a logic of identity. The certain principle or harmony of an objective truth is that upon which 'it is impossible to be mistaken'[75] and the basis of all logic, all certainty, and all truth, is this: 'it is impossible for anyone to believe the same thing to be and not to be ... [for] it is impossible that contrary attributes should belong at the same time to the same subject.'[76] This has to be presupposed as 'the starting-point for all other axioms,'[77] but it cannot be demonstrated by anything prior to it, for if there had to be a demonstration of everything 'there would be an infinite regress'[78] and nothing would ever be demonstrated at all. This positing of truth as that which in-itself is its own most simple being, and of error as that which is compound and always changeable in being of-and-for-another, is the logic underpinning not only the necessity of first principles in liberal arts but also of metaphysics, nature and freedom up to the late 18th century.

Aristotle also discerns a hierarchy of intellectual virtues. Because the natural philosopher 'deals with things that have *in themselves* a principle of movement ... [so] natural science must be neither practical nor productive, but theoretical.'[79] In the *Physics* he explains that of all things which exist, there are those such as animals and plants which exist 'by nature'[80] and have a principle of movement and rest within them, whereas products of art or skill have no such innate principle and cannot (re)-produce themselves. In the *Metaphysics* he notes that natural science deals with things which have just this principle in themselves, but sees also that the principle cannot exist outside of the matter of the object. With regard to mathematics there is an ambiguity as to whether its objects are immovable and separable from matter.[81] In fact Aristotle decides that in mathematics objects are only partly unmoved and unlikely to be able to exist independently apart from matter.[82] If neither physics nor mathematics, which are both theoretical or speculative, deal with things which are both immovable and independent, then they cannot be considered to be the highest sciences, for they are not dealing with first causes or first principles. If 'there is no substance other than those which are formed by nature, natural science will be the first science; but if there is an immovable substance, the science of this must be prior and must be first philosophy.'[83] And this too must be 'the divine.'[84] There are, then, three kinds of theoretical sciences – natural science, mathematics and theology. 'The class of theoretical sciences is the best, and of these themselves the last named is best; for it deals with the highest of existing things, and each science is called better or worse in virtue of its proper object.'[85]

There is also a discernible shift in Aristotle's thinking regarding the relation of theory and practice. In the *Protrepticus* Aristotle sees *phronesis* as Platonic *nus*, an intuitive divine philosophical knowledge. But in the *Metaphysics* and especially in the *Nicomachean Ethics*, *phronesis* is no longer *nus*. It is no longer mere speculation. Instead it is now 'a practical faculty, concerned both with the choice of the ethically desirable and with the prudent perception of one's own advantage.'[86] The prudent here are not *sophoi*, but *phronomoi*. When Aristotle moves away from his teacher, the necessities and harmonies of theoretical and practical reason are separated, and the liberal arts will play its part in turning this into a division between sciences (the *quadrivium* of disciplines) and arts (the *trivium* of virtue).

In Aristotle, then, the three types of knowledge, speculative, practical and productive, become the three realms of metaphysics, ethics and the illiberal arts. This is the categorisation that comes to define not only what is to count as liberal arts education. It also reinforces the divide between speculative philosophical virtue and political rhetorical virtue which, as Kimball says, defines the central struggle of liberal arts education thereafter.

*   *   *

Kimball works with this sharpened opposition between the closed fist of scientific truth and the open palm of creative rhetorical expression. He sees two ideal camps which, in the history of liberal education, represent the open rhetorical ideal of the *artes liberales* and the closed dogmatic philosophical or theological truths. To the ideal *artes liberales* tradition belong the Sophists, the school of Isocrates, the emerging *trivium* of Roman education including the *studia humanitatis* of Cicero, the retrieval of Greek literary sources in the humanist Renaissance, the defence of classical literature against the emerging empiricism of the natural sciences in the 17th and 18th centuries, and the defence of classical education against the specialism of University research. To the philosophical tradition belong Socrates, Plato and Aristotle, the early Christian educators, Augustine and Aquinas, and the modern era of enlightenment philosophers. Kimball argues that the Enlightenment saw a shift from the liberal arts ideal to the liberal-free ideal where the oratorical virtues of breadth and public engagement are threatened by the new critical spirit of individualism, specialisation (including in philosophy), education and research which, practised for their own sake, are detached from responsibility for the good. We will follow this path in the remaining chapters of Part I, around tensions that define the dualism of the closed fist of philosophical discipline and the open palm of rhetorical freedom.

2
The Seven Liberal Arts: Varro's Secret Path

While there is little clear idea of a 'liberal arts' education in Greek antiquity, the idea takes clearer shape in Latin antiquity, and thereafter in early Christianity. I now follow Varro's path on which liberal arts education is formed on its journey to the European universities. Again I draw attention to the tension between the iron fist of necessity (philosophy and theology) and the open palm of freedom (rhetoric, education and faith). What emerges clearly is the struggle for dominance between rhetoric and philosophy, and the hierarchy that is at stake between them.

In the first century BCE, Varro classifies nine disciplines:[1] the seven liberal arts of grammar, dialectics, rhetoric, geometry, arithmetic, astrology[2] and music, and we know from Vitruvius, that he added architecture, and, it is assumed, medicine.[3] Parker states that the seven liberal arts 'started from Greece [and] ... travelled to the universities in Varro's secret path.'[4] Cicero (106–43 BCE) was a contemporary of Varro and paid tribute to him (in *Academia* I.9) as something of a polymath – writing on poetry, Latin literature, religion, morality and philosophy. Cicero was more interested in the liberal arts as a preparation for oratory, but the Roman view of the liberal arts more widely is as a preparation for higher education in philosophy, medicine or law. This idea of education as the handmaid of higher truths is found consistently on Varro's path.

Cicero names geometry, music, grammar, poetry, natural science and moral and political philosophy as examples of the liberal arts that prepares one for oratory. Prior to Varro and Cicero, Cato the Elder (c. 234–149 BCE) drew up a Roman curriculum for his son's education to stand against the Greek curriculum. With rhetoric came ethics, medicine, military science, agriculture and law.[5] In the first century CE,

Seneca (4 BCE–65 CE), while retaining Stoic philosophy as the highest wisdom, lists as the *liberalia studia* grammar (literary scholarship), music, arithmetic and astronomy.[6] Philo the Jew (c. 20 BCE–c. 50 CE), living in Alexandria in the first century CE, holds to the Greek idea of the encyclic arts (*enkuklios paideia*), including, in the main, grammar, rhetoric, dialectic, arithmetic, geometry and music, but not astronomy. Parker refutes entirely the suggestion that the liberal arts were ever the same as the Greek encyclical or general education, lacking as the liberal arts did, agriculture, medicine, fine arts, history and architecture.[7] Historians seem agreed on the lack of any definitive list of the seven liberal arts in Athens, Alexandria or Rome;[8] indeed, 'the number 7 is the least important thing in the system.'[9] Classical Rome did not have 'even the *trivium*, still less the *quadrivium*.'[10] Seneca makes it clear that no definitive list of seven liberal arts existed and suggests that in fact any such lists may well be arbitrary and based merely on opinion.[11] The arbitrary figure of seven was only arrived at along Varro's secret path and established for the first time at the beginning of the seventh century.[12] There is no known single author of the definitive seven liberal arts, but the path is occupied, amongst others, by Augustine, Boethius, Capella and Cassiodorus.

Rhetoric and *humanitas*

Latin antiquity preserves the tensions in first principles between discipline and freedom in the relation between philosophy and rhetoric. As Kimball observes, for Cicero oratory meant the open palm of creative and imaginative nation-building as it had done for Isocrates, opposed to the totalities and idle speculations of the philosophers. In *De oratore* he says that the greatest sin is for the orator to depart from the common sense of the community.[13] The orator needs more than the philosopher. The philosopher can have wisdom, but the orator needs wisdom and the moral perfection of its public expression. Socrates

> separated the science of wise thinking from that of elegant speaking, though in reality they are closely linked together... [Hence arose] the undoubtedly absurd and unprofitable and reprehensible severance between the tongue and the brain, leading to our having one set of professors to teach us to think and another to teach us to speak.[14]

This divorce of knowledge from eloquence lies at the heart of the separation of philosophy and rhetoric and again here the logic of the closed fist stands against the creative expression of the open palm.

But Latin antiquity also preserves the tension of this dualism within the ambiguities of the work of *humanitas*. *Humanitas* comes to be defined as the universality or first principle of the virtue of each political citizen, although the Roman conception of humanity is not quite that of the Greeks.[15] *Humanitas* was a closed fist, a 'message of universalism, of the essential unity of the human race, that had come down in philosophical form from the Greeks, but needed the pragmatic muscles of Rome in order to become a [more open palm of] practical reality.'[16]

Aulus Gellius (second century CE) in *Noctes atticae* defines Latin *humanitas* in contradistinction to Greek *philanthropia*. Diogenes Laertius[17] describes three types of philanthropy: courteous address, helping those in distress and hospitality. It also carries the aristocratic idea of the goodwill of a superior to an inferior. Plato describes this aspect as characterising the age of Cronos, a golden age of peace and harmony where divine spirits governed philanthropically over man, distributing laws, justice and harmony 'among the races of the world.'[18] This becomes the model for the human government of the Republic, where the mortal leaders are to imitate this *philanthropia*, 'in obedience to what little spark of immortality'[19] lies in them.[20] *Philanthropia* could also refer to the civilised training that one might have in order to overcome savage behaviour, or to the working of justice. In each case, *philanthropia*, by definition, is in the gift of the master.

Gellius argues that those who use Latin correctly understand that *humanitas* has its root not in any abstract (closed) necessity but rather in the openness of *paideia* or in education in the liberal arts (*bonas artes*). This relates closely to Jaeger's idea that *paideia* signifies human self-education over and above that provided by nature. *Humanitas*, like *paideia*, nevertheless carries the ambiguity of being an expression of the universal nature of human being lived as an individual political citizen.

Richard Bauman shows how Roman *humanitas* is caught in the tension between two competing drives: human cruelty and human affection arising at the time of the destruction of Carthage and Corinth in second century BCE.[21] *Humanitas* thus carries an ambivalence that one can be universally virtuous even if one is being individually cruel because the cruelty has as its justification the universality of virtue, that is, *humanitas*. This ambivalence in *humanitas*, of trying to use the universal good to justify particular cruelty, remains a dilemma within the notion of humanity to the present day.

In the middle of the second century BCE an intellectual circle grows around Scipio Aemilianus in Rome working on synthesising Greek and Roman thought, including the synthesis of severity and morality as *humanitas*.[22] For Bauman, however, the term *humanitas* is not introduced until Terence's *Heauton Timorumenos* (*The Self-Torturer*, 87 BCE) in which are the lines 'I am a man, I count nothing pertaining to man foreign to me.'[23] Here is possibly the first expression 'of common humanity, of universalism.'[24]

But it is Cicero who 'takes almost complete control'[25] of the concept of *humanitas* by moving it 'out of the ivory tower.'[26] Cicero carries the ambivalence of *humanitas* by holding universal human sympathy and individual cruelty and severity in tension to one another. His universalism is illustrated in *On Duty* (I. 50–2). The human community is established on natural principles of reason and speech which distinguish it clearly from the realm of animals. But even here the human bond is graded such that blood relations exhibit the strongest bonds, then marriage, state, language and finally universal fellowship of the whole human race. One should always contribute to the common benefit, and at times this would involve being cruel. He told his brother Quintus, who governed Asia, that *humanitas* allowed justice to be administered 'with the utmost severity, as long as you are consistent and impartial.'[27] *Humanitas* includes severity and cruelty for its own sake, and in the interests of the governed, but it means as well that in commanding 'there is nothing harsh or cruel, always clemency, leniency, humanity.'[28] Clemency can be replaced by severity when the interests of the state require it – we must 'recommend gentleness on the understanding that we may exercise severity for the sake of the Republic.'[29] He laments the destruction of Carthage but could see that it served the national interest.[30] The dividing line here between *humanitas* and *inhumanitas* is not clear and may lie in 'the eye of the beholder.'[31] What is clearer is that *humanitas* as a first principle contains the tension between the necessity and discipline of the universal and the freedom of the individual. This ambiguity will reappear in the culture of Renaissance humanism and in enlightenment *Bildung*.

The seven liberal arts on Varro's path

The oratorical tradition enjoys prominence in Latin antiquity, while the philosophical tradition of the Greeks will be reclaimed in neoplatonic Christianity. Between the fall of the Roman Empire and the early Renaissance liberal arts is more clearly defined in various educational encyclopaedias, and also more firmly kept in its place by the speculative sciences of philosophy and especially theology. Education will recover its essential humanism in the Renaissance when philosophy and theology will come to be seen as formulaic or as scholastic.

On Varro's path of the liberal arts one finds among others Capella and Boethius, as well as Augustine, Cassiodorus and Isidore.[32] West suggests that Boethius, Cassiodorus and Isidore were to become 'the acknowledged authorities'[33] in the schools of liberal arts of the Middle Ages. Parker notes that in the period between Capella and the foundation of the universities, Cassiodorus, patronised by Charlemagne, 'hallowed the list [of liberal arts] for future generations.'[34] But the list of liberal arts was never intended to be a comprehensive suite of all knowledge. Nor was it intended to be comprehensively available to all, and severely restricted the access of women in order to match the restricted role they were expected to play.[35] Lacking a science of the aesthetic, painting and sculpture were excluded. Architecture could be closely associated with music[36] but like medicine it was seen as an art of the material world and thus not liberal. Weisheipl concludes that 'St Augustine, Boethius, Cassiodorus and St. Isidore served as the principal sources for all later discussion of the seven liberal arts.'[37] Between them they were the path by which the liberal arts 'travelled to the universities.'[38] This path, briefly described now, illustrates the difficulties faced in trying to maintain the logic of necessity of first principles in the relations between the holy books, philosophy and the seven liberal arts. It is a tension that has its actuality in a struggle to assert Aristotle's hierarchy of the theoretical sciences, especially theology, over the more practical aspects of liberal arts education.

The dates of Martianus Capella are not agreed upon, and therefore it is not known for certain when his book *The Marriage of Philology and Mercury* was written – the fifth or sixth century, before 439 CE, or before 330 CE.[39] Despite its paganism there is some agreement on the part played by Capella in compelling 'the mediaeval ecclesiastics to do homage to the seven liberal arts.'[40] The book tells of the marriage between Mercury, the inventor of letters and representing Greek divine arts, and philology, representing school learning.[41] Each of the seven liberal arts is a bridesmaid and gives a discourse explaining their individual natures. There are nine books, perhaps in tribute to Varro's earlier work, and after the two opening chapters each of the liberal arts has a separate chapter in the order of grammar, dialectic, rhetoric, geometry, arithmetic, astronomy and music. Again with an eye on Varro, Capella explains that medicine and architecture are on standby, but are deemed to be concerned with earthly, material and changeable things, and as such, having nothing in common with the divine guests at the wedding.[42] Capella refers to the seven liberal arts as the *enkuklios paideia*[43] of ancient Greece, the name giving rise to the impression not just of seven liberal arts, but of their being something of a *tota philosophia*, a complete human knowledge.[44] The result was that Capella 'made the seven arts immortal'[45] and influenced all who wrote about liberal arts thereafter.

Even though Boethius (c. 475–7 CE–c. 524–6 CE) is credited as the first to use the term quadrivium,[46] he leaves 'no general account of the seven arts, nor is there to be found in his writings any indication that he thought the number noteworthy of this connection'[47] nor does he mention Capella's *Marriage*. Boethius holds himself within the classical tradition of the liberal arts, preserving the ideal of 'the classical Roman tradition when the Roman world was crumbling.'[48] He is probably best known in this regard for the textbooks he wrote on the liberal arts, which were used in liberal arts education for the next 600 years. Adding to Roman works on grammar and rhetoric, Boethius wrote on logic, music, arithmetic and geometry (and may have translated Ptolemy's *Astronomy*). He planned to translate the works of Plato and Aristotle, but completed only two Aristotelian logical works. Still, 'this work, plus half of Plato's *Timaeus* was to provide the sum total of classical Greek philosophy known to the early Middle Ages.'[49] He orders the subjects of the *quadrivium*, perhaps coining the term *quadrivium* as the place where four roads meet.[50] According to his model of philosophical speculation, Boethius gives priority to number which is in itself a whole, then to music which is the harmony of wholes in relation to each other, then to geometry and astronomy which explore magnitude without motion and with motion respectively. The order of the quadrivium sees the learner move from material in motion to the immaterial and unchangeable, or to theology/philosophy, repeating the hierarchy in which freedom or education is the handmaid of discipline and science. This order differs from the quadrivial disciplines in Capella in that in the former music aligns with mathematics while in the latter it bestrides astronomy.[51] It is the Boethian textbooks on number and music (and possibly geometry), not Capella's *Marriage*, which 'by the later Middle Ages became almost standard as the textbooks for those disciplines.'[52]

With regard to the higher studies Boethius divides philosophy into theoretical (speculative) and practical (active) and divides theoretical philosophy into three classes of being: intellectibles, intelligibles and the natural. This is in line with the Aristotelian logic of necessity that harmony cannot be compound. The intellectibles exist beyond matter and are eternal forms studied by dialectics. The intelligibles are intellectibles 'that have fallen into bodies, such as the human souls.'[53] The natural beings are those which cannot exist separate from material bodies. Fifteen years later, Boethius in his *De trinitate* divides speculative philosophy into physics (nature), mathematics and theology according to a hierarchy of bodies, abstractions and divine substance without matter or motion.[54] He divides practical philosophy into personal, political and domestic morality.[55] 'Three other disciplines make up the trivium: grammar, rhetoric and logic'[56] and are concerned with the exposition of knowledge rather than its acquisition. Weisheipl notes that Boethius offers a fusion of Platonic and Aristotelian philosophy. The Platonic holds to the tripartite nature of the speculative (nature, mathematics and theology, as in the *Republic*) while the separation of the theoretical and the practical, and the scientific nature of physics and the inseparability of bodies and sensible forms are Aristotelian.[57] But one can add here, according to an insight that will be explored in Part II, that in struggling to work with the divide between theory and practice Boethius not only holds Plato and Aristotle in creative tension but also he does so through (liberal arts) education.

Cassiodorus (c. 480–c. 575) begins his description of dialectic in the *Institutiones* (or *Introduction to Divine and Human Readings*[58]) with a description of the division of philosophy along the Platonic lines seen above in Boethius. The primary division is between speculative and practical philosophy. The former contains natural philosophy, doctrinal philosophy and divine philosophy, again based on a hierarchy rising from material, through abstraction, to the ineffable. The quadrivial disciplines are the four sciences which explore quantity, sound, space and the motion of the heavenly bodies. Practical philosophy divides into moral, economic and political philosophy.

In his *Exposito Psalorum* the Psalms are interpreted pedagogically, revealing his view that the trivium and quadrivium had 'a scriptural origin'[59] offering them a higher logic of necessity in the harmony of first principles. O'Donnell says here, Cassiodorus was 'so far from embracing the classics he could abandon them all together.'[60] The second book of his *Institutiones* is divided into seven chapters, one each on grammar, rhetoric, dialectic, arithmetic, music, geometry and astronomy.[61] O'Donnell describes it as a textbook in which the seven subjects are not recommended by Cassiodorus to be enjoyed for their own sake or as an end in-itself. Education may serve science but it is not truth in-itself. Cassiodorus distinguishes the arts as the *trivium* and the disciplines as the *quadrivium*, suggesting that the arts are that in which the palm is open, while the disciplines are those in which the fist is closed because the outcome is unchangeable.

One final list of the seven liberal arts comes from Isidore of Seville (c. 560–636), in his *Etymologies*. He too tries to define the logic of necessity in the tension of the relations between Scripture, philosophy and the seven liberal arts. He defines philosophy in two ways. First in the Platonic (and Stoic) division into physics, ethics and logic, noting that Plato divides physics into arithmetic, geometry, music and astronomy; logic into dialectic and rhetoric; while Socrates divides ethics into the four virtues of the soul, prudence, justice, temperance and fortitude.[62] He also divides the Holy Scriptures into these three philosophies: nature as Genesis and Ecclesiastes, ethics as Proverbs; and logic as the Song of Songs and the Gospels. His second definition of philosophy is that of Cassiodorus.[63] Specifically on the liberal arts he lists seven, and again notes the distinction between the disciplines, in which what is true cannot be otherwise, and the arts, which concern that which is possible of more than one outcome.

Summing up this period Kimball states that the handbooks of Martianus, Cassiodorus and Isidore, in trying to accommodate the liberal arts to Christianity, employ the oratorical tradition in doing so. By this Kimball means that Cassiodorus, for example, draws heavily on Cicero and employs the metaphor of the closed fist and the open palm. Isidore too promotes grammar over other arts including those of the speculative disciplines. In contrast he identifies Boethius as evidence of the persistence of the philosophical tradition, subordinating rhetoric to dialectic, and composing treatises on the mathematical liberal arts. As consolation, philosophy is the discipline which, through speculative dialectic, can liberate the mind from both literal and figurative prison. But it remained the case that the key factor by which liberal arts commended itself to theology was as handmaid, in that it offered study in the *trivium* which was a precondition for the skills needed to read and interpret the sacred texts.

Seen in this way, Varro's path shows the continuing tensions between the closed fist of speculation in theology and philosophy, and the open palm of language in at least part of the curriculum of the seven liberal arts. These tensions are nowhere better illustrated than in Augustine. He finds discipline and freedom to be an educative tension between divine knowledge and human faith. Here the ancient logic of the necessity of first principles is again in a difficult relation to the finite understanding.

Augustine (354–430)

The logic of necessity grounding Christian theology is the tranquillity of harmony and perfection in the absolute identity of the one God with

Himself, leaving the unrest and the imperfection of the composite and the contingent to the sinful city of man. When liberal arts are deemed to be the handmaid of religion it is because even though they can have a theoretical knowledge of God – they can know logically that He exists – they overstep the mark if they think they also know what He is. Here logic is in a sense trumped by religion which makes a virtue out of the logic of the necessity of God, the virtue of faith. The faith of the contingent creature knows God and knows this knowledge to be imperfect because it is not self-animation, not its own principle. To live this relation of faith is to mediate logical knowledge with the appropriate humility that belongs to all finite knowledge.

Augustine is exemplary in living with this tension and struggle. Not only does his own personal life play out its divine comedy, he manages to hold philosophy, liberal arts and theology together in a creative and educative tension. He has at times been seen as one source for the seven liberal arts. His *Retractions* (1.5) notes that prior to his baptism he had attempted to write books on the liberal arts,[64] completing one on grammar and six on music. Five more were begun, on dialectic, rhetoric, geometry, arithmetic and philosophy (replacing astronomy/astrology).[65] In *De ordine* (II.16) Augustine speaks of the order of liberal arts, referring to the study of formless matter, motion, time and space, and in the *Confessions* he says that in his youth he read 'all the books I could get hold of on the arts which they call liberal.'[66]

Kristeller notes that before becoming a bishop and theologian,

Augustine had been a rhetorician, a philosopher, and a heretic who underwent conversion, and all these elements and experiences left their traces in his writings. Augustine is a preacher, a moral teacher, and a political thinker, an expositor of the Bible, an autobiographer, a skeptic and neoplatonic philosopher, a rhetorically trained writer who finds a justification for the study of the pagan poets, a systematic theologian who continues the work of the Greek Fathers, a vigorous opponent of heresies who formulated or sharpened the doctrines of original sin, grace, and predestination.[67]

But through all this, he finds a 'process of education'[68] in an individual's history, like that in a people's historical epochs, raising each from the visible and the temporal to the invisible and the eternal.

His early work reflects his own pagan education in liberal arts at Carthage, and in Manicheanism, in which he perhaps gains an outlet for the dualistic nature of his own emerging thinking. This dualism helps him to maintain the relationship between pagan philosophical education and Christianity, although at this early stage he finds the Scriptures to be lacking somewhat in depth and style. By the time of his *Retractions*, he is able to say that 'as far as the nature of man is concerned, there is nothing in him better than mind and reason – and yet the man who wishes to live happily should not live according to this... "He should live as God lives" (I Peter 4.6).'[69] Whereas at the age of 30 he held that the highest good of man lies in the intellect[70] by the time of the completion of his *Retractions*, aged 73, he corrects himself; the highest good of man lives in God.[71] But these retractions are notable not simply for placing God higher than philosophy and liberal arts education, but for retaining both philosophy and the liberal arts as stages on the way to truth and as weapons to be used for the sake of that truth.

One example of this comes from *On Christian Doctrine* where he says that eloquence is not to be blamed for making the false seem true – a charge levelled against Socrates 800 years earlier, and against the Sophists in particular – rather the blame lies with those who use it in such ways.[72] He emphasises here that 'the theory of reasoning in particular runs like a system of nerves through the whole structure of Scripture.'[73] In Book IV he makes the case that the defenders of Christian truth should not make this unnecessarily difficult by avoiding knowledge of liberal arts. Why, he asks, would not good men study rhetoric in order to 'engage it on the side of truth, when bad men use it to obtain the triumph of wicked and worthless causes, and to further injustice and error?'[74]

Specifically, in his defence of the liberal arts Augustine states that there are seven stages to wisdom: fear of the Lord; piety in relation to sin or ignorance; knowledge of God in contrast to knowledge of earthly things; strength and resolution to pursue the eternal; compassion which cleanses the soul; a view of God in which the believer dies to this world, but still only through a glass darkly; until finally, the seventh stage finds peace and tranquillity in divine wisdom. He then concentrates on the third of the steps to wisdom, that is, knowledge. Being open to the more ambiguous messages in Scripture requires knowledge of Hebrew and Greek, in addition to Latin, so as to read different translations. Arithmetic is required to understand some of the divine significance of key numbers in Scripture. Music opens up the understanding in relation to number. Reason will overcome superstition, including astrology and divination. History is essential for a knowledge of God's authorship of past events. Natural sciences can aid in solving difficulties of Scripture. Even a knowledge of the mechanical arts is deemed necessary in order to understand the part they play in Scripture. Dialectics can unravel questions that arise in Scripture, always being careful not to degenerate into wrangling and sophistry. The lesson to be learned in understanding all of these arts is that they display the order and harmony of God's creation. The liberal arts do not create God's universe, but they do discover it. In sum, he states, 'if those who are called philosophers, and especially the Platonists, have said aught that is true and in harmony with our faith, we are not only not to shrink from it, but to claim it for our own use from those who have unlawful possession of it.'[75] These liberal arts contain falsities and superstitions which are to be avoided, but 'they also contain liberal instruction which is better adapted to the use of the truth, and some most excellent precepts of morality; and some truths in regard even to the worship of the one God are found among them.'[76] It is clear that, although the liberal arts are not to be studied for their own sake, neither are they merely a mechanical skill set. Augustine argues for the ambivalence and, I would say, for the education carried in this ambivalence, as the path to wisdom.

Perhaps the most incisive comment on the relation between liberal arts, philosophy and the divine science from Augustine is this: 'we must believe before we understand.'[77] He tells us it was part of God's plan for him to read Platonic philosophy before the holy books, in order for him to find 'those who see what the goal is but not how to get there.'[78] This is an argument based on the order of philosophical and divine education. It is the educative journey of a philosophical spirit – 'To perceive and to grasp the order of reality proper to each thing, and then to see or to explain the order of the entire universe by which this world is truly held together'[79] – who remains dissatisfied with sceptical and stoical refusal of assent, only to find that all these same philosophical mysteries were to be found in the Scriptures but with the addition of the grace of Christ, none of which 'is in the Platonist books.'[80] Even though the philosopher can, at best, be only 'bravely miserable,'[81] there is the suggestion here that liberal arts and philosophy and theology can walk the same path and achieve the same end.[82]

In the *City of God* (written between 414–26), Augustine defends key aspects of Platonic philosophy from within the division of the three philosophies: natural philosophy (physics), reason (logic) and moral philosophy. The pre-Socratics had given attention to the natural sciences, their leader being Pythagoras, while Socrates had turned philosophy towards the question of morality, and Plato, by classifying reason as the method of knowing truth from falsehood, therein created the three philosophies – natural, moral and logical. Natural and moral philosophy both employ logic, but it is speculative philosophy that 'has a special claim to insight into the truth.'[83] Together, these three philosophies offer a unified conception of God as the cause of existence, the principle of reason and the order of human life. The three philosophies can teach Christianity that it is right to seek God in whom the universe is a unity, in which all things are certain, and in whom all is goodness. Augustine repeats his own commitment to the Platonic (and Aristotelian) view of God as unchangeable, uncreated and immaterial, and that the whole material universe 'could only come into being through him who simply *is*.'[84] As with liberal arts, so with philosophy, 'they raised their eyes above all material objects in this search for God.'[85] As such, 'there are none who come nearer to us than the Platonists.'[86]

Augustine does not avoid the difficulty of the relationship between the unchangeable and the changeable, between knowledge and faith, and between discipline and freedom. His thinking is remarkable for the ways in which he refuses to abstract one from the other. By keeping liberal arts education close to faith and theology he is able to express the tension of first principles as education. In Augustine, perhaps, learning has its most profound expression as the realm in which truth appears on Varro's path. He did not of course have a modern logic available to him in which this learning could become its own first principle.

3
Renaissance Humanism

Philosophy and rhetoric revive their opposition in the Renaissance as the closed fist of (theological and Aristotelian) orthodoxy and the open palm of (classical rhetorical) humanism. But there are different arenas in which this opposition is played out: in the battle of the books; in the ambivalence inherent in the growth of rational method; in the opposition of dogma and interpretation, of Empire and Church and of speculation and observation; and of course in the opposition between scholasticism and humanism. Again, my interest here is not with a comprehensive historical account of these developments, but rather with the way they illustrate the continuing tension between rhetoric and philosophy, and between freedom and discipline.

The character of liberal arts education is reconfigured in the 10th to the 12th centuries across Europe by the growth of monastic, urban, parish and cathedral schools. The teaching in these schools is labelled scholastic. Originally it meant submitting all disputes to the established authorities of the dialectical method which 'systematized subject matter into genera and species by identifying and categorizing points of consistency and, when faced with a *contrarium*, searching for a *solutio* by making new *distinctiones* (categories) or citing an *exceptio*.'[1] The pejorative sense of scholasticism is usually illustrated by the ability of scholars to make distinctions and exceptions ad infinitum leaving the actual experience of the world a long way behind. Nevertheless, as the new translations of Aristotle's work become available, this logic becomes the *organon*, the instrument, of judging truth from falsehood. This logic remains grounded in the old Aristotelian logic of necessity of harmony, positing truth as non-contradiction, and positing the absurdity of infinite regression be resolved by a Prime Mover.

Kimball points to considerable ambivalence in the 12th century regarding the meaning of philosophy, and the *artes liberales*. The term *moderni* gradually becomes used to describe those who embrace the new Aristotelian logic, but with it comes a certain suspicion that they were throwing aside education in the classical or rhetorical tradition, and casting the *authores* adrift. As such, 'liberal education and its rationale were being transformed.'[2] As John of Salisbury laments, he who eliminates eloquence from the study of philosophy 'destroys *omni liberalia studia.*'[3] At stake here is the definition of a liberal arts education, important because its definition would determine its relationship to theology. If it was grounded in the new logic, the new kind of philosophy, then, the method of knowing truth might be separated from revelation as a truth in its own right. If it held allegiance to a more Platonic metaphysics it could be because it was suspicious of the new logic becoming a heterodoxy, choosing instead to give emphasis to revelation over reason.[4] In the end, the question of whether liberal arts prioritised reason over revelation, or revelation over reason, became less important than the reaction against its neglect of the classical authors, a reaction against intellectualism per se, and a demand for a return to the rhetorical and ethical tradition.

The battle of the books and the ambivalence of method

Latin antiquity is key in perpetuating and reinforcing the Isocratean version of liberal education. Platonic metaphysics and Aristotelian logic were not excluded, but, says Kimball, Roman liberal education and liberal education for 500 years or more 'involved something very different from the pursuit of critical speculation and learned contemplation.'[5] Learning in the Middle Ages 'had its foundation in Roman, and not in Greek antiquity,'[6] not least because during this period 'the Latin West was largely cut off from the richer Greek tradition.'[7] The 12th century challenged the domination of the rhetorical tradition, where *antiqui* came to refer to the classical education of Latin and Greek authors, and *moderni* to the new Aristotle. By the 13th century the battle of the books was being fought, symbolised in d'Andeli's poem where Orleans, the centre for classical study, fought with Paris which moved with the times and turned to the new Aristotle. The 'humanistic studies'[8] defended themselves against 'the labyrinth of Aristotle.'[9] While Paetow blames the *ars dictaminis*, law, philosophy of nature and medicine for the decline in interest in the classics, Kimball notes the paradox of grammar, rising in popularity through the *grammatica speculativa* – the search for universal grammar – alongside a declining interest in the traditional grammatical handbooks of Priscian and Donatus. In d'Andeli's poem logic defeats grammar. The tide of interest in Aristotle 'was irresistible and easily swept away all obstacles.'[10] Kimball's conclusion here is that philosophy now rises above rhetoric, and 'the concern for moral training is de-emphasised, while rhetoric practically drops from sight...Grammar is even more sharply torn from classical writings and transformed into a linguistic and formalised tool for specialized research.'[11]

D'Andeli's poem *The Battle of the Arts* (c. 13th century) laments the victory of logic, blaming divinity for abandoning study and retiring to France for the wine, leaving education dominated by argument, by Scholastic dialectic, and the new Aristotelianism.[12] John of Salisbury joined the lament: 'whereas dialectic furthers other studies, so if it remain by itself it lies bloodless and barren.'[13] On one level logic as intellectualism comes to dominate teaching in the newly forming guilds or universities at the cost of grammar and literature. Ethics and metaphysics 'attained the status of elective courses only.'[14] By the middle of the 13th century the writings of Aristotle became 'the basis of philosophical instruction at the universities.'[15] This new intellectualism would, in time, move from the books to the arena of experience and observation. In this respect, Aristotle provides a 'notion of a science as an organised body of knowledge with its own defining principles and conclusions.'[16]

In a sense, the later phase of his own philosophy, the one which prioritises empirical experience and observation over Platonic speculation, the one in which there is no corner of nature where 'one cannot find absence of haphazard and conduciveness of everything to an end,'[17] usurps those who worshipped Aristotle's written word as if it were sacred. This is the beginning of the end of the vision of speculative first principles that can explain everything regardless of the appearance of the universe, and the emergence of rational self-defining intellectual principles of academic subjects. Despite papal bans on aspects of Aristotelian metaphysics and other paganisms, philosophy becomes increasingly dominant,[18] and the main disciplines each begin 'the gradual formation of an established body of texts and authorities.'[19] Gradually in the 14th century the old ways of philosophical speculation on overarching first principles give way to 'a more restricted view of epistemology, bounded by more strictly defined notions of evidence and demonstration.'[20] In time this leads to separate arts faculties and separate chairs in order to represent the growing areas of specialism.[21] Albertus Magnus and Thomas Aquinas distinguish the separate territories of theology and philosophy, and this helps to establish the autonomy of each as subjects in their own right. Now philosophy in particular is free to reason merely from scientific principles, that is, from rational first principles and not from scriptural authority.

Gilson argues that education here loses itself somewhat to intellectualism as method, for example, in the way the popularity of the question as a method of teaching enacts a 'technical'[22] approach to university education. Indeed, Aristotle's natural philosophy brings about 'a new and universally applicable method.'[23] Dialectics is seen as a shortcut to the thinking of first principles in the arts. It is 'the art of arts.'[24] This, in turn, re-defines art, science, teaching and learning into the one activity of teachable method, laying down the doctrines of principles and causes. 'For the schoolmen the best method of teaching was a reasonable re-creation of the original discovery. Thus the order of teaching (*ordo doctrinae*) was said to follow the order of discovery (*ordo inventionis*).'[25] Theology, like the other arts, assumes the shape of 'an objective exposition and interpretation.'[26] Each art/science becomes 'impersonally teachable.'[27] This leaves behind the educational ambiguities of *The Confessions* and the *Commedia* and moves to a scholasticism of rational self-evident principles and demonstrable natural cause and effect. Gilson suggests that Aquinas plays his part in this development by accepting 'the general notion of science, the empiricism and the intellectualism'[28] of Aristotle. Ballard argues that the Renaissance was the rebirth of ignorance, casting the long shadow of science over the trivial arts, and bringing about the division of the two cultures – humanities and sciences. The sciences, he says, fail to integrate themselves within liberal learning and remain abstract.[29]

Richard McKeon argues that intellectualism in liberal arts education takes a new form in the Renaissance. While medieval liberal arts are universal disciplines that apply to any subject matter, Renaissance liberal arts are particular subject areas. This is a reaction against the way that universal disciplines, or necessities, tended 'to become universal, abstract, verbal and to lose connection with the particularities of circumstances, subject matters, and problems.'[30] Nevertheless, these 'subjects' take it upon themselves to offer methods 'capable of universalization in organizing and ordering the subject matters of all arts and sciences.'[31] By the 20th century, these have become fragmented from each other and have lost connection to the 'common problems and matters of daily life,'[32] something, he says, whose implications 'we are still engaged in working out.'[33]

Humanism

The dualism of the iron fist and open palm has its most distinctive shape in the Renaissance in the opposition between scholasticism and humanism. Campana argues that *umanista* appears in Latin only in the second half of the 15th century and in Italian only in the 1530s. Those who revived classical learning in the 13th century reverted to Cicero's phrase *studia humanitatis* to collect together those studies 'which integrate and perfect the human mind and which are therefore the only ones worthy of man.'[34] Campana shows that the term 'humanist' has its roots firmly in education. It describes a teacher of classical literature, a chair of *humanitas*, and also a student of classical learning. In carrying the two elements of education – teacher and student – the 'humanist' also carries the ambivalence of the master/slave relation in Roman *humanitas*, even though '*umanista*' is restricted in Renaissance Italy to the practice of education in Renaissance schools.[35] Campana argues for keeping the term 'humanist' within this limited and technical sense of teacher/student.

Dante's book on *Monarchy* illustrates some Renaissance thinking on the quality and quantity of humanity. The human race as a whole has an essential nature which no single person, household, city or kingdom can achieve. This essence is the potential intellect which is only found in the great variety of potential pertaining to the vast number of human beings in the human race. Here Dante conjoins the universal or theoretical with the particular or practical, or with the actualisation of the potential. Thus, the 'activity proper to mankind as a whole is constantly to actualize the full intellectual potential of humanity, primarily through thought and secondarily through action ... [and] it is apparent that mankind most freely and readily attends to this activity ... in the calm or tranquillity of [universal] peace.'[36]

Dante argues that 'mankind is most a unity when it is drawn together to form a single entity ... by one ruler.'[37] Mankind 'is in its ideal state when it is completely free.'[38] Freedom is the greatest gift God has bestowed on human nature[39] but only when 'living under a monarch, is it supremely free.'[40] He concludes, 'Mankind exists for its own sake and not for the sake of something else only when it is under the rule of a monarch, for only then are perverted forms of government (i.e. democracies, oligarchies and tyrannies) which force mankind into slavery, set right.'[41] This is a view also found in the *Convivio*: 'to perfect the universal social ordering of the human species, there must be one individual, who should possess ... universal and undisputed authority ... the Emperor ... and his word is law and should be obeyed by all.'[42]

Dante's difficulty here is that he is working with the Aristotelian logic of necessity of non-composite and harmonious first principles translated into the changeable sphere of human political culture. It requires positing the monarch as the first principle of all the people, or as the harmony of *humanitas*. He argues that the love of the monarch works only for the good and freedom of the people. The contradiction between divine harmony and its being enacted on earth leads him to suggest that, 'although a consul or a king are masters over others with respect to means, with respect to ends they are the servants of others; and this is especially true of the monarch, who is considered without doubt the servant of all men.'[43] Gilson says of humanity in Dante that 'If the *genus humanum* ("human race") of Dante is really the first known expression of the modern idea of Humanity, we may say that the conception of Humanity first presented itself to the European consciousness merely as a secularised imitation of the religious notion of a church'[44] or as freedom under the authority of a humanistic monarch who is 'the spiritual father of mankind,'[45] and compelled to practice charity and justice. Authority over mankind is, at one and the same time, servant of humanity. It is in the ambiguities of this relation of master and slave that eventually the hierarchy of the ancient logic of necessity yields to a modern logic of freedom in equality.

The influx of new translations in the Renaissance period creates a new front for the dualism of philosophy and the ideal of humanity carried in the rhetorical or *artes liberales* tradition. The latter is reinvented as the *studia humanitatis*, while the *via moderna* is the new Aristotelian philosophy. In addition, Kristeller also suggests that the liberal arts and the philosophical and scientific disciplines compete with the *authores* of the great Latin texts. Either way, classical learning is re-formed into the humanist revival of Latin and Greek texts which stands opposed to the dominance of Aristotelian philosophy in the universities. As such, Kristeller argues that Renaissance humanism 'must be understood as a characteristic phase in what may be called the rhetorical tradition in Western culture.'[46] Cicero is seen by the humanists as something of a synthesis between wisdom and rhetoric to the extent that 'Renaissance humanism was an age of Ciceronianism.'[47]

The humanists oppose 'the culture of scholasticism'[48] and deplore its approach to learning and scholarship as merely over-specialised and pedantic, and its 'taking refuge in an esoteric jargon.'[49] Petrarch provides evidence of the way in which the decline of liberal arts is perceived by the emerging humanist movement. In a letter to Francesco Nelli (Simonides), Prior of the Church of the Holy Angels in Florence, Petrarch bemoans the decline of the pursuit of virtue into the new necessity of a set of technical skills. There are the dialecticians who sacrifice virtue for victory in syllogistic skill; the mathematicians and geometricians who measure everything except their souls; the musicians who pursue sounds rather than morals; and the philosophers who seek the causes but not the creator of all things. 'Finally, note the great fall of those who also usurped a more noble name and professed a knowledge of divine things: instead of theologians, they are dialecticians, sophists at that; instead of lovers of God they are knowers of God.'[50] This latter is a 'corrupt vanity.'[51] Against this, the humanists believe learning should deal primarily with the social relation, with learning that moulds human character through moral purpose; an education in which

> learning was translated into positive and active practice and conduct, whether of the citizen and participant in public life, of the private individual seeking both cultivation and ethical conduct, or of the scholar, philosopher, and teacher. Knowledge should have to do with human life and how it should be lived, not with spinning out abstractions remote from the concerns of life in the world.[52]

Kimball finds Renaissance humanism here to be the retrieval of the tradition of rhetorical humanism, noting that the humanists label the period which lacked classical education the 'middle' between the glory of Rome and its modern Renaissance. What unites the Renaissance humanists 'was primarily their common commitment to an educational ideal based on the classical literature of antiquity, especially the writings of Cicero and Quintilian.'[53] Humanism here is traced back to classical *paideia* via Varro, and the *studia humanitatis* is equated with the *artes liberales* which 'by the 15th century, had come to mean the disciplines of grammar, rhetoric, poetry, and history, often combined with moral philosophy.'[54] It continues the educational ideal of the (open palm of) 'refinement of human personality'[55] that characterised ancient virtue, in contrast to the scholastics who continue to concentrate on (the iron fist of) philosophy and logic.

The *studia humanitatis* also begins to dominate the curriculum of the grammar schools which prepared for University entry. In these schools, 'Under the influence of Renaissance humanism, grammar came to mean training in both language and literature more and more often including Greek in addition to Latin as time passed. In grammar and in rhetoric, which followed, the universal paragons were Cicero and Quintilian.'[56] However, a sign of impending change was that, while the grammar school student could thereafter study the arts at University, the Faculty of Arts 'especially in Germany, was coming to be called the faculty of philosophy.'[57]

In addition, civic humanism challenges the contemplative life of the medieval university, and the newly emergent self-confident 'international republic of learning'[58] is restless in its dependency upon ecclesiastical authority.[59] A new professional class has increasingly secular humanist interests, reflecting on human political society and educating its future leaders. The earthly world here is growing separate from the world beyond. In addition, Plato is rediscovered; poetry, art, sculpture, architecture and music are retrieved, even if they are not ascribed to liberal arts; books are printed; America is 'discovered'; and in cosmology, the Earth is 'asked to waive the tremendous privilege of being the centre of the universe.'[60]

By the mid-1400s humanism was finds its way into 'all areas of Renaissance culture'[61] including philosophy. Humanist teachers effect a humanist secondary education for most scholars including those who would become philosophers. Even though humanists are not philosophers, 'both traditions developed side-by-side [in Italy].'[62] After the Renaissance, Aristotelianism is displaced by modern science and modern philosophy, and humanism 'became gradually detached from its rhetorical background and evolved into modern philosophy and history.'[63]

Renaissance subjectivity, history and universalism

The Renaissance also demonstrates the tension between discipline and freedom in the emerging sense of self-awareness in the Renaissance individual. This has significance too for the Renaissance notion of 'history' in which humanism reconciles the parts – the different ages of history – within the harmony of the 'whole' of human history.

If *paideia* is the beginning of Western human being becoming the object of its own thinking, creating culture from out of nature, the Renaissance has its own version of this self-awareness. Kristeller observes something similar in the meaning that humanists give to their own activities, in terms of it being a 'renaissance.' This term has a subjective meaning for them, for they recognise that they are involved in a 'revival or rebirth of the arts.'[64] If the ancient ideal of the rhetorician includes the creativity required in interpreting and communicating wisdom, this is part of the subjectivity that Renaissance humanism rediscovers.

This subjectivity has one of its most profound expressions in the concern for the education most befitting the idea of the human being. This is a continuity with Jaeger's conception of *paideia*, including expressing the universalism of *humanitas*. Petrarch calls on Seneca and Augustine for the idea that 'nothing except the soul is worthy of wonder.'[65] Ficino's revival of Platonism, and of Platonic love, re-values both the conception and the dignity of human being. In addition, Ficino expresses the universalism of *humanitas* as 'the conscious awareness of a solidarity of all men which imposed definite moral and intellectual obligations upon each individual.'[66] Demonstrably 'a humane man [should] persevere in the service of humanity [because] . . . individual men, formed by one idea in the same image, are one man.'[67] As such, 'of all the virtues, wise men named only one after man himself: that is humanity.'[68] Pompanazzi revives the Aristotelian virtues, intellectual, practical and technical, arguing that in the rhetorical tradition practical virtue is the only one that belonged to man alone and which enabled his perfection while on earth. Pico della Mirandola holds that God's great gift to humankind was that it be 'the molder and maker'[69] of itself into whatever shape it prefers. There are here not just the standards for human conduct of each individual but also 'a very strong sense for human relationships and for the solidarity of mankind.'[70]

Robert Proctor takes this observation further. He argues that in antiquity human being looks for perfection in the external cosmos while the Renaissance individual looks for perfection within himself. The moulding and making of oneself is only possible 'if one posits the existence of an individual subjectivity which experiences its consciousness as an autonomous centre of thought and feeling which it can objectively act upon, and compared to other such autonomous centres of consciousness.'[71] As with Burckhardt's famous treatise on the birth of the individual in the Renaissance, so Proctor finds the development of 'a unique, autonomous, personal self.'[72] This is not, however, a revolution against the logic of the iron fist of necessity, only in the means for its achievement. Perfection, whether in the heavens or in the individual or in humanity, remains defined according to the ancient harmony of self-sufficient necessity. What is important here, however, is that it is from within subjectivity that reason will learn of freedom as thinking for-itself.

Despite this, Kristeller argues that the universalism of *humanitas* in the Renaissance is still most apparent in the universal man. There are treatises on the ideal gentleman and courtier, and the preferred forms of biography and letter writing illustrate the attention being given to individuality. The universal man, through study and writing, would have excellence in a variety of pursuits, and this was never more true than in art where the artist needed to combine 'moral stature and a general education with the technical competence appropriate for his profession.'[73]

In sum, Renaissance thought and literature aim at 'the expression of individual, subjective opinions, feelings, and experiences.'[74] However, this did not extend to an interest in being especially original. Authority lay with the classical authors, and quotation was a form of imitation used frequently in speeches and in writing. Even if great attention is paid here to the moral individual, the *uomo universale*, there is no great sense that this could be achieved by anything other than imitating the examples from antiquity. This morality is held to be best imbibed through its beautiful presentation in speeches and treatises which emphasise the mind or human virtues most perfectly. Even though it comes about essentially through literary and scholarly work, its universalism is carried in the continuity of human being from antiquity to the age of the Renaissance. Machiavelli, for example, in comparing the Roman Republic to contemporary ideas assumes that 'human beings are fundamentally the same at all times, and therefore it is possible to study the conduct of the ancients, to learn from their mistakes, from their achievements, and to follow their examples where they were successful.'[75]

There is also a sense of universalism, perfection, necessity and harmony in the view that Renaissance humanists have of their own place within a universal history.[76] Even though the retrieval of ancient authors had begun in the reign of Charlemagne, something new to Renaissance humanism is the idea of distinctions between ancient and modern, past and present, being assigned to different historical epochs. Petrarch is generally credited with giving rise to a view of European history that went from the civilisation of ancient Greece and Rome to a dark age, an age of 'barbarism, ignorance, low culture.'[77] Mommsen notes a changed conception of the metaphor of darkness and light here. After the death of Christ the medieval historians of the Holy Roman Empire used darkness to describe the pagan civilisation of ancient Greece and Rome up to the reign of Augustus. They contrasted this with the light brought by Christ into the world. The Renaissance reversed this. It labelled as dark anything after Greece and Rome and before the 1300s, dark because all the great literature was lost and dark because ancient freedoms had been replaced by tyranny. In a letter of 1359 Petrarch distinguishes ancient pagan history from the history of the Christian Roman Empire, an epoque which he called an era of *tenebrae* or darkness. He sees his own time as 'modern' but still part of the decline of the Roman Empire. He is pessimistic that things will return to the golden age of antiquity, but still hopes that 'there will follow a better age...When the darkness has been dispersed, our descendants can come again in the form of pure radiance.'[78] There is here a delineation of ancient, modern and future times, where the modern corresponds to a middle age. Petrarch laments the neglect of the ancient writers by later generations which have 'robbed posterity of its ancestral heritage.'[79] But this whole view of history as having a necessity or *telos* of universality is itself grounded in the Aristotelian logic of first causes. The golden age of antiquity serves to block any infinite regression that a search for historical origins might throw up – a block that is still employed today when trying to avoid the implications for Western identity of contingency upon prior traditions and civilisations.

Bruni's *History of the Florentine People* also displays universalism in the humanist conception of history, one which 'has dominated European historiography ever since.'[80] It is a tripartite division into ancient, medieval and modern periods, the latter beginning with the demise of the Holy Roman Empire and the beginning of the emergence of national states. A similar delineation of history is attempted by Vasari in his *Lives of the Artists* (1563). He differentiates between the arts of antiquity, the decline in the dark ages and the renaissance of the arts. Here too he draws attention to a universalism, observing this same pattern or necessity in other fields of learning, suggesting a relationship between all the liberal arts.[81]

Richard McKeon draws attention to the work of Jean Bodin (1529–96) whose art of history sought to place a universalism of *humanitas* over and above the laws of individual republics. Bodin is of particular interest here because he returns to Plato's threefold model of philosophy, something which will be important for us in Parts II and III. Bodin defines history as 'the true narration of things,'[82] and divides it into three relations of the human, the natural and the divine, of which history is respectively probable, inevitable and holy, and whose virtues are prudence, science and faith. Together they provide for true wisdom. He rejects the philological exposition of laws and returns to first principles, a rejection that is, of style for substance. Again of interest is that philosophy and the rhetorical tradition are conjoined in the nature of the three philosophies. His art of history is grounded in the metaphysics of the question which arises when human beings, struggling for self-preservation, experience the 'awe of nature's workings.'[83] Bodin states that from this awe mankind seeks to understand causes, or first principles, which takes it to the question of God and to the idea of truth in contemplation. But Bodin has a pedagogical point to make here which establishes contemplation as an education in the relation between truth and thought, matter and mind, and master and slave. Philosophers can never totally overcome the mediation of the senses. As such, they should not teach as if they had overcome human affairs or natural science. From the other direction, first-time learners move from human affairs on earth to the natural causes that exceed the earth, to the order and harmony – first principles – of the universe; 'so that by these steps we may sometime return to that intimate relationship which we have with God to the original source of our kind, and again be united closely to Him.'[84]

Melanchthon (1497–1560) also seeks to negotiate the necessity of philosophical first principles with the freedom of rhetorical liberal arts education. He not only reforms the University of Wittenberg in the 1530s, but he does so by combining humanism, civic humanism, philosophy and theology into a liberal arts education. He writes textbooks on Latin and Greek grammar, rhetoric, dialectic, moral philosophy and natural philosophy. His inaugural speech at Wittenberg, 'On Correcting the Studies of Youth,' confirms a commitment to restoring classical learning and to driving out scholasticism. Thereafter he rebuilds the liberal arts curriculum.[85] He defends the seven liberal arts arguing that the lower faculty is a necessary preparation for higher faculties, and especially for theology. He sees the liberal arts as gifts from God, given so that He might be known through his wondrous creation. Languages are needed for any understanding at all, requiring grammar and eloquence; dialectics is the road to truth provided it avoids scholastic or sophistical quarrelling and remains connected to Aristotelian logic and method; arithmetic and geometry are the sciences by which God created the universe, and as such they are 'the wings of the human mind,'[86] lifting it to the truth of the heavens; astronomy is what men were given eyes for when lifted from material pursuits.[87] It seems music was more of a school subject than a university subject. The three philosophies also feature in this curriculum. As well as dialectics, natural philosophy offers an understanding of the nature of man, of God and of the good. As such, it is important for moral philosophy, which is itself of divine significance, to reveal the truth of men's lives 'restrained by civic discipline.'[88] The Gospel remains 'the forgiveness of sins and the promise of reconciliation and eternal life for the sake of Christ, and human reason by itself cannot apprehend any of these.'[89] But within the liberal arts and the three philosophies, and within theology too, there is an overwhelming importance attached to education as the preparation for and practice of humanity. 'By these subjects the mind will be shaped towards both pleasantness and humanity,'[90] and the professional without such studies is 'without any humanity.'[91] Philosophy, and ethics in particular, is 'the workshop of humanity.'[92] The teaching of virtue is 'to be called humanity.'[93] His educational philosophy warns that 'if the arts I have recounted here were to be consigned to oblivion and annihilated, it would be sadder than if the sun were taken from the world.'[94]

* * *

In sum, Renaissance (rhetorical) humanism sets itself against the dialectical scholasticism of speculative and universalist Aristotelian philosophy and method and accepts instead rigorous rational interpretation grounded in observation and experience delineated into separate subject disciplines. But the logic on which validity or truth are based does not change. The sovereignty of an ineffable first cause is not challenged, nor is the ancient logic of non-contradiction or of harmony as self-sufficient necessity. The methods of achieving harmony change, but the goals do not. Even in the fragmentation of speculative unity into a variety of academic subjects, the idea of what counts as truth – the simple, tranquil, non-composite, non-contingent necessity – is unmoved.

The battle of the books continues through the Renaissance and the Reformation, where the *antiqui* of classical education opposes the *moderni* of the new Aristotelian translations of logic and philosophy. Kimball names Petrarch as the key player in retrieving the *studia humanitatis* from Cicero and Gellius, which would culminate in a humanist curriculum of grammar, rhetoric, poetry, history and moral philosophy. Vergerio, da Feltre, Valla, Erasmus, Vives, Melanchthon and Luther all give priority to liberal training over scholastic logic and philosophy and aim at the 'continual refinement of the human personality.'[95] Thomas Elyot's *The Book named the Governor* (1531) combines knightly valour, humanism and Christianity into the ideal of the 'gentleman.' His education included Erasmus, Quintilian, Cicero and Isocrates. This was the kind of model of the gentleman that would cross the Atlantic to the colonial colleges in the 17th century, where Kimball finds the seven ideal characteristics of liberal arts in the early Harvard, Yale, and William and Mary Colleges.

4
Bildung and the New Age

Thomas Mann defined *Bildung* in the following way:

> The inwardness, the culture (*Bildung*) of a German implies introspec-
> tiveness; an individualistic cultural conscience; consideration for the
> careful tending, the shaping, deepening and perfecting of one's own
> personality or, in religious terms, for the salvation and justification
> of one's own life; subjectivism in the things of the mind, therefore, a
> type of culture that might be called pietistic, given to autobiograph-
> ical confession and deeply personal, one in which the world of the
> *objective*, the political world, is felt to be profane and is thrust aside
> with indifference.[1]

But how does this deeply personal and individualistic education relate
to the universal idea of humanity, to the notion of neohumanism and
to the ancient logic of necessity of first principles?

The neohumanist concept of *Bildung* once again throws into sharp
relief the themes being pursued here in Part I, namely the dualism of discipline and freedom. In this chapter discipline refers to the traditional
authority of universal and eternal truths which will in time come to
be associated with the classical curricula that, as we saw above, previ-
ously opposed inclusion within scholastic Aristotelian form. Freedom
now refers to the emancipation of the critical individual mind from
accepted truths and dogmas. This is one of the modern versions of the
dualism of *ars and liberalis*. It still has its source in the ancient logic of
necessity as harmony and unity, even when (as we will see in Parts II
and III) it is opposed to this necessity. *Bildung*, in particular, carries the
difficulty of the dualism, especially in trying to reconcile the perfection
of the inner person with the harmony of virtuous social relations. It also

unfolds the contradictions that will educate modern consciousness to a modern logic of necessity, and thereafter a modern conception of liberal arts education. I will explore *Bildung* now in Humboldt, Herder and Hegel, and very briefly in Fichte, Kant and Gadamer.

Wilhelm von Humboldt (1767–1835)

Humboldt's concern was that 'a great deal is achieved around us, but only little improved within us.'[2] In his *Limits of State Action* (1791–92) he fuses Stoicism, aesthetics, Rousseauian education and sociological insight to create a version of neohumanism encompassed in the term *Bildung*.[3] In it he advocates an inner development grounded in freedom and spontaneity, one that has its roots in the ancient logic of necessity as harmony, tranquillity and moderation in all things. Nevertheless, it is the role of *Bildung* to hold in tension two elements which have a spontaneous reciprocity. On the one hand, there is the inner formation of the individual self, constituted by self-mastery, freedom of the individual and the growth of an inner harmony that is an end in-itself. On the other hand, this inner harmony needs social relations of a kind that will allow it to express itself as also in harmony with what lies outside. At the heart of *Bildung* here is the synthesis of inner and outer, creating true originality, for the man of *Bildung* knows 'his way of life is harmoniously in keeping with his character.'[4] Only in expending his energy into the social world, with others, could an individual achieve self-perfection or inner harmony. Achieving 'unity in diversity'[5] lay at the heart of Humboldt's *Bildung*. He meant by *Bildung* 'the fullest, richest, and most harmonic development of the potentialities of the individual, the community or the human race.'[6]

Humboldt discerns humanism here in both quality and quantity. State control can reduce individuals to 'an agglomerated mass of living but lifeless instruments of action and enjoyment, rather than a multitude of active and enjoying energies.'[7] The individual should not be subordinated to the citizen. Instead, the human being should think of and work on 'his own character as though it were a free-standing work of art.'[8] This is the quality of humanism. With regard to quantity, the inner life is inauthentic if it is solipsistic. Inner harmony draws individual humanity towards others such that they 'flow together into a single complete whole in which individuality is resolved.'[9] Man is 'naturally more disposed to beneficent than selfish actions'[10] and the man who is his own work of art, 'suffused by a deep feeling for his own individuality [is also] deeply familiar with the universal ideal of humanity.'[11] The quality of humanism, the one found in the universal quantity of all, is the absolute standard of humanity.

> Since it is supposed to apply to all men, it must be something general,[12] but since it cannot be anyone's serious intention to make all the different human natures over into a single model, it must not violate the differences between individuals. It must therefore be something which always remains one and the same, but which may be carried out in manifold ways.[13]

This contains the fundamental ambiguity of the relation between (the freedom of) the I and (the discipline of) the We, the one and the whole, that has accompanied *humanitas* from its inception. *Bildung* 'elevates humanity in general and strengthens each particular individuality, and does this in all men regardless of character differences.'[14] This is 'the spirit of humanity,'[15] and the greatest human being is 'consequently he who represents the concept of humanity in its greatest strength and widest extent. To judge a man means nothing other than to ask: what content does he give to the form of humanity?'[16] From this, Humboldt concludes that 'the universal law...that reason dictates to all human community is this: each man and each community must respect the morality and culture of the other.'[17] And of himself Humboldt wrote, 'I am a thoroughly inward-oriented person whose entire effort goes to transform the world in its most manifold shapes into his own solitude.'[18]

This is no longer a *humanitas* based on slavery; it is possible for all men. All men have sensuous impressions which act spontaneously upon the soul, animating it to reconcile the inner and outer in a harmony grounded in this free spontaneity. The visible and invisible worlds combine in an aesthetic that is home to the harmonious and the tranquil. Man 'creates an image in the depths of his creative imagination which he then works to give validity to in his inner and outer life alike.'[19] As the man changes, so does the state in which he lives. The role of the state is not to give priority to any particular interpretation of this harmony, but rather to 'produce a balance'[20] between itself and the individual in order to effect a balance between the individual and his external life. This balance is tranquillity found in 'the proportion that exists between his energies and the sum of his inclinations.'[21]

For Humboldt, the discovery of God is an important contribution to the history of *Bildung*. Spontaneously, sensuous religion is hope and dread. But when culture (*Kultur*) emerges, then the soul has a new idea of perfection in something outside itself. This wonder develops the

religious idea. When this religious feeling becomes 'true spiritual culture' (*wahrer geistiger Bildung*)²² then purpose replaces senseless chance.
This *Bildung* has a stoical flavour; man's 'unalterable dependence on
external fate no longer daunts him... and no freak of destiny can disturb the calm, inner life of the soul.'²³ But religion is not necessary for
Bildung, here, and its efficacy depends on the character of each individual. The state, like marriage, will be transformed by the self-educating
individual, to which the state must fit itself, rather than fitting the person to the state. Humboldt's school reforms therefore aim at 'a general
education in an atmosphere of freedom.'²⁴

Sorkin comments that the duality of inner and outer in *Bildung*
has its roots in 18th-century German Pietism's conception of the relation between moral character and good works. It was secularised by
Shaftesbury and Rousseau, both of whom treat the relation of the I and
the We as an educational tension. Humboldt's *Bildung* is neohumanist
in holding the inner education of the individual to be a means of self-
improvement and in demanding that self-improvement have actuality
in the social world as moral action.²⁵ *Bildung* brings civic humanism
to state humanism. But, for Sorkin, as the nationalistic demands on
German education grew after defeats by Napoleon, so the humanistic prioritisation of individual over citizen was reversed, and *Bildung*
became both a state training and an elitism. An example, over 100 years
later, might be Abraham Flexner who aligns *Bildung* with the educated
elite of Oxford and Cambridge 'who have governed England and the
dominions honestly, efficiently, and like gentleman.'²⁶

Johann Gottfried von Herder (1744–1803)

Herder speaks of three kinds of inner *Bildung*: the earliest is a
Rousseauian type of natural education, teaching 'freedom and dependence on oneself'²⁷ by means of 'uncompelled self-observation, and
independence from other's judgements';²⁸ the second is a moral *Bildung*
which should not preach virtue to an individual's understanding but
'only to his conscience,'²⁹ in order to learn morals from hearts and not
from antiquity; third, political *Bildung* requires education for citizenship
and patriotism. He adds a note too on the importance of women being
educated, learning 'to feel virtue.'³⁰

This subjectivism is further emphasised in his theory of language
which relativises ideas and concepts to their own time and form of
expression. Together, his relativising of morality and language upon sentiments and sensations gives rise to a specific form of *Bildung* as inner

development. This has its roots in Shaftesbury's notion of inner form which was translated into German as *Bildung*. Herder emphasises the inner as the site of the growth and development of the human being. He means to show 'what man should become'[31] and takes from Kant both a new science of what individuals can become and a new philosophy of what humankind can become.[32] But he was suspicious of too great an emphasis on the nature of mere speculation. Herder criticises Kant for 'having left out a third great exemplar of "human philosophy," the Earl of Shaftesbury.'[33] As such, for Herder right or moral action depended on arousing the appropriate sentiments in the individual and this would contribute towards 'the ultimate goal: the *Bildung* of humanity.'[34] The idea that rational first principles could achieve morality in each person is an illusion. It is a mistake to think that ideas have such influence. It is a delusion for ideas to believe that 'they form "humanity." '[35]

But Herder's notion of *humanitas* exhibits an ambivalence that comes across in his *This too a Philosophy of History for the Formation of Humanity* (1774). Herder gives credence to the idea that humankind is developing from the childlike patriarchal authority of the Orient, the boyhood of the Egyptians and Phoenicians, the youth of Greece, the manhood of Rome, and the northern invasions which stood between the Romans and the Enlightenment Europeans. It is in opening up the conceit of the latter that Herder displays the ambiguities of *humanitas*. From the barbarian, the Christian and the scholastics comes the idea of brotherhood, higher and more abstract than at any previous time. But such a conception of *humanitas* also betrays its arrogance and conceit. For one thing, perhaps the passage of history is due not to humanity, but to a mechanics of all forms of social life, in which the individual is little more than a puppet. This over-rationalising of the modern age may mean that a form of humanity is being lost, that of 'inclination, drive, activity for living.'[36] The Greeks spoke 'in an applied way, every word had a role.'[37] However, the moderns speak of 100 human races at once 'so as to say for each of them nothing.'[38] As Nietzsche conveys so powerfully 100 years later, so Herder says, 'Dear, weak, annoying, useless free thinking – substitute for everything that they perhaps needed more; heart!, warmth!, blood!, humanity!, life!'[39] The arrogance of the idea of enlightenment as the zenith of humanity, the idea that it has exhausted 'all common principles of what is right and good... for all times and peoples'[40] defeats itself. To suppose there is more virtue now than there ever was in the whole world, 'I believe that just for that reason there must be less.'[41]

But perhaps of most significance is Herder's treatment of the ambivalence in enlightenment reason regarding its claims to universality. For example, 'between every universally stated, even the most beautiful, truth and its least application there is a gulf.'[42] More powerfully still, actions justified in the universal interest suffer through 'a natural law of the imperfection of human beings';[43] with thrift comes poverty, with philosophy comes unbelief, with 'freedom in thought always slavery in action.'[44] Asked what effect 'love of humankind, justice, moderation, religion, well-being of subjects'[45] will have on posterity and which way they will tip the scales, Herder says, 'how do I know?'[46] And in the separation of the universal and particular achieved within modernity, the gap is so large that Herder is forced to ask whether a 'Socrates of humanity'[47] is any longer possible. The Socrates of modernity plays on a stage so much bigger than the Socrates of Athens that any relationship between individual virtue and the idea of universal truth are stretched beyond breaking point. A modern Socrates would need to be at the heights of Newton, effecting the whole human spirit, raising the whole species. But such nobility and wisdom would require Socrates to take flight to the heavens. For posterity he would not just be a single name, but an 'angel of God'[48] to his own age and to future ages. Such a messenger would understand the operations of fate over rationalised outcomes. But if all this sounds too unlikely, Herder's message remains clear: 'do not despair in the dregs of the age!, whatever may threaten and impede you – educate.'[49] It will be hard, harder than educating, where 'all ethics are the same and all equally even, right, and good.'[50] It requires 'the shining star in the night'[51] who can educate and form humankind for a virtue that is 'quiet, reticent, mostly unrecognized, but so high, so fast spreading!'[52] It is nobler 'to sow into hiddenness and the whole wide world without oneself expecting a harvest . . . entrust the seed to the wafting zephyr.'[53]

Immanuel Kant (1724–1804) and Johann Gottlieb Fichte (1762–1814)

Kant's idea of *Bildung* appears within the tension between discipline and freedom (as does his distinction between subsumptive and reflective judgements). His use of *Bildung*, in distinction from *Erziehung* and *Kultur*, contains elements of the *humanitas* explored above. Discipline, care, instruction, culture and development (*entwickelt*) are all able to contribute to the essence of education, which is formation or *Bildung*. Only *Bildung* achieves the formation of the moral citizen, the person who understands the cosmopolitan nature of the highest good. Discipline and instruction can take the place of the wild in human nature, while culture can replace the rule; but it is *Bildung* that unfolds the universal good that forms the human spirit. Scholastic formation (*Scholastischen Bildung*) teaches the principle of the individual in-itself; prudential formation (*Bildung zur Klugheit*) teaches the individual to be a citizen; moral formation (*Moralische Bildung*) elicits the value of 'the entire human race.'[54] This *humanitas* is grounded in 'common human understanding'[55] learned through the necessity of rational principles, within the freedom of Socratic learning, rather than heteronomous discipline. Kant notes too that he lived in an age of discipline, training and culture 'but not by any means'[56] in an age of *Bildung* or moral formation. Lacking this, he wondered whether mankind would not be happier in a raw political state.

Fichte even more clearly employs the ancient logic and discipline of necessity to ground his idea of the education of mankind.[57] In the fourth lecture on the *Purpose of Higher Education* he outlines a theory of inner education arriving at harmony. There is a 'feeling for truth in all human beings,'[58] but its development requires the scholar whose vocation is 'the teacher of humanity.'[59] It is the vocation of all human beings to understand how the self is determined in relation to the alien which exists outside the self. This relation is sensuous and also rational; while the empirical self is changeable and therefore empirical, the pure self is unchangeable, it is the true self. 'The ultimate vocation, then, of all finite rational beings is absolute unity, constant identity, and complete agreement with themselves.'[60] This requires that all human faculties 'should be in perfect harmony with each other.'[61] In turn, this requires that external things should be modified in order that they too 'will harmonise with the pure form of the Self.'[62] The modification of the external self, and the empirical self, in pursuit of such harmony is 'culture' (*Kultur*).[63] The goal is the 'complete identity of a rational being with itself,'[64] for one exists 'to become morally ever more perfect, to improve the world around one's self physically and, with regard to society, morally.'[65] This means that the natural should become subject to rational human laws.

Hans-Georg Gadamer (1900–2002)

I include Gadamer here not only because he provides one of the most interesting philosophical descriptions of *Bildung* at the start of *Truth and Method*, discussing broadly the humanism and human sciences of the 19th century but also because his comments take us back to Hegel. Taking up the creativity of humanism, Gadamer sees the human sciences not seeking instances of general rule, but as a more artistic instinctive induction that, in Herder's phrase, knows to reach up to humanity. This reaching up becomes encapsulated in the 18th century as the concept of self-formation or cultivation, that is *Bildung*,[66] and it becomes the air breathed by 19th-century human sciences. The original use of *Bildung* had been to describe the appearance of a natural shape, for example, a well-formed body or a mountain range. From Humboldt came the use of *Bildung* to mean something more inward, something where knowledge and feeling shape character, in distinction from *Kultur* which is the development of talents and skills. Within the ancient logic of necessity, self-formation forms itself; it does not have its end in anything else, anything external. Gadamer turns to Hegel initially for the exemplar of *Bildung*. Taking a line very similar to that which Jaeger did regarding the Sophists, Gadamer sees Hegel arguing that humanity breaks with the immediacy of nature by means of self-consciousness and reason. *Bildung* is the becoming of this intellectual being, while the *ungebildet* individual has not raised itself to this rational state, nor, therefore, to reaching up to humanity. Being raised to the universal, out of nature, is the task that defines one's humanity. It requires the sacrifice of selfish desires, because freedom from the object of personal desire is freedom for the universal. The universal interest limits the particular, but since the individual gains humanity, it is not really a limitation at all.

Gadamer interprets Hegel here in terms of alienation and return. The intellectual attitude is already alienated from nature as it has nature as other or alien to it. The alienation from natural or immediate being means the mind being called into the social world of language, custom and social relations, a world which the student is now required to make his or her own. *Bildung* is this self-cultivation, out of the alien, and into the new human world. The move into the human world is no more than a 'return to itself from what is other.'[67] In leaving nature, humanity returns home, and the return journey is *Bildung*.

Gadamer goes this far with Hegel but no further. He finds in this humanism an openness of self to other, an openness akin to an aesthetic capacity, a *sensus communis*, an understanding of humanity which, from Shaftesbury, means 'love of the community or society, natural affection, humanity, obligingness.'[68] Gadamer argues that this openness to humanism was lost to the human sciences in the age of Goethe and Kant, and the German Enlightenment instead saw the 'emptying and intellectualising'[69] of the *sensus communis*.

This is part of the problem that Gadamer finds in Hegel's notion of alienation and return. For Gadamer, return in Hegel is too complete, too final, too finished. In Hegel, experience leads to 'a self-knowledge that no longer has anything different or alien to itself. For him the perfection of experience is "science", the certainty of itself in knowledge.'[70] For Gadamer, instead, complete experience does not mean that 'experience comes to an end in it and a higher form of knowledge is reached.'[71] As such, 'experience itself can never be a science.'[72] Gadamer's notion of experience is 'always open to new experiences'[73] while, he believes, Hegel's is not. As such, Gadamer's *gebildet* individual is a man of experience who is 'radically undogmatic,'[74] aware of human finitude, master neither of time nor of the future, knowing 'the limitedness of all prediction and the uncertainty of all plans.'[75] Gadamer's essay on *Bildung* traces its humanism as far back as the Sophists, including to the tension between Plato and Isocrates, exploring how this humanism is adapted to rhetoric, to the humanities and to 18th-century human sciences. As such, he sees *humanitas* as a continuity of the educational tradition of *artes liberales* from antiquity to the present day.

Georg Wilhelm Friedrich Hegel (1770–1831)

There are several aspects to Hegelian *Bildung*. First, as Gadamer noted, as a Head teacher in Nuremberg Hegel describes the process of education in which the young are drawn away from, or alienated from, a natural existence. Studying the world of antiquity, with its language and culture, is just such a way of removing students from their natural comfort zone. However, while antiquity is sufficiently unfamiliar to make students aware of their loss, it is also familiar enough to begin the journey of the students returning to their true life in human culture. Here, the students' self-formation will be an education in which they find themselves for the first time, each in their own individual truth. Formation here is estrangement from the self in order to return to the self differently. Like art, education in Hegel is seen as an improvement upon nature.

A long note on *Bildung* accompanies paragraph 187 in the *Philosophy of Right*. Here education is the journey from self-interest to the understanding that one's needs and their satisfaction are social affairs. The impossibility of getting everything one desires is a formative experience in the limits of universal freedom, in which the needs of the one are re-formed according to universal needs. In the *Philosophy of Right* this opposition is concrete in the 'dispassionate, upright, and polite demeanour'[76] of the civil servants who will have enjoyed a classical education, opposed to a mechanical education.[77] Against Gadamer's version of a closed education in Hegel, Hegel says the true vocation of education

(*Bildung*) is the liberation from nature and from the particular and is the work towards a higher education regarding the hard work of spiritual life.[78] The fact that it is such *hard work* is the reason why it is so unpopular.

But in order to understand the nature of such educational experiences one needs to turn to the *Phenomenology of Spirit*. Here subjectivity has the same experience of alienation, this time as the unhappy consciousness in which self-consciousness is separated from the pure divine mind, which is beyond it, and is forced to live as the composite earthly mind. The separation is *Bildung* because it is the alienation that will allow self-consciousness to re-discover its own truth, its own self. Self-consciousness will find itself for the first time in its own truth only because it has been torn from its immediate life. This is why, even though antiquity may be a wonderful resource for educating the modern mind, nevertheless it would be anachronistic to assume that one could be Platonic or Aristotelian again.[79] What self-consciousness will learn is that the two separate minds – man and God – have their *relation* in (and as) the subjectivity of the unhappy consciousness. As such, 'the goal of Culture is to produce a universal self-consciousness that has no *need* of that estranged selfhood standing at the seat of Judgement in the Beyond.'[80] This universal self-consciousness will be returned to itself in the Enlightenment, but will again have to suffer this seeming contradiction between thought and deed, or between private motive and public duty. This is the return of the question of the ambivalence of *humanitas*, but this time within the realm of modern reason.

There is one further meaning to draw upon here. In the *Philosophy of History* Hegel says that *Bildung* is related to form, and especially to the production of the form of universality, a production which is thought.[81] To think the truth of anything is its culture in the specific sense that it will be torn from its natural appearance and re-formed according to its being humanised or made known in-and-for-human thought. This re-formation is also the character of *Bildung*; for something to become a culture is for it to be re-formed in being known. This affects the unhappy consciousness just as much as it affects, say, democracy which is re-formed as non-democracy in measures that aim to protect it (e.g. from terror attacks), or Marxism, which is re-formed as non-communitarianism in measures which aim to realise it. To be a culture here is to have one's intentions opposed by the very means used to achieve them, or to be part of the divine comedy. Theory and practice re-form each other, just as self-consciousness seeking to know the truth of something, leads to becoming self-conscious of the impossibility of its being known. Education or *Bildung* in Hegel is the culture in which the search for truth is also the barrier to truth. This contradiction is one that underpins the modern logic of necessity of modern metaphysics, explained now in Part II.

*   *   *

The Renaissance humanists had re-established the authority of the ancient authors such that liberal arts education by the 16th century was 'grounded in texts thought to contain an essential unity of truth'[82] and which assigned 'overriding authority to tradition, to the legacy of the past.'[83] But by the middle of the 17th century classical and humanist culture suffered 'the same fate which it had prepared for Scholastic and mediaeval culture at the opening of the 16th; it becomes old-fashioned and ridiculous'[84] in relation to the new metaphysics of nature which comes to underpin enlightenment reason.

This new rational metaphysics unites logic and nature. Conformity with natural principles is to be regarded 'as the basis for theology, politics, law, or claims to property.'[85] Natural philosophy is the new home of first principles, and its overriding logic of necessity is that harmony and perfection are now to be found in the equality of each individual. This challenges one of the foundations of the liberal arts tradition. *Paideia, humanitas,* virtue, eloquence and nation-building had all been associated with an elite, educated according to a distinctive and protected curriculum, and certain of the virtue of their leadership. The new spirit of equality demands that all should be masters. What faces liberal arts education here is seemingly an oxymoron. How could a curriculum designed for leadership serve all citizens equally? In addition, how could a curriculum designed to foster virtue be relevant to the new scientific world which demanded a plethora of specialist skills and trades across many sciences? Finally, how could the exclusively theoretical curriculum contribute to the practical business of creating a modern industrial economy? Economic success requires the free use of reason for scientific and technical innovation. In the face of this, liberal arts education and its associated *humanitas* look scholastic, esoteric and somewhat redundant in the new world. What lay ahead now, especially in the United States, was the battle between the discipline of the classical, rhetorical college education and the more modern open Humboldtian-type university of research, scholarship and specialisation.

When the latter crosses the Atlantic it brings with it a new concept of liberal education, one defined in sympathy with the freedom rather than the discipline of *Bildung* as liberating, as freeing the mind from unexamined opinions and assumptions to think independently and exercise critical judgement, to question conventional doctrines and inherited claims to truth, to gain some skill in analysis and some capacity to deal with complexity, to embrace a certain scepticism in the face of dogma, and to be open to many points of view.[86]

Not only is this the spirit that will underpin the new universities in America, it is a redefinition of liberal arts education as liberal education.

This re-configured view of liberal arts education 'came increasingly to shape the directions of liberal education in the universities and colleges.'[87] Kimball notes that the oratorical tradition had always sided with breadth in the humanist curriculum over specialisation, including in speculative philosophy, and that it was 'natural therefore, that in the American liberal arts college the oratorical tradition of civic and polite learning militated against the specialised research of the University.'[88] However, freedom and discipline are re-configured in this new landscape. Now discipline and necessity come to represent the outmoded core curriculum of rhetoric and its associated disciplines, while the freedom for individual research comes to represent freedom from the iron fist of the compulsory curriculum and its timeless truths.

Death rites have been and continue to be offered regarding the traditional liberal arts education. Not only, as Hanna Holborn Gray says, was the old collegiate model 'now vigorously challenged as failing to produce truly educated graduates, as a thin and atrophied form of rote learning of little use, as unsuited to meeting the needs and interests of a new age, and as ludicrously unresponsive to the requirements and developments of the contemporary world.'[89] It also did not survive the challenge. Spurred on by the freedom of the elective system and the professionalisation of distinctive academic subjects, specialism gained ground over the idea of the discipline and necessity of universal man. By 1901, Rudolph argues, 'the classical course was dead,'[90] the mediaeval curriculum 'passed into history'[91] and 'vocationalism enlarged its domain.'[92]

Even if this is overstated, it is clear that the new freedoms in higher education threatened classical liberal arts in the most fundamental way possible, for it undermined not just its content, but its *raison d'être*. The idea that, as Arnold said in 'Literature and Science' (1882), liberal arts education concerned 'the best that has been thought and said in the world'[93] was now revealed to be something like an imperialism of a particular idea of universal truth carried by a particular set of liberal

UNIVERSITY OF WINCHESTER
LIBRARY

gentlemen. The new freedom defines the old freedom as a tyranny that requires to be overthrown. Kimball argues that this marks the transition from the liberal arts ideal type to the liberal-free ideal type. The seven characteristics of this new liberal-free ideal of freedom are intellectual rationality, critical scepticism, tolerance, egalitarianism, an ethic of individualism and personal growth and pursuit of knowledge for its own sake. This revolution, says Kimball, 'can be considered the catalyst for engendering the liberal-free ideal in America.'[94]

From the 1920s, liberal education and liberal arts in the United States carries on the opposition between individual choice and conformity to tradition, between freedom of enquiry and ancient wisdom and values, and in essence, between the two demands that have named liberal arts education from its inception: freedom (*liberalis*) and discipline (*ars*). I have shown in Part I how, in antiquity, freedom belonged within the hierarchy of the master over the slave, who had the discipline of truth and virtue as his own; in the Renaissance, how freedom belonged to the humanists who protected virtue and *humanitas* from the iron fist of Aristotelian scholasticism; and in the enlightenment that freedom moved its base to the equality of independent thinking individuals away from a notion of conformity to received wisdom packaged in a predetermined universal curriculum. In the United States, the paradigm of choice became the power base of departmental strength, status and popularity within the University. Clearly what this new education most risked was the idea that a set of first principles underpinned and held together all branches of knowledge within the divisions of University faculties and departments. Perhaps the voice that most challenged this perceived fragmentation was that of Robert Hutchins.

Conclusion to Part I

The end of humanity

In Part I we have followed the dualism of discipline and freedom both within the field of liberal arts education and occasionally beyond it. We have seen that this can be illustrative of the core dualism within liberal arts of the iron fist of *episteme* and the open palm of *oratorio*. It has revealed how education itself plays out the tension between a core of what is to be known and a creative and interpretive freedom of individual judgement. Three of the key players in this dualism have been metaphysics, humanism and subjectivity. Metaphysics is the resolute and steadfast bastion of discipline. Humanism, grounded in a metaphysical notion of human essence, at times represents an education in human freedom, especially the freedom of the creative individual against the universalism of theology or scholasticism, while at other times, notably as classical education in modernity, it represents the discipline of truth carried in and by the canon. Finally, subjectivity (again with a metaphysical grounding) often opposes rigid formulas and methods, accepted dogmas and assertions, and impositions at a structural level, all of which give impersonal universalist knowledge priority over individual creativity, imagination, abstraction and, most recently, freedom of expression.

But the landscape has changed dramatically over the last century. Each of these three players in the dualism of freedom and discipline, and rhetoric and philosophy, has been criticised to the point where its continued existence is now uncertain, to say the least. The death of metaphysics has been announced; with it, the hypocrisies and double standards of humanism have been laid bare; and subjectivity, at times the core of humanism, has been exposed as an essentialist prejudice of Cartesian self-consciousness. The end of metaphysics spells the end of first principles. In response, an open and 'inclusive' liberal arts education, embracing relativism and pluralism rejects the search for first principles, seeing it as a merely Western prejudice, and a particular type of Western prejudice – metaphysical, humanist, white, male – at that. It is not clear what present or future is left for liberal arts in this age of the end of metaphysics, the development of post-humanism and the deconstruction of subjectivity.

Heidegger's version of the end of metaphysics exposes the presupposition of the essence of man as rational consciousness. This is a metaphysics created by consciousness, which then makes itself the centre of the universe, and assumes the knowledge of everything from this privileged position. As such, consciousness-centred humanism is 'either grounded in a metaphysics or is itself made to be the ground of one,'[1] because the whole philosophical tradition from Plato onwards believes that essence precedes existence. Heidegger seeks to avoid the humanistic and Cartesian implications of this privileging of consciousness and its essence by reversing the priority, and arguing that essence is dependent upon a prior state of being, that of *Dasein*. He describes this Being as likened to standing in a clearing, in the nameless, and as an ecstatic moment in being and time. This does not abolish thinking; it simply acknowledges that thought is what lets Being be. The thinking that is Being is primordial and precedes all contemplation. Humanism, as Heidegger acknowledges, comes from the Roman *humanitas*, being a translation of Greek *paideia* understood as scholarship and training in good character. But this humanism, like all humanism – Marxist, Christian, or existential – is metaphysical. This is replaced in Heidegger by the 'quiet power'[2] of Being's own possibility. But it is at least questionable as to whether Heidegger's quiet power of *Dasein* fares any better as a non-metaphysical notion of existence than do the metaphysical ones. His membership of the Nazi party in the 1930s warns of the dangers in releasing spirit from its accountability to its self-conscious metaphysical contradictions.[3]

Perhaps just as powerful is the critique of the *ambivalence* of metaphysical humanism, an ambivalence which, as we have seen, accompanies it from its ancient beginnings. *Paideia*, whether it be of Isocrates, Plato or the Sophists, reproduces the tension between universal wisdom and self-promotion for reward and esteem. Roman *humanitas*, for example in Cicero, practises cruelty against some in the cause of humanity for all. The Renaissance, as Kristeller points out, for all its humanism is still 'a period of political ruthlessness, of crimes of violence and of passion.'[4]

The Terror of the French Revolution displays the ambivalence of fraternity for all, while the powerful stakeholders in the United Nations continue the tradition that the idea of humanity – its values, its laws, its economic system – is forged in the eye of the beholder and, in a very modern way, in the 'I' of the beholder.

This point is made forcibly by Franz Fanon among many others. Fanon, known for his support for Algerian liberation from France in the 1950s, holds a mirror up to Western *humanitas* to remind it of the contradictions that were present at its conception and which remain so today. He cites the European project of humanism as one in which its proponents 'are never done talking of Man, yet murdered men everywhere they find them, at the corner of every one of their own streets, in all corners of the globe.'[5] It is this same Europe 'where they never stopped proclaiming that they were only anxious for the welfare of Man: today we know with what sufferings humanity has paid for every one of their triumphs of the mind.'[6] As Sartre states in his Preface to Fanon's *The Wretched of the Earth*, Fanon speaks of European humanity in order to 'reproach us with our inhumanity.'[7] 'It was nothing but an ideology of lies, a perfect justification for pillage; its honeyed words, affectation of sensibility, were only alibis for our aggressions.'[8]

Sartre himself offers an example of the critique of Western metaphysical subjectivity as the expression of a universal and timeless essence. He argues for a relationship between existentialism and humanism, claiming it as a hopeful and optimistic expression of genuine human freedom in the world. The key characteristic of this existentialism and humanism is the death of God and the crisis of choice that therein befalls man. Without God, there can be no conforming to a preconceived ideal of human essence. Man simply exists first, and then is free to make of himself whatever he chooses. In the abandonment of God, man is 'condemned to be free,'[9] condemned to legislate for himself. Sartre finds no universal human essence, but instead finds the 'human universality of condition.'[10] This is Sartre's notion of humanism, for in making choices, the human being realises 'a type of humanity,'[11] and in choosing the human, there is always 'the possibility of creating a human community.'[12] This is not the humanism of an a priori human essence, *humanitas*; it is instead existential humanism or truly free human existence, free especially from the chains of an all-powerful transcendental model.

In the post-humanist age, even this Sartrean notion of conditioned subjectivity is rejected in favour of the ungrounded play of narrative, difference and *différance*, and in the undecideability and deferral of meaning. For Karen Barad, 'Representationalism [representation of an object by the self-conscious subject], metaphysical individualism, and humanism work hand in hand'[13] to protect the prejudices of the essential subject. For Deleuze, 'difference and repetition have taken the place of the identical and the negative, of identity and contradiction'[14] because identity and contradiction are prejudices of subjective consciousness. Against this, he proposes to 'think difference in itself independently of the forms of representation which reduce it to the Same.'[15] Liberal arts education is left here with the challenge of a world without identity, without the same, without dialectic and without first principles, in which 'Repetitions repeat themselves, while the differenciator differentiates itself,'[16] or with only 'a Cogito for a dissolved self.'[17]

For Fanon, Sartre and many others, whatever good the West may wish to claim for its concepts of humanism and humanity, it has always been prepared to use violence and oppression both military and economic, in the name of humanism and humanity. Emmanuel Levinas says of this, that Western history announces 'the realization of a humanist ideal while ignoring the vanquished, the victims and the persecuted ... They denounce the violence ... without being concerned by this contradiction.'[18] But, as we have suggested above, perhaps there has not been a time when *humanitas* did not contain such contradictions.

When *humanitas* passes into the ideals of the Enlightenment, and into *Bildung*, it brings its contradictions with it. Kant and Hegel do not escape these contradictions, defining humanity in less than 'inclusive' terms. This should not surprise us regarding antiquity for there was no concept of universal sovereign reason, and *humanitas* exhibited precisely the oppositions that reflected this. But in an age of enlightenment, when Kant can dare all human beings to be free by thinking for themselves, what excuses are there for Kant and Hegel differentiating common humanity into a hierarchy of 'races'? Kant supports *humanitas* in the form of cosmopolitanism, arguing that whatever shape individual acts may take, the necessity or iron fist of all actions may 'in the history of the entire species be discovered.'[19] Inevitably, this posits *Bildung* as the self-formation of the species acting according to its own necessity or end, even if this is unknown to the actors. But for Kant it is antagonism within and between communities, with all its attendant violence and opposition, which is the step from 'barbarism to culture (*Kultur*)'[20] and leads to moral formation. The resistance to sociability is nature's way of ensuring *Bildung*; it is the discipline in which freedom is learned. The antagonism between nations will have the same educative effect, leading to a federation which will act with a united will. If this seems fanciful, Kant reminds us that wars and revolutions are just such reforms of relations within and between nations. Humanity's natural end is to live within the law of self-determined freedom.

Indeed, Kant can be said to practice some of these antagonisms. Robert Bernasconi, for example, finds in Kant a racism where the white races are considered to be 'humanity at its greatest perfection,'[21] and who are 'the only ones who always advance to perfection.'[22] Or, again, Kant saw Native Americans lacking in *Bildung*, and whose cultural necessity was limited to slave culture. Bernasconi also draws attention to the silence of Kant regarding the slave trade, despite his cosmopolitanism, and his definition of freedom as thinking for oneself which 'would seem to be a perfect instrument with which to combat chattel slavery.'[23] Hegel seemingly fares little better. Negroes, he said, 'are to be regarded as a race of children who remain immersed in their state of uninterested *naïveté*.'[24] They let themselves be bought and sold seemingly without reflecting on the rights or wrongs of this, and in their own countries 'do not show an inherent striving for culture.'[25] Hegel too assigns various shapes of *Bildung* to the characteristics of different 'races'; black races, for example, are seen at the level of immediacy, awaiting alienation from natural life that will mark the beginning of culture and rational life.

In principle, Kant and Hegel both defend humanity as the one human race; for Kant, race is an attribute of the one common humanity; 'there are no different kinds of human beings';[26] while for Hegel if there is a natural difference between races, it does not change the fact that 'man is implicitly rational; herein lies the possibility of equal justice for all men and the futility of a rigid distinction between races which have rights and those which have none.'[27] What compromises the principle of *humanitas* here is the same fundamental problem that has always accompanied *humanitas* – that the content or substance of the idea of humanity lies always in the eye and the I of the beholder; and in the modern world the eye/I of the beholder is, to varying degrees, white, male and an owner of and a considerable benefactor from private property. The idea of humanity remains as compromised now by the antagonism between necessity and freedom, the iron fist and the open palm, as has always been the case.

It might seem that liberal arts education here has reached an impasse. Even where it is critical of the ambivalences of metaphysics, first principles, humanism and subjectivity, seemingly it is not prepared fully to abandon them for the post-humanist and post-metaphysical world of difference and repetition in which there can be no first principles. It is perhaps prepared to accept that it is the source of the best and the worst that the Western mind has achieved, but nevertheless it does not wish to discard the good for its complicity with the bad. Still, it has to face up to the fact that this ambivalence carried within humanism undermines liberal arts education as the *telos* of humanity, collapsing under the weight of its own all-too-easily identifiable contradictions and hypocrisies. Perhaps, for all its best endeavours, noble aspirations and fine words, rational enlightenment *humanitas* is no longer able to avoid either the range of differences that it fails to contain or the implications of trying so to do. It seems unable to offer an inclusive history of mankind. This is perhaps the exhaustion of *humanitas*, and therefore of liberal arts education, ending in failure.

Yet from the other side, it is by no means clear that post-metaphysical theory, in fact, is post metaphysics at all. If metaphysics is, as I will now show in Part II, the relation of the relation between thought and truth, then it has never been just the dualism or the dialectic that Deleuze and others believe. In *Theaetetus*, Socrates dissolved the subject two and a half thousand years ago, arguing that we get rid of the verb 'to be' because nothing is ever solid or stable. The metaphysical relation both acknowledges and works with this instability, as do the natural and social relations. Post-metaphysical work does not do justice to the integrity of these relations, and what it misses, fundamentally, is that the post-metaphysical viewpoint is just another shape that the metaphysical relation takes. It is to the educational subject and substance of the instability of these relations, metaphysical, natural and social, that Part II now turns its attention. Liberal arts education will be returned to, not just in these relations, but as these relations.

Discipline and freedom

Kimball's analysis of the history of the *artes liberales*, because it consistently sustains the centrality of the dualism between the iron fist and the open palm, keeps open the possibility of exploring this relation as something existing in its own right.[28] In my view, which I now begin to outline, this relation can be called education, and specifically liberal arts education. Even more dramatically perhaps, I will argue that this education has developed into a modern first principle wherein can be found education as an end in-and-for-itself. The closed fist and the open palm are two ends of the relation in which learning or education happens. This relation, I will also argue below, is always already a shape of subjectivity. Subjectivity is a third partner in the experience of discipline and freedom. It is the experience of their difficulty. But I will argue that this difficult relation does not just exist in the experience of each subjectivity. I will argue that this relation is subjectivity, and that subjectivity is this education.

My claim can be made first as a set of brief responses to Kimball's history of the *artes liberales*. I am in complete agreement with Kimball when he says, 'The efforts by so many academicians to deny the paradox and to recover the strengths of either ideal [philosophy or rhetoric] without the attendant liabilities contribute to the confusion in current discussion about liberal education.'[29] But while he is right to argue that the relation of each ideal could be sustained even in these paradoxes and contradictions, I will go further. I will say that these paradoxes and contradictions have a meaning of their own, a meaning that is fundamental to developing a modern metaphysics of education as a first principle, and upon which I will base a conception of a modern liberal arts education.

Kimball argues that wherever one side of the tension between *ratio* (reason) and *oratorio* (speech) has been prioritised, then 'the dialectical balance between the two sides has been lost.'[30] This balance, which Kimball calls *logos*, is judged according to the ancient logic of harmony. But the modern logic of relation re-defines *logos* not as dialectical balance, but as the relation of the relation between *ratio* and *oratorio*. This does not posit their relation to be 'perfectly complementary,'[31] but instead opens up the question of what relation – here *logos* – means when it relates to its own conditions of possibility. If reason and speech are philosophy and rhetoric, and therein discipline and freedom, then they are not the mutual relation or perfect balance suggested in the art of becoming the gentleman. They are instead the *logos*, the subjective experience of the substance of their separation. Kimball is right to support 'dialectical tension'[32] here over the sacrifice of its 'systematic integrity for the sake of comprehensiveness'[33] but the integrity of the tension is not maintained either in the logic of harmony whose desired goal is 'balance'. It is found in tension learning of its own truth from itself.

Part II now presents the history of liberal arts education not merely as the dualism between rhetoric and philosophy, but as the education that inheres in the relation – the tension – between them. It is always tempting to say here that this education is 'beyond' the dualisms that are its relation. But modern first principles are not defined beyond the dualisms that commend them. They are still in the dualisms, but deeper within them than observers most often care to look. The ancient logic of necessity expresses itself in three such relations: metaphysical, natural and social, or as they have already appeared above, as the three philosophies. In these relations, I will argue, is to be found the modern notion of educational truth. It is here, I believe, in these depths of learning about the educational truths that live in dualisms that we can find the best defence against the delusions of grandeur of metaphysical first principles and of the all-too-easily taken-for-granted authority of their rejection.

What will such a strange and unfamiliar notion of truth as education offer? Living first principles as education will not satisfy those who seek some kind of ethical certainty or moral imperative for action in the world. Education as human freedom works in a much more difficult and at the same time more profound way than to tell everyone what they must do in order to be human. At root, education can only reveal what the truth of metaphysics, *humanitas* or subjectivity teaches in the learning of them; and this learning is everywhere, but it passes one by unless one learns how to recognise this learning. Human freedom is learning because freedom is: 'humanity: know thyself.' What else can the culture of humanity be but its own education? What such education can reveal here is that the profound difficulties – difficulties that human freedom creates regarding the relation of freedom and discipline, or of the I and the We, or of the self and other – do not mean that one should resign oneself to the impossibility of human freedom; nor, even to the comfortable position of just criticising the mastery that always inheres in Western freedom, that is, its imperialist, colonialist, racist and sexist prejudices. Education invites us to continue to learn of human freedom from within all of these difficulties.

R. M. Hutchins

It might seem precipitous to end Part I with R. M. Hutchins here, but I have a specific reason for doing so. While President of the University of Chicago (1929–45) he attempted to retrieve the idea of first principles, and at a time when modern reason would interpret this as hanging onto the authoritarianism of the discipline of a core curriculum, 'with its metaphysical underpinnings and faith in the unity of knowledge.'[34] Such a concept of unity looked to some like a demand for an 'ideological conformity'[35] to the imperialism of the faculty, threatening 'the intellectual freedom at the core of the University.'[36]

Hutchins champions the intellect over the technical, the core curriculum over electives,[37] a hierarchy of truths over relativism, the whole over the parts, general education over specialism and permanent studies over the merely contemporary. He also rehearses themes that are raised within liberal arts education and does not hesitate to place things within a hierarchy. The curriculum of pre-university general education is to consist of the *trivium* – grammar, rhetoric and logic[38] – and mathematics from the *quadrivium*. The learning of other languages is not considered vital.[39] Students are to read the Great Books of the Western World, discerning what is timeless from what is fashionable, and what is common from what is accidental. 'The liberal arts are the arts of freedom. To be free individuals must understand the tradition in which they live. A Great Book is one which yields up through the liberal arts a clear and important understanding of our tradition.'[40] Hierarchy will be mediated somewhat by the variety of methods employed[41] and the independence of the student will be aided by being able to choose when to take exams. In addition, he is clear that general education is for everyone and that devotion to the liberal arts and liberal education has been 'largely responsible for the emergence of democracy as an ideal.'[42] Access to liberal education for all is perhaps 'the most important question in the world'[43] for 'we all practice the liberal arts, well or badly, all the time every day.'[44]

The key to Hutchins proposals is the view of metaphysics that underpins it. He leans most heavily on Aristotle and Aquinas. A general education will discipline the mind in the five intellectual virtues, leaving the student able to know and to demonstrate truth, and to produce and to act according to reason. In doing so, he implicitly separates *phronesis* from the Platonic forms and leaves open the question, the *aporia*, of their re-unification. When Hutchins says he is not arguing for any specific 'metaphysical system'[45] he is nevertheless working with a specifically Aristotelian notion of metaphysical logic, quoting, for example, from Newman, regarding the beautiful, perfect and noble mind in contrast to the useful and mechanical mind. He takes his metaphysics of general education from the Aristotelianism of Aquinas. Aquinas accepts that truth is what cannot be otherwise and takes this as a principle of universality. Where Aquinas says 'in speculative matters truth is the same in all men, both as to principles and to conclusions,'[46] Hutchins rewrites this as 'Education implies teaching. Teaching implies knowledge. Knowledge is truth. The truth is everywhere the same. Hence education should be everywhere the same.'[47]

Hutchins defends Aquinas as one among others in the mediaeval University who gave the University 'a principle of unity.'[48] They did so by making clear statements 'in due proportion and emphasis of the truths relating to man and God, man and man, and man and nature,'[49] or according to the three philosophies, a strategy Hutchins replicates in his own definition of unity, noting that theology is no longer able to fulfil this function. As such, America is left 'trying to discover a rational and practical order for the higher learning of today.'[50] He suggests that it should look to the Greeks for the principle of unity, namely the study of first principles which, as liberal arts education, is the ordering and proportioning discipline. For Hutchins metaphysics seeks the causes of the things that are; it is the first science, and as first, it is universal. Without either theology or metaphysics, 'a unified university cannot exist.'[51]

Many were suspicious of this return to the tradition of the *artes liberales*. It seemed to be weighted too heavily in favour of discipline over freedom. Kimball's conclusion is that Hutchins' real weakness was that he 'never explicitly identified'[52] his metaphysical principles. 'He never finally presented a system... other than that everyone ought to be liberally educated in the Great Tradition so as to become smart enough to find first principles.'[53]

What makes *The Higher Learning in America* so appropriate to my own project of *Philosophy and Modern Liberal Arts* is that I can now respond to an invitation that Hutchins offers at the end of his book. 'With theology has gone metaphysics. It is now but a shrunken shadow of its former self... in sadly mutilated condition.'[54] But 'if we can retrieve metaphysics and restore it to its place in the higher learning, we may be able to establish rational order in the modern world as well as in the universities.'[55] This would be nothing less than a 'miracle.'[56] I take up the challenge of this miracle in what follows.

Part II

Introduction

Difficult Educational Truth

From the history of liberal arts education as the dualism of philosophy and rhetoric, I now retrieve a different concept of liberal arts education from within the oppositions that express this dualism. I will, at different times, refer to the relation of oppositions as work, tension, difficulty and struggle. They all refer to the one truth: to the learning that calls itself education.

The three broad shapes that this relation takes in the Western tradition are metaphysical, natural and social education, or the three philosophies. The way these relations or this education is known is as difficulty, specifically as our own experience of the difficulties, the *aporias*, concerning first principles of truth, nature and society. I distinguish now between the logic of dualism, which knows difficulty only as opposition, from the logic of relation which knows opposition as our difficult education. It is this educational logic, and this logic of education – this work of education – that constitutes modern first principles and modern metaphysics. I will present this educational logic as a re-conceptualised notion of education for its own sake.

Perhaps the most appropriate introduction in the next few pages to the first principles of difficult education is with something difficult. There is no better candidate for this than the difficulty of describing the logic of this education, including, like it or loathe it, the logic of the property relation within it. Then, in chapters 5, 6 and 7, I will explore ways in which this educational logic of relation expresses itself in ancient and modern first principles in metaphysics, natural philosophy and social and political philosophy. A modern liberal arts education has its curriculum partly in the form and content of these three philosophies or in the difficult oppositions that are expressed in their three philosophical educations.

Difference is the relation of relation

The three philosophical educational relations – metaphysical, natural and social – share an illusion. They each appear to register the separation and difference between two elements. Metaphysics registers the separation between truth and experience. Science registers the separation between mind and matter. Social theory registers the separation between master and slave. But to 'register' these separations or relations is also to relate to them. Each philosophy – speculative, natural and social – is therefore in relation to the relations. The register of difference is a relation of relation. As we will see below, the relation of relation is the modern logic of the thought of thought (metaphysics), the movement of movement (nature) and the freedom of freedom (social relations), each of which are actual as education. It is the logic in which infinite regression is neither sinful nor nihilistic. Instead, it is where vulnerability to infinite regression is its own self-determining truth. This vulnerability and its self-determination of its truth is the relation of the relation: namely, learning.

The illusion the philosophies share, then, is that the relation of the relation only registers difference. As such, each fears that it can only ever register difference in a *reductio ad absurdum*. To conquer this fear of infinite regression each philosophy creates virtue out of such necessity – a tranquillity which resists eternal negation – and defines as barbarian the unrest which resists first principles and perpetuates the chaos of regression. In this illusion lies the truth of ancient liberal arts education: that virtue is the in-itself, the one and the master; and that the barbarian is the for-another, the composite and the slave. What the illusion so powerfully resists is learning of the way that the logic of virtue and the barbarian within first principles is also the logic of the illusion. Modern metaphysics, as I will explain it below, learns of a different logic from within this resistance, an educational logic.

Metaphysics, science and social theory have often immunised themselves by the ancient logic of necessity from the turbulent unrest carried in the contingency of composite thoughts and objects. Recently however, they have been challenged to work with this turbulence without a safety net. Two points are fixed only in relation to a third party (e.g. a Euclidean grid map) which is also considered fixed. But this is never the case. Kant and Hegel, and Galileo, Newton and Einstein understand that the third party is fixed only in relation to another fixed point, which is in relation to another fixed point, and so on ad infinitum. Everything is relative to everything else all the time(s). The cost of this adventure in the total relativity of movement is the demise of truth in metaphysics, objectivity in science and humanity in social theory.

The weapon of mass destructive relativity is infinite regression. Resistance to infinite regression and chaos takes two forms that are inextricably linked: religious and sceptical. If regression is truly infinite then there is no first cause, and nothing would actually exist. Therefore, for Aristotle, 'the series must stop somewhere.'[1] The Prime Mover is a positive logical and religious necessity, countering the purely negative logic of infinite regression. Or, alternatively, the logic of infinite regression really is negative and resists positing a first principle just to solve the problem. Here is the scepticism in which absolute truth is impossible.

What is significant here is that both responses employ the same logic to arrive at their conclusions. Both judge mediation to be error. Both protect truth from this error, one by means of a Prime Mover whose truth in-itself in eternal tranquillity is necessary but still unknowable in finite thinking, the other by a scepticism which judges mediation in finite thinking to be both unavoidable and always error. Religion and scepticism both resist the corruption of truth within the error of earthly time, and in doing so protect truth, motion, and freedom from their own difficulty. God and (mediation) the death of God share the same logic of necessity – that experience is error compared to truth – even in the modern world of quantum mechanics, of *différance* and of the end of metaphysics.

The property relation as subjectivity

Why does the experience of relation, or infinite regression, legislate against itself? Why does thinking prefer to be in (dualistic) error than in (educational) truth? Why, instead of affirming itself, does it prefer to have truth beyond it, or to have no truth at all? Freud asked a similar question of consciousness – why does it sabotage its own recovery from psychosis? So, why is consciousness resistant to being its own truth? It is because it thinks it finds security and stability in the dualisms of oppositions, which offer it both God and the death of God as immunity from chaos and dogma respectively.

This illusion of stability in dualism has one of its most powerful shapes in the property relation. The illusion is that the property relation (only) separates and differentiates property from its owner. When the object is for thought, when matter is for mind and when the slave is for the master, then truth is protected from error by ownership. Property serves a dual function here. It preserves the owner from the chaos of infinite regression because ownership defines what it owns as pure error, as barbarian, or as that which fails to have its own truth in-itself. As such, ownership also assigns virtue to the owner, for he takes upon himself the virtue of ownership, that is, a benevolent dictatorship of the object for its own sake. Truth and virtue are protected from the relativity of the barbarian other by ownership per se and also in protecting the other from its own relativity and barbarism. The property relation stacks the deck so that property can appear as the safeguard of freedom, but the appearance is due to it pre-determining the rules of the game in its own image and its own interests. Virtue and barbarism, separate and together, are the subjectivities of property relations.

Because of his relation to his property, the master does not meet his own criterion for truth and virtue. His independence is not its own first principle, for it is contingent upon owning the slave. He does not have his own principle in himself. Thus his virtue is also barbarian. The barbarian aspect of virtue is hidden within the property relation that appears to protect virtue from the barbarian. But the protection – the very fact that it needs protection – corrupts what it protects. It protects the master from being his own first principle.

The answer to the question, why thinking resists its own truth is akin to the question 'why does mastery sabotage attempts to resist its own barbarism?' In both cases, subjectivity is the private property relation, protected from unprincipled infinite regression by the illusion that pertains to relation seen only as dualism. Opposition to the object confers both security and virtue on the owner. Why would he sacrifice the truth of this 'relation' for something like the relation of the relation which, from the viewpoint of this subjectivity in the private property relation, could only be error? Besides, the property relation offers so much and asks so little in return. What is the incentive to risk the difficult logic of education when the illusion of virtue is so strong? One answer might be, education pursued for its own sake. And why would anyone choose that? Why would anyone pursue truth when the lie is rewarding in so many ways? The answer to this is perhaps that living a lie is not its own truth. But is this enough for the master to bite the hand that feeds him, and to resist his own sabotage of truth? If truth is enough for him to resist his resistance to truth, then there is a logic of education as resistance that applies here. Education, as its own logic of necessity, resists the resistance of the master to truth. It resists his resistance to learning by learning first of the resistance to learn.

However, as part of this learning, the logic of education resists the strategies used to protect the illusion of virtue, [next word in italics] and it resists the logic of this resistance. As such, it makes few friends. Here it finds that both supporters and detractors of private property are wedded to the one, ancient logic of necessity, grounded in a propertied and therefore illusory notion of virtue and the barbarian; and grounded too in an intriguing mix of religion and scepticism.

In the periods prior to the Enlightenment the master used the Prime Mover and the barbarian slave to protect against the infinite regression of his own experience. In modernity, reason believes it grounds its own principles, and so the master grants equality of mastery to all in law. How, then, is reason to keep infinite regression at bay if there is no slave? It does so by belief in a personal God that must exist in order to protect from infinite regression, but which cannot be known by us in-itself. If it could be known by us, in-itself, then this would be the secularised death of the personal/ineffable God, and the undermining of private property and the master as the principle of freedom. The religion of the personal God, involving the scepticism of His being truly known, is the modern property relation defending itself, protecting itself against infinite regression on earth and above. As such, the virtuous property owner defends his own individual and private truth being illegitimately collectivised into a knowable universal truth in-itself. Here private property defends itself in the scepticism that any universal, any collectivism, is merely an illegitimate positing of truth in-itself as knowable. This scepticism is religious in knowing that God is necessary – to protect the property-owning individual against infinite regression – but not what God is.

The barbarian slave does exactly what the virtuous individual detests. He creates a collective truth, seen as in-itself – be it history, or materialism, or class consciousness and so on – to protect against the error of merely finite and particular interests of each master. For the barbarian, this collective truth in-itself is a knowable universality; it is the in-itself which is also for-itself. It is sceptical regarding God because it sees His necessity as motivated by private (bourgeois) interests, but it is also religious because this communal consciousness posits universality free from the error of mediation, or free from (bourgeois) infinite regression. This is the source of its becoming an earthly terror.

The personal God of the property-owner and the death of God in the collective share the sceptical religious prejudice against truth as mediation. The property-owner requires a personal God who cannot be collectivised, while the communist requires the death of precisely this personal God and of the property rights over objects that He defends. Both overcome the posited error of mediation, and both are the cause of immeasurable suffering in doing so.

Here, then, both defenders of and protesters against private property presuppose the same (ancient) logic of necessity. Both presuppositions are grounded in the logic of necessity which guards truth against the infinite regression of its being known educationally, that is, as true when 'corrupted' in and by the composite mind. To argue for the preservation or abolition of private property is the same logical case: the difference amounts to whether one defends (ancient) truth best under the guardianship of the bourgeois individual or in collective class consciousness. Whether for or against private property, the logic of the private property relation determines the shape of such differences because it determines the shape of 'difference' per se.

Question and answer

A further powerful example of the illusion of relation as merely separation and difference is that of the dualism of question and answer. As claims for and against private property are fought out on the terms set in advance by the relation of private property, so the educational practice of question and answer is predetermined according to the ancient logic of harmony (virtue) and the barbarian, and not in the modern educational logic of their relation. The integrity of questions is that they do not have the answer in advance. They are required to be independent from each other. Yet this is merely the illusion of their relation. In fact, the question is pre-determined by the sovereignty (or mastery or ownership) of the answer over the question. For the answer, the question is in fact the spectre of barbarian infinite regression – the child's persistent 'why' to every answer it receives. There is seemingly no first principle in this persistent 'why.' It is the chaos that has no principle of its own. The terminus of this infinite questioning is provided by the answer. The answer puts an end to the infinite regression of the question. The answer therefore has chaos as its other, kept at a safe distance. As such, the answer owns the question even before it is asked. This control is what defines what is to count as an answer and guarantees the status of the answer. It is an end in itself because it is master of the question and by being master of the question it is safe from infinite regression.

In ancient logic the answer is tranquillity, self-complete and moved in and of itself to be its own truth. Yet, of course, the answer is dependent upon the question. The answer to barbarian continual questioning turns out in fact to be equally barbarian, another lack of independence, and not a first principle after all. The barbarian aspect of the answer is hidden within the relation that protects the answer from continuous (barbarian) questioning, that is, within the relation in which the question and answer appear only as opposed to each other.

The answer (like the master) sabotages attempts to question itself because it has its identity grounded in overcoming the question. What is the incentive for the answer to question itself and risk undermining the security, the subjectivity, the tranquillity and the civility provided by owning the question? The 'answer' here might be to learn the truth of itself rather than continue to protect the illusion of its independence. But what would be strong enough to induce the answer to undermine itself? Perhaps only the integrity of learning, if learning, somehow, is the truth of the answer's relation to itself as a question.

If we employ the characteristics of the property relation here, then the defenders of answers over questions will be 'religious' in positing the integrity of the answer to lie in the personal or the universal while supporters of the question will be nevertheless 'sceptical' in denying that any question is definitive or eternal or complete in-itself. They share the same ancient logic of necessity here. Both see the chaos of mediation as error. The question is never given an educational logic of its own by which it can re-define the relation of question and answer, and with it re-define what is to count as education and learning within this relation. If it did, it might see that learning is truth's own affirmation in the negation that is carried by the question.[2]

Freedom as education

There is a shorthand I employ in what follows which illustrates the change from the old logic of necessity to a modern one. I hope that what will draw educators towards the latter is that this modern logic of necessity and this modern shape of a first principle is education. I hope what will draw others towards education is that it has its *telos*, its own inner (and outer) necessity as freedom. The terms 'truth,' 'nature' and 'freedom,' each expressing the truth of the three philosophical relations – metaphysical, natural and social respectively – are in this sense interchangeable. To do metaphysics is to enact the culture of the metaphysical relation. This concerns, in different ways and at different times, the shape of the relation between the in-itself, the for-another, the for-itself and the of-itself. To do natural philosophy is to enact the culture of the natural relation. This concerns the shape of the relation between animate mind and inanimate matter in the macrocosm and microcosm. To do social and political philosophy is to enact the culture of the social relation. This concerns the shape of the relation between master and slave. All three share the same logic of necessity. Truth in-itself is the self-moving master, while error, being truth only for-another, is the slave whose movement is not its own principle. It is from within these three philosophical relations that I will seek to re-invigorate liberal arts education as the story of freedom's own education.

The logic of necessity has taken three distinctive shapes, or cultures, in the history of Western societies. My shorthand for these three shapes is: freedom is to think; freedom is to think for itself; and freedom is to learn. Each is a stage and a shape of subjectivity, and each is an expression of its own educational conditions of possibility. I briefly describe these now, but they are dealt with again below in Chapter 7.

Freedom is to think

Socrates, Plato and Aristotle between them plunge Western life into the question of relation. Plato seeks to restore the relation between the soul and the city to a divine integrity, and against the imbalance of the relation between them which, among other things, led to the execution of Socrates. Aristotle discerns a logic in the necessity of identity wherein the uncertainties – sometimes dialectical – that accompany relation can be overcome. But Plato and Aristotle together are in a relation which lets neither of them settle. If priority in the relation is given to transcendental forms, the cost of this imbalance is the truth of each individual thing. If priority is given to empirical truth then the cost of this imbalance is the loss of an overarching universality, truth as an idea in its own right. Repairs to the broken relation do not restore harmony and balance. They only repeat the sovereignty of the standpoint of the repairer.

The remarkable outcome of the Plato–Aristotle relation is that the relation comes to know itself as the work of the human mind. This is Western philosophy, where thought not only thinks about objects, it also thinks about the effect that thinking has on the appearance of the object. This is the birth of the idea of human culture, that is, that ideas have a life, a substance and a meaning of their own. Once the mind creates its own culture, it becomes an object of its own enquiry, as much as it is an enquiry into the universe and the *polis*. The response to this discovery of the power of the mind is Stoicism. Stoicism is the relation of thought to itself, finding no distinction between the activity of thinking and the identity of the thinker. In the ancient logic of the necessity of harmony, Stoicism is the truth of the relation of thought to itself: here freedom is to think, and to do so undisturbed by events, misfortunes or emotions that would disrupt this harmonic relation.

Freedom is to think – and it is uncomfortable to read this phrase now and the two that accompany it below, as a noun, and as a concept in its own right, and especially a concept of Western subjectivity, but I hope the reader will persevere despite the apparent clumsiness – is the first subjective shape that the three relations of subjectivity take. Its metaphysics is that thinking is in-itself and not for anything else; its physics is that movement must not be seen as other to the natural universe, but rather part of and therefore undisturbed by that nature; and its freedom requires that virtue must pass the barbarian – being only for something else – to the slave, for whom thinking can never be freedom. Chapter 7 describes the various stages that freedom is to think takes in its struggles to contain this freedom against the threat posed by becoming alienated from itself.

Freedom is to think for itself

The collapse of the relation of freedom is to think occurs under the weight of its own contradictions. Stoic freedom cannot remain immune to the implications of being a universal principle of freedom. This promotion, as it were, requires that freedom not only think, but think for itself. This is a new universal rational truth for it, and a new shape of the relation or culture of Western human subjectivity. It is the autonomy of the mind which, in thinking for itself, is sovereign, and equal in the dignity and freedom of all such minds. This enlightenment reason is the shape of the relation that provides the ground for equal rights, for equality and for individual freedoms.

However, this relation will also suffer at its own hands and will play out the shapes that the relation takes in trying to be its own truth, its own freedom. Again, the relation will oppose itself, by being itself. At its most dramatic, this relation will destroy itself, calling this the end of metaphysics, the end of classical physics, and the end of Western freedom as a template for the freedom of the world.

Freedom is to learn

Freedom is to learn is the shape that the relation or culture of Western human subjectivity takes when it understands the logic and necessity of education as a first principle. This is the logic and the necessity of education as relation (or more accurately as the relation of the relation). Freedom is no longer merely thought in-itself (Stoicism), nor in-itself because it is all otherness (enlightenment reason). Freedom now is in-itself when it is for-another and for-itself. To learn this is to learn of-itself; and it is a freedom that can only be learned because freedom is the educational experience. Freedom is the education; freedom is to learn.

Most challenging here perhaps is that each of the three shapes of freedom are three shapes of human subjectivity. Freedom is to think is the ancient subjectivity, the free man who is untouched by nature, slavery or mediation by another. Freedom is to think for itself is the rational enlightenment subjectivity, the autonomous person who has legal rights of person and property, and who is defended from any particular other by the universal law of generalised otherness, that is, by the law of all. Freedom is to learn is the subjectivity that knows of itself as relation. It knows itself as the education regarding its composition as relation, and it knows the truth of this relation to lie in education.

In what follows now I try to define a modern liberal arts education according to education as a modern first principle. It requires a different and modern idea of metaphysics, of logic and of necessity, not imposed from without, or presupposed from within, but according to the relation between them which is (a re-definition of) how any beginning is made. What modern metaphysics does is bring first principles face to face with themselves so that they can enact the same sovereignty over themselves that they enact on everything else. This is to challenge experience with experience, motion with motion and freedom with freedom. The challenge is to know their relation as education. I note, again here, Hutchins who said, 'if we can retrieve metaphysics and restore it to its place in the higher learning we may be able to establish rational order in the modern world as well as in the universities.'[3] I will undertake to retrieve metaphysics, but the order or rationality or necessity that comes with it would, I think, surprise Hutchins. He said that to retrieve metaphysics would be nothing less than a 'miracle.'[4] If modern metaphysics also reforms the idea of what constitutes a miracle, then in this new meaning, perhaps, I can agree with him.

5
Metaphysical Education

What is metaphysics?

To study metaphysics is to bring thinking to the study of thinking. In regard to liberal arts education metaphysics is the search for first principles. For the ancients, a first principle is where harmony and necessity meet. Harmony refers to that which is at one with itself. Necessity is the logic of this harmony – something is what it must be – and logic is the necessity of this harmony – what must be is itself. Together they constitute the identity of truth. The most elemental division in metaphysics is between that which is 'itself' – a simple oneness, or harmony – and that which is other than itself – compound and reducible to a simpler form. As such, harmony, as its own necessity and as its own first principle, becomes the criterion by which all first principles are to be known. If one asks, justifiably, why should harmony and necessity be presupposed to conjoin in such a way as to produce truth, the original answer from Pythagoras is that it is to be found in nature, as a natural law of the universe. Cosmology, mathematics, geometry and music all reveal this natural harmony and necessity. It is not of man's invention. It is not an accident. As a law of nature and the cosmos, it befell the Greek mind to try to emulate this harmony and necessity in speech and action, in one's soul and in one's social relations.

The claim that harmony and necessity are the very stuff of a first principle is a claim based on logic. Where, then, does the idea of logic come from? Does the logic of a first principle emulate the order and coherence of nature and the soul, or does the truth of the soul and nature emulate the logic of a first principle? Modern metaphysics does not fear the infinite regression that lies at the heart of this question. Instead, it finds a necessity and a logic hiding within the question.

To ask the question – which comes first, harmony or logic? – presupposes the two elements as fixed points for a fixed observer. This is the logic and necessity of the dualism of question and answer, the safeguard already established against infinite regression. The question and the answer carry the ancient logic within them. Whatever the answer to the question might be, the logic of question and answer, the logic of non-contradiction, the logic that defines itself against anything being called an answer which does not defeat infinite regression, always wins. It wins because it expresses its sovereignty as the pre-existing structure of question and answer. Whatever the answer, the sovereignty of this logic is reproduced. But when thought explores the conditions of the possibility of its asking and answering questions, or the conditions of the possibility of the logic and necessity it employs, it is working as the relation of opposites to itself. As such, metaphysics is the question of the condition of the possibility of the question of logic and necessity. This, as we will see, is where the logic of modern first principles is to be found.

I will return to Hegel in due course, but here it is helpful to look ahead to one of his most fundamental observations regarding metaphysics as the question of its own condition of possibility. In responding to Kant, Hegel says that when Kant uses the critical method to try to discover the truth, he assumes that the tool he uses for the enquiry – thought – must not be allowed to corrupt the truth in-itself. Hegel opposes this by arguing that it is thought which introduces the prohibition in the first place. The tool cannot be laid to one side. It is the condition of the possibility of the enquiry. Thought is its own necessity here but assumes that in being so it cannot also be its own harmony. This, I will show below, is the culture of error that defines ancient metaphysics for 2,500 years. Hegel's point here is crucial for modern metaphysics, for logic and for the idea of first principles that can inform a modern liberal arts education. If thought is the condition of its own possibility, then thought is its own logic and necessity. If it re-defines what we are to understand as harmony or truth or logic, then so be it.

Part I began the task of following liberal arts education around the three philosophies of truth, nature and society, and the ways in which, grounded in the logic of necessity and harmony, they play out the relation between discipline and freedom. The philosophical relation of truth is the metaphysical relation or metaphysical education. In this chapter I want to discern the difference between the ancient and modern shapes of this metaphysical relation.

Ancient metaphysics

The relation between Plato and Aristotle can be represented by the fate of *phronesis*. Socrates inherits *phronesis* as divided between the ethical and the religious, and employs *phronesis* as 'the ethical power of reason.'[1] Plato argues for *phronesis* as wisdom, or as a unity of knowledge of the good and of good actions, a unity called the Forms. In contemplating the Forms, 'knowledge and action coalesce.'[2] But when Plato divides this unity into dialectic, ethics and physics, 'from then on there were several *phroneseis*.'[3] Plato retains the term *phronesis* to illustrate the relationship between the Forms and the harmony of the universe (*Timaeus*) and between the Forms and values by which individuals should order their lives (*Republic*). Aristotle holds to something like this unity as *nus* in the *Protrepticus*. But later, Aristotle divides metaphysics from ethics, and *phronesis* comes to belong exclusively to the latter. In short, Plato strives to illuminate harmony between thought and action, whereas Aristotle separates them into pure intellectual harmony and pure practical wisdom. This defines the opposition between theory and practice, between the ideas of philosophy and rhetoric within liberal arts education and between the closed fist of method and the open palm of creative, virtuous character. Jaeger sees this as a seminal moment in defining the Greek legacy. 'When the theory of the Forms was abandoned being and value fell apart, and dialectic thereby lost its direct significance for human life, which to Plato was an essential feature of it.'[4]

Aristotle in the *Metaphysics* and the *Nicomachean Ethics* rejects the dialectical version of a first principle. The *Metaphysics* grounds itself in the rationality where dialectical contradiction is the criterion, precisely, of that which is not true, because it is not in-itself, not independent and not unchangeable. Where the sun in Plato depends upon the sight of others for it to be seen, in Aristotle's logic it simply undermines its credibility as an independent first cause in-itself. Opposed to Plato's dialectic of sun and sight is Aristotle's conception of the first cause or Prime Mover. There are then two versions of metaphysics competing here, and not only do they come to define the tension in liberal arts education between philosophy and rhetoric but they also open up two logics, and two different ideas on the nature or harmony or necessity of a first principle.

Book 2 of the *Metaphysics* contains Aristotle's definition of a first principle, a definition that shapes the ways in which Western intellectual life judges truth from error.[5] He says, 'We do not know the truth without its cause...That which causes derivative truths to be true is most true. Therefore the principles of eternal things must always be most true; for...they themselves are the cause of the being of other things.'[6] This definition is open to the threat of infinite regression where one cause is caused by another, and that by another, and so on ad infinitum. Aristotle has a theological backstop here which incontrovertibly makes infinite regression impossible. Efficient causes cannot form an endless series because 'if there is no first there is no cause at all.'[7] As such, an infinite series of causes is absurd, and 'the series must stop somewhere and not be infinite.'[8] This appears to be faultless logic on five counts. If regression is infinite there can be no first cause;[9] if there is no first cause then nothing has ever been caused, and the actual world around us proves that this cannot be correct; if there is a first cause that is itself not caused by anything prior, this first cause must itself be eternal; an eternal first cause could not be destroyed by something finite; a first principle is its own end and is therefore also its own limit. The purpose, or *telos*, or *entelechia* of a first principle is that it is its own end, an end in-itself, and limited only by itself. This is also the logic used in liberal arts education to claim an idea of education as its own end, or for its own sake.

The result is that Aristotle creates a logic of first principles in which the dialectic is registered as error against the truth of the unchangeable. Where in Plato the dialectic could hold truth, nature and society together – in the difficulty of the dialectic as education[10] – Aristotle separates out different independent identities from each other and offers an alternative threefold division of philosophy as speculative, practical and productive.[11] Each has its own notion of virtue, or of necessity, according to the means by which the soul possesses the different realms of truth. The five intellectual virtues are knowledge (*episteme*), comprehension (*nus*), philosophical wisdom (*sophia*), practical wisdom (*phronesis*) and art (*techne*).[12] Within the speculative intellectual virtues, *nus* comprehends first principles and causes, *episteme* demonstrates them in science, and *sophia* is the wisdom that comes from the combination of understanding and demonstration. The logic of this combination is self-fulfilling. A first principle which cannot be otherwise cannot have itself as an object; it cannot therefore demonstrate itself, for that would mean being compound, divided between itself and its being demonstrated.

The question that separates Plato and Aristotle is, 'Does mediation/negation/dialectic corrupt or create truth?' For Plato it somehow enacts the truth; for Aristotle it corrupts it and makes it compound. For

Plato, as for Socrates, knowledge is virtue because the dialectic is not just a knowing of truth, it is a knowing of the production of truth in the soul as in the world; the logic of metaphysics demands that the understanding of truth be exercised over the soul and the city. This is why of the Forms, the good is the highest. Equally Plato can hold *techne* within metaphysics because the sciences, especially mathematics, are *technai* and can lead from the senses to the intellectual world. Aristotle protects first principles from mediation or production, and as such, *techne* is not part of the speculative virtues, nor of the practical virtues, but only of the virtue of knowing how to produce an artefact. *Phronesis* can avoid *techne* because it is a praxis of moral and political action, and not a *poiesis* that has its object external to it. In the hierarchy of virtues Aristotle has to hold *sophia* supreme because it alone is the divinity of pure first principles, causes and movers.

The two approaches therefore differ on the relation between the three philosophies. Plato can hold *phronesis* (the social relation) within metaphysics because he does not posit truth as independent from mediation. Aristotle has to hold *phronesis* completely separate from metaphysics (speculative virtues) so that judgements do not corrupt the oneness and simplicity of scientific necessity.

Cultures of error[13]

To the mediaeval scholar Aristotle, not Plato, was the logician[14] and Aristotelian logic was the dominant force in Western intellectual life after the fall of the Roman Empire and, most especially, in Christianity, Judaism and Islam.

The three religions did not really stray from the definition of the truth of a first principle that Aristotle had laid down. This meant that the three religions were united in their view that God was ineffable, rationally necessary and unchangeable. The idea that human thought could presume to know God in Himself was deemed an arrogance, and each time thought claimed to do so, it repeated the error of infinite regression in relation to truth. From Aristotle to Kant, the history of Western philosophy as of the history of the religions is constituted as a variety of cultures of error and errors of culture.[15] A culture of error judges thinking always to corrupt the purity of its object, that is, when an object in-itself becomes mediated as an object for-another. The contingency of being for-another is always error compared to the in-itself of a first principle. The error of culture, therefore, is that it presupposes that this culture, this education, this experience of contradiction, is always wrong and has nothing in and of itself to teach us that would challenge the ancient logic of necessity, or that it has no educational substance of its own.

Here, in the chiasmus of the culture of error and the error of culture, there is not only the Platonic difficulty of metaphysics but also the logical Aristotelian resolution of the difficulty. For example, Stoicism and Scepticism sought universal harmony in reconciling the particular to the natural necessity of the universe. The Church Fathers separated the cities of man and God according to the error of human thought in relation to the perfection of the divine. The Islamic philosophers of the 9th to the 12th centuries CE held to the notion of perfection in the necessity of a first cause and to the error of the compound. In the Judaism of Maimonides God can only be known indirectly, and simplified images of God are necessary to ensure faith among the multitude. The question of how God could be one and many without becoming changeable and compound was one which dominated mediaeval philosophy and theology. Aquinas's defence of single individual intellects against Averroes' continuum of a single intellect would lead to the divide of church and state in the West, and the lack of such a division in the East.[16] Faced with the contradiction that God was whole yet also present in each living part of the universe, considerable ingenuity was required to square this circle. God had to be universal and particular, yet in no way divided from Himself.

The rationalist philosophies of the 17th century, in particular Descartes, Spinoza, Leibniz and Locke, reject the ambivalence associated with dialectical thinking in favour of clear, unambiguous self-evidence of reason, and therein protect the true from the threat of mediation and infinite regression in relation to thinking. The rationalism of Locke, even though it believed that reason had finally escaped the need for such ingenuity, in fact created the ground for the most dramatic confrontation between the in-itself of the universal and the for-another of particularity. Having demonstrated the sovereignty of reason over everything else, having shown that reason is the in-itself because everything is known by reason and everything is for-reason, this still did not produce the direct experience of the truth of things in the way that he hoped. God's gift of reason, as Locke saw it, had given man the means by which to know Him, but still only up to a point. The gift of the idea of the in-itself is divine, but the limits of this gift are human; the in-itself remains perfect when it is for-itself, but when in the finite human and essentially rational mind it is for-another, then for its own protection against error it must be deemed ineffable. Locke's under-labourer replaces the Scholastic obfuscations of the rhetorical philosophers, and with this Locke argues that reason does not need Aristotle. This is near to the Kantian gateway through which one passes on route to modern metaphysics.

Kant and Hegel

The idea that truth mediated by thought is the error that must be overcome if the true is to be protected from corruption by contingency within infinite regression reaches its height in Kant. But this is not because Kant thought of dialectic as an illusion practised by 'metaphysical jugglers'[17] who mistook rules of the employment of reason for objective principles. Instead, Kant's synthetic a priori expresses a necessity between experience and objects of experience which mark his Copernican revolution in metaphysics. This necessity establishes two contradictory necessary truths: that all understanding of objects in the world are necessarily in conformity with their being experienced; and that, in line with truth as self-determining necessity, free from heteronomy and enjoying its own identity and autonomy, truth must be exempt from just that necessity. It is nothing new in the history of Western philosophy that these two necessities are in opposition, but it is the first time that the culture of error knows itself as necessity and totality, and therefore as true. Everything else is dependent on being experienced, but pure a priori reason is exempt from such dependency. It remains, for Kant, the unknowability of the in-itself. But it is not strictly Aristotelian, because Kant establishes the synthetic a priori as a metaphysical difficulty in its own right. It is this difficulty that Hegel takes up.

Hegel's response to Kant is as straightforward as it is dramatic. In a sense, it embraces Kant's Copernican revolution and brings to it the universality of an Einsteinian relativity. Kant famously says that, in maintaining the true as unknowable, he had denied man complete knowledge 'in order to make room for faith.'[18] For Hegel this is the last stand of the ancient and mediaeval cultures of error. They had always presupposed that thought was error in relation to the true, meaning that they presupposed that the true stood on one side, and the thought of truth on the other. This was the basis and the necessity of Aristotelian metaphysics. But for Hegel, as for Plato, the real necessity of the true is not found in complete and unchangeable identity and stability. Instead, the real necessity is in the instability and lack of identity that always accompanies the idea of truth, even, or perhaps especially, when this instability is being explained away as the fault of the thinker, against the perfection of its object. Perhaps, says Hegel, it is the fear of this error, of thought corrupting the perfection of the true that is the real error. Perhaps the true has never been perfect or stable or unchangeable. Perhaps, within the ancient logic of necessity, what had been labelled error for 2,500 years was really the true, and the true, in turn, was really only the error.

I have explained this in the most straightforward way I can. But this must not mask the fact that Hegel's observation is not just difficult to think through. It also claims that truth now is precisely the difficulty of doing so. I think that this difficulty has its own truth, its own necessity, as education. Further, this is what education as its own first principle looks like; it is the truth understood as the difficulty of the learning of truth. If we take this difficulty seriously, it changes how we are to think about truth and about education because it finds education to be truth and truth to be education. It changes also how we are to think about the meaning of understanding something. To understand truth as education is to know the truth of understanding as a difficulty, and not as the resolution of difficulty, not as a question owned by an answer. Education can overcome everything that opposes it, everything, that is, except itself. With regard to itself, education can only become its own difficulty. When education is doing itself, when it has itself as its subject and its object, or its thinking and its doing, then education is its own re-defined necessity, its own re-defined harmony and its own re-defined virtue. This is a modern logic of necessity as education. This is therefore modern metaphysics and is the logic of a modern liberal arts education.

There is a sense in which modern metaphysics is not different from ancient metaphysics. It still takes the harmony of self-determination, or of freedom, to be the criterion of truth. It is still a metaphysics of the identity of necessity. But in holding to this, it finds necessity to be true in exactly the opposite way to ancient metaphysics. Harmony is re-defined as the universality of disharmony; what is unchangeable is the fact that everything changes; the only identity that is stable is the identity of instability. The necessity that is universal is that in which nothing escapes the mediation of thought. To call this necessity of modern metaphysics dialectical is to risk the term 'dialectical' becoming immune from itself. Modern metaphysics precisely defines itself by subjecting dialectics to its own necessity, and the necessity of dialectics means that it must learn of itself in the same way it learns of everything else, in the educative experience of mediation. Within ancient metaphysics this is at best confusion, at worst the end of truth altogether in infinite regression. What modern metaphysics does is to find truth in the totality of opposition and not in the totality of the resolution of opposition.

Education as the modern logic of first principles

In liberal arts education, the claim is sometimes made that the free self-education of the free man is education in-and-for-itself. Modern metaphysics now re-defines how education as a first principle is formed in relation to these philosophical terms. This will be difficult for those with and without a philosophical background. But in modern metaphysics the difficulty is the education.

To explain the logic of the educational structure of a modern first principle, I need to employ four philosophical terms: in-itself, for-another, of-itself and for-itself. These four terms can display the logic of the history of Western metaphysics up to and including the present day. Aristotle's metaphysics established itself on the notion of truth in-itself. This term carried the simple non-privation of the One, independent of change caused by anything heteronomous or external. It carried the idea that what was in-itself was true and that what was true was in-itself. The circularity of this definition lies in the notion of harmony as the necessity and logic that express perfection. It is summed up in the shape of the circle. The circle is its own beginning and end, its own continuity and movement; it is unaffected by anything outside it; it has nothing in excess, nothing that is less than the whole; it is a perfect whole; it is entirely its own necessity. It is, therefore, the self-establishing logic of the whole, the One, the simple and the perfect. I will show in Chapter 7 the social and political values carried by this logic. But for now I observe that the idea of truth in-itself is embodied in the idea of self-mastery, self-discipline, self-control and self-definition. As such, the in-itself can be totally distinguished from its opposite, that which is not in-itself and is, therefore and by contrast, only for-another.

But, as Socrates demonstrated, everything that is deemed to be truth in-itself is relativised in the recognition that everything that is known is not only in-itself but also in-itself for-another. Metaphysics is the effect of the uncertainty generated when the in-itself is compromised by being for-another. Metaphysics is not the assertion of the sovereignty of the in-itself as transcendent. It is, instead, the question of sovereignty prompted in having truth as an object of thought. Metaphysics is what holds assertions of sovereignty – for or against the in-itself – to account by placing claims for sovereignty back into the difficulty that each opposing camp tries to resolve in its own way. Modern metaphysics is where metaphysics learns of this difficulty as its own truth.

The education of metaphysics in the European Enlightenment re-forms the relation of the in-itself and the for-another. The universality of enlightenment reason lies in the way that every object is for reason, that is, nothing is known that is not mediated by reason and judged by reason. Reason takes itself to be the criterion of truth because its necessity is universal; nothing can escape the gravity field of the black hole of enlightenment reason. What is it, then, to be true as rational? It is to pass the test of consistency. But what is the consistency of reason? That everything known passes through it. How do we know if something has passed through reason or not? If it has, then its claim to be universal is justified within the reasoning of reason. The tautology here is unavoidable. Reason is defining itself as all rationality because infinite regression is absurd, and reason is what curtails infinite regression. By the very nature of the justification, the justification has to be self-completing, or else it would fall prey to infinite regression and be 'illogical' and 'irrational.' All that falls outside of reason – superstition, dogma, tradition and prejudice – belongs to the irrationality of infinite regression and is undermined by rationality. Now, everything that is true is so only because it is for-reason. This is to defeat the contradiction that something can be in-itself and for-another, because now the 'other' (thought) is also the truth of all 'otherness' (rational thought), that is, it is rational that everything is for-reason. This totality defines the universality of rationality. Reason is now its own consistency and truth against the error of infinite regression. The buck stops with reason.

But something very interesting and of immense significance happens here. The colour and character of such reason undergoes profound changes. Enlightenment reason rises to power by demonstrating the non-identity, the non-truth of everything which avoids the universality of the rational. But in one sense all that has happened is that Aristotle's metaphysics of non-contradiction and identity has finally established itself as the universality of everything, or as the first principle of all first principles. The Enlightenment makes all laws rational, consistent and non-self-contradictory. Further, it defines each human mind as having rational capacity and as such being potentially free. Aristotle's metaphysics of identity becomes, in the Enlightenment, the sovereign identity and freedom of each rational mind and each rational universal law.

Here, then, is the Janus-face of enlightenment reason. It overcomes everything other to itself by mediating everything and convicting all otherness of being non-identical with itself. Yet, when reason establishes its own sovereignty as a principle, it is not as the non-identity of mediation that it does so, but as its identity. The poacher turns gamekeeper here; the slave (mediation) that fights against the master (truth) becomes the new master. It falls now to modern metaphysics to resist this new master by convicting it of non-identity with itself and to resist reason's own resistance to self-mediation. Modern metaphysics mediates the master of mediation and establishes new forms of reason, of freedom and of truth grounded in the instability of education.

To return to the philosophical terms, in the Enlightenment the in-itself that is for-another becomes the sovereignty of rational experience. But this sovereignty avoids its own implication of being for-another and takes for itself only the idea of reason in-itself. In Kant, reason in-itself becomes reason in-itself and for-itself in the totality of the synthetic a priori. In Hegel, reason in-itself that is also for-itself is invited to change the meaning of this universality. Hegel returns mediation to reason, bringing its weapon of totality now against itself, to show that the sovereignty of enlightenment individuality in-itself is illusory, for it too is mediated, and mediated by the experience of itself. In other words, the in-itself of modern reason becomes for-itself in the experience of itself as an other. It looks clumsy, but the first principle of modern metaphysics as education is that modern reason learns that reason in-itself is undermined by being for-another, and that this other is itself, but now changed in the experience of-itself which is also for-itself. Or, succinctly, the metaphysics of a modern first principle is the in-itself which, being for-another, is an education of-and-for-itself. These terms will have a particular significance when employed within the social relation in Chapter 7, with regard to the liberal gentleman in Chapter 8, and for the teacher/student in the work of education in Chapter 9. For now, they expose themselves as the definition of modern metaphysics having its first principle in education.

Retrieving subjectivity in and from method

One of the most challenging aspects of a modern first principle, and of modern metaphysics, is that the logical relation of truth in-itself, for-another, of-itself and for-itself is actual as modern subjectivity, as you and me. This notion of subjective logic also re-forms or re-educates us about the meaning of objective logic. Common sense grounded in the ancient logic of non-contradiction tells us that subjectivity and objectivity are abstractly separated. Modern metaphysics unsettles the logic and stability of these identities. In this instability subjectivity comes to be comprehended as the logical relation which knows itself as education. It is what is happening when identity in-itself, now for-another, is also its education for-itself and therein of-itself. Subjectivity here is the logic of education. This is a very long way from the caricature of subjectivity as logic that is portrayed in *Star Trek* as Mr Spock. Spock is the subjectivity only of abstract logic, characterised as cold, calculating, un-human, all the things that Dr McCoy is able to chastise him for. But as we know, Spock is half human and at times he is allowed to reveal the difficulty and struggle – the education – of being so. The subjectivity of modern metaphysics is this logic of learning, having its identity consistently re-formed by being undermined by the logic in which subjectivity is related to truth, or related to its learning of itself, though always capable of revealing the cold, hard inhumanity of its abstract (Vulcan) side. To say that subjectivity is logic, and that this relation is modern metaphysics, is to say that the truth of modern metaphysical subjectivity is to live not only in the dualism of objectivity and subjectivity but to live also in the educational truth of relation. Subjectivity, or subjective substance, is the way this relation is known and lived. The implications of this for the ideas of freedom and nature, I will explore below.

There is no solipsism in this logic of subjectivity. Reason has to be for-another if it is to experience the infinite regression of this mediation. When everything is for reason and reason is also for itself, then it has the two elements needed to learn of infinite regression as educational subjective substance. Whenever it seeks the comfort of resolving this difficulty, thought will trouble its thoughtlessness, and demand, again, the learning of truth in the truth of learning. There is only education; more or less understood, more or less embraced, more or less the truth of subjectivity. Where liberal arts education has always claimed that it stands for education as an end in-itself, education for its own sake, it has not had the logic or the metaphysics that would sustain this claim. Modern reason offers this logic and this metaphysics to education by making the relation of truth and its other an educational truth. Not only does this re-define logic and metaphysics, and the modern rational subject, it re-defines the idea that modernity has of itself.

God

We saw above that the personal God and the death of God share the same logic and necessity of truth judged as in-itself and mediation judged as the error of infinite regression.[19] As such, the question as to whether liberal arts is either secular or religious misrecognises this shared logic. I want now, briefly, to ask what the notion of modern metaphysics and of education as a first principle mean for the idea of God and for the misconceived opposition of religion and scepticism.

Modern metaphysics will not be able to sustain the idea of God, or truth, as a man in the sky with a beard making decisions and intervening in the fate of His creation. Picture-thinking of this kind does not experience deeply enough its own contradictions, particularly with regard to (rational) experience being the condition of the possibility of any object. But in many cases reason also avoids its own implication in these conditions of its own possibility. Were it to yield to this implication and this complicity it would become subject to its own totality and destroy for itself any secure idea of being independent and purely in-itself. The question is, then, in the collapse of picture-thinking, and in the collapse of reason in-itself, what is left? Is there a kind of truth which somehow exceeds the totality of reason which is perhaps undecidable or unknowable, and which should in any case be deferred? Or, is there some kind of truth within reason which, even in its collapse, will serve now as a religious truth, perhaps something like an ecstatic moment of pure negation in which the whole makes itself known?

Modern metaphysics holds onto neither of these responses. Ecstasy, like the belief in an ineffable God, is grounded in the culture of error which says that while absolute truth does exist, it cannot be known in and by composite thought. The death of God, the end of metaphysics and religion and post-foundational thinking in general practise the error of culture, presupposing that composite thinking makes the absolute not just unknowable, but impossible. But the idea of truth that is denied by these post-men and post-women is not the truth that is known in modern metaphysics. The truth that is decried is only an abstract notion of truth, one that is neo-Kantian in the sense that because all knowledge is contingent in one way or another, so absolute truth is deemed impossible. It matters not whether the conclusion is that absolute truth exists but cannot be known (religion), or cannot exist per se (scepticism), for the presupposition of the nature of truth – abstracted from its being known – is the same in both cases. The truth of modern metaphysics is different altogether. It includes within it both the ineffability of absolute truth and the impossibility of its existing at all. It includes them as part of the educational relations that are comprehending themselves as true within ineffability and impossibility, within religion and scepticism. Assertion and denial of absolute truth have their truth in their relation, the relation that constitutes modern metaphysics. The term 'absolute' will look very dangerous here, pointing towards fixity and dogma. But the very meaning of the term 'absolute' is re-formed from being an abstract assertion or denial, to being the educational relation of such assertions and denials; not just their negation, but the truth of such negations as our difficult education.

If education in modern metaphysics is true, then it means that education, as a first principle, is a modern conception of God. This has to sound strange, even nonsensical, to the mind which posits God as a man in the sky with a beard, whether that is to affirm His existence or irrefutably to deny it. But modern metaphysics diverges from this depiction of absolute truth. It would be easy to say that this is just an anthropocentric representation of God, but in fact, being for or against God is always already anthropocentric. It is always a reflection of how subjectivity understands itself; specifically it is the representation of the logic of freedom and property that defines subjectivity. In this sense God is always already a self-education about one's lack of freedom. If humanity were absolutely free (within the ancient logic), then God would no longer be either the resolution or the repetition of finite error. Modern metaphysics understands the nature of the need for God, the need to name the lack of freedom in human social life. In this sense subjectivity, by definition, is always already religion, and since modern metaphysics does not claim to have resolved incompleteness, only to be open to learning its truth, so a notion of God survives. What one can say is that for 2,500 years the learned tried to encourage the *hoi polloi* to think of God in the most simplistic ways so that the difficulties that theologians wrestled with would not be allowed to undermine the simple faith of simple people. Modern metaphysics now opens up these difficulties to all modern minds and refuses to do so simply by means of simple or familiar representations.

The idea that God is education means that it is not something that is exclusive of human form. Truth in modern metaphysics is educational logic as subjectivity. Truth is in learning, and the learning is the instability of the individual. God is therefore subjective by being the logic, the *logos*, of this education. He is present as the logic of modern metaphysical education. As a rhetorical flourish, one might say here that schools and universities are the new churches; teachers are the new philosophers and theologians; education is the new form of prayer. But still, modern metaphysics is not a religion in any usual sense of the term. It is not a doctrine. It is an experience of how all the usual meanings of religion, doctrine, prayer, church and so on are re-formed in the difficult learning of (the instability of) the self.

What is perhaps most challenging in the idea of education as truth, as a first principle and an end in-itself is that it changes the usual set of questions that are asked about God. Does God exist? Is there life after death? Is their heaven and hell? If there is a God why does He allow suffering? These and many other such questions posit the ancient logic and necessity of truth as self-completing harmony. But each of the questions collapses under the weight of presupposing the logic of what is already predetermined to count as an answer, and as *The Answer*. The *aporias* of this logic are where the modern conception of God is to be found – not in answering these questions, but in opening them up to the metaphysics, to the learning and to the education that their presuppositions contain.

6
Natural Education

What is nature?

To study nature is to bring motion to the study of motion.[1] Natural education and natural relations are not unreflective or instinctual. They are not 'water in water,'[2] as Georges Bataille puts it. They are motion known to itself. For us this appears as the relation between, and an education about, mind and matter. What education as a first principle reminds us here is that relation is also movement and that trying to understand the laws of motion is already to participate in the motion of laws. Observation, as quantum physics knows well, is already intervention.

In the ancient logic of harmony the natural relation redeems an infinite regression of change by means of a first principle of all motion. Of the ten kinds of motion that Plato lists in the *Laws*, the two fundamental types are those which can move other things but not themselves, and those which can move other things and themselves. The latter is the most powerful because 'the motion which can generate itself is infinitely superior'[3] to that which can only impart motion to others. The logic of this superiority is that it is its own necessity, where necessity means harmonious self-completing. Plato rehearses the argument against infinite regression here, stating that all motion must have a source that is self-generated. 'Self-generating motion, then, is the source of all motions, and the primary force in both stationary and moving objects.'[4]

This marks the beginning of the Western rational form of the natural relation, which seeks to overcome fear of the power of natural motion by bringing it within human understanding so that it can be explained, harnessed and controlled. It remains to be seen whether 'nature' can hold itself immune from being in relation to its own laws of motion.

The two ways in which this natural relation has expressed itself in liberal arts education have been in relation to the macrocosm of the cosmos and the microcosm of the atom. We will follow both briefly now in order to illustrate the struggle of the Western mind to understand the movement of nature as a first principle. We will see that this struggle is most often expressed as the attempt by the intellect to protect the integrity of its models of the universe by saving the appearance of nature that seems to contradict them. Natural education, in this sense, is the history of attempts to redeem the natural world according to intellectual models of the ancient logic of the necessity of harmony.

The cosmological narrative

There is a well-established narrative of the history of Western cosmological thinking, or the history of the understanding of the macrocosm. Aristotle reports that Xenophanes (Sixth century BCE) 'contemplates the whole heaven and says the One is God.'[5] The name given to the oneness of the heavens was *kosmos*, originally meaning the beauty of arrangement and order on Earth, but being applied also to the order and harmony of the motion of the heavens.[6]

Pythagoras was perhaps the first to unify the cosmos within the perfection of a sphere.[7] Adding *logos*, meaning the rationality of the logic of necessity, proportion and harmony, we arrive at cosmology as the order and proportion of the motion of the one universe. The Platonic model forms the spherical universe of Pythagoras into the geocentric model of the universe with the Earth stationary and fixed at the centre, the seven rings carrying the seven known planets, and the eighth sphere of the fixed stars. Thus begins the challenge to make the observed movements of the planets, including their irregular motions, agree with the mathematical or theoretical model or to save the appearances of the universe by successfully incorporating them into a logical scientific model. Eudoxus, a student of Plato, devised a model of 26 spheres.[8] Heraclides perhaps suggested that Mercury and Venus rotate about the sun, while the sun and the other planets orbited the Earth. Aristotle suggested that motion in the universe must be eternal and that this motion belonged to the substance whose principle is actuality, or actually to be.

This first principle of movement and actuality is the Prime Mover. He is uncaused and eternal, and he is the first cause of all that is in the universe. The path of infinite regression – where X moves because of Y, and Y moves because of Z ad infinitum – stops at the Prime Mover. Here, Aristotle's logic is that if infinite regression were true, then there would be no universe, because its cause would never be reached, and if it is never reached, then there would never be any actuality at all. The very fact that the universe actually exists shows that infinite regression is logically and necessarily impossible. This logic is the logic and harmony of the fixed and unchangeable necessity that moves itself, and which is the cause and principle of the moving universe. Only the Prime Mover can be this harmony in-itself for it is the simplicity of being its own necessity. Everything else that moves in the moving universe is compound because everything else is moved by another and is not its own necessity, its own identity.[9] In short, the Prime Mover, in safeguarding against infinite regression, protects nature (and logic and society) from the relativism of total motion.[10]

The Renaissance enacts the rebellion against saving the appearances of the objects for the sake of speculation. Petrarch leads the way with his withering attack on Aristotle and Aristotelians in, for example, *On His Own Ignorance* (1368). Here he asks a simple and direct question in relation to natural philosophy. How could the ancients and the scholastics presume to know so much about nature having seen so little of it, and to know so much about specific things in nature which they have never seen? How, asks Petrarch, could Aristotle have known 'something for which there is no reason and which cannot be proved by experience,'[11] for example, the blindness of the mole or the deafness of bees.[12] It seems to Petrarch that the Scholastics assume to know what they cannot experience and decline to know what they can experience.

This re-forms the natural relation, for now motion is expressed in the relation between observation and its object. Where speculation gave priority to intellectual models, observation now gives priority to the object, and to an objectivity that is not affected by doctrinal dogmas. Leonardo da Vinci powerfully argues for just such a reversal of this priority within the natural relation. The truth of nature for him derives from observation, not speculation[13] and he claims the eye and not the speculative intellect as the 'window of the soul'[14] and as 'the chief means whereby the understanding can most fully and abundantly appreciate the infinite works of nature.'[15] The logic and harmony of sound rules come from experience which is 'the common mother of all the sciences and the arts,'[16] with painting able to create harmony with lasting and permanent effect over time.

Galileo employs the new shape of the natural relation to the most dramatic effects regarding the laws of motion. Where Aristotle had speculated that heavier objects would fall more quickly than lighter ones, Galileo observes this to be incorrect. Where Aristotle held that the Earth stood fixed at the centre of the universe, Galileo in 1609 saw moons orbiting Jupiter. And where Aristotle could conceive of a universe of fixed positions, Galileo observed that the ideas of being at rest and in motion are relative to each other, and that there is no such thing as absolute motion or position. Here observation begins to out-rank the ingenious speculative attempts to save the appearances in nature which, left only to observation, would undermine the intellectual defence of nature against illogical infinite regression. Now the natural relation demands that the laws of motion conform to what makes sense for direct and observed experience. Truth in the natural relation is to be found in observable and testable order and regularity, even if it threatens the stability of the ancient canon. The logic of the necessity of objectivity is now grounded in the scientifically observable laws of natural motion. The abjuration of Galileo in 1633 reveals the struggle between speculation and observation for authority over motion in the universe. Here, motion begins to express a new logic of necessity, one where, even though the church says the Earth is fixed, nevertheless, *Eppur si muove*, still it moves.

Newton and Einstein in motion

As Kant and Hegel are faced with the absolute persistence of thought's mediation or movement of the object, so Newton and Einstein are faced with a similar problem, the absolute persistence of motion mediating things deemed fixed and immutable. As truth and thought lose and re-find each other differently in modern metaphysical education, so now truth and motion lose and re-find each other differently in modern natural education.

The ancient logic of necessity – Aristotelian in prioritising speculation, and Renaissance in prioritising observation – still held truth to be immune from the infinite regression of mediation. Truth had to be protected from corruption by ensuring that movement could never be known in-itself by that which only mediated it. Motion, being mediation, was disqualified from knowing itself as motion. But after Galileo motion is able to slip the chains of the in-itself and roam free, moving everything and fixing nothing, least of all itself. Motion here is the barbarian who brings chaos and disorder to the logic and theology of the Prime Mover.

Newton observes that the laws of motion are the same for all freely moving observers. The question that modern metaphysics poses, however, is do the laws of motion apply to themselves? Do the laws of motion, applying their own truth to themselves, mean also the motion – and therefore the relativity – of laws of motion? The metaphysics of the natural relation here suggests that when the laws of motion are understood, in fact they are moved or mediated by the thought which knows them. What is the implication, then, of the laws of motion succumbing to the motion of laws? According to the ancient logic of necessity, the result is the absurdity of infinite regression, for the laws of motion will be moved ad infinitum without a first mover. According to the modern metaphysical logic of necessity, this absurdity can be understood differently, as the truth of motion. In the logic of modern metaphysics, motion is in-itself (law) and also for-another (moved), and in this difficult relation it is motion of-itself for-itself. The truth of the motion of motion is a self-determination in and through otherness or contradiction which, in modern metaphysics, is the truth of learning and education. A similar necessity is opened up by the laws of gravity. If the star-souls are no longer credible as ways to explain the harmony of the spheres, another explanation is required which will save the planets from disharmony. But Newton's conception of gravity opens up not just the relativity of motion to the relation of an object's gravity and mass but also the relation of this relation as the motion that is the universe. The conditions of the possibility of the relation of gravity to mass in general are likewise the conditions of the possibility of the relation or motion of all objects to each other.

When the laws of motion are applied to themselves, they put the laws in motion. Laws become what they are not supposed to be, contingent and dependent upon a relation to an other. The same effect is achieved by the observer of motion. As is often remarked, the observer of motion relativises motion by means of the motion of observation. The question is, does the universe have to be saved from this relativity of the motion of motion? Immunity from relativity was granted in the Aristotelian logic of necessity, but this logic is now also within the natural relation of law and motion. Thus, despite the obviousness of an apple falling to the ground, the laws of motion and of gravity bring unparalleled uncertainty into the logic of necessity of the natural relation.

Newton seeks the solution to the relativity of position in the traditional religious notion of divine intellect. He finds in the relativity of place and movement the dangerous implication of also relativising the absolute place of God. Against this, Newton holds to the idea of God who is always and everywhere, who is all time and place and whose substance man cannot know. In keeping with a traditional metaphysics, the natural relation for Newton is that, given the order and necessity of the natural laws of the universe, there must still be a first cause of the universe. In correspondence he says that to make such a universe required 'the counsel and contrivance of a voluntary Agent'[17] skilled in mechanics and geometry. And in the General Scholarium at the end of *Principia*, Newton reiterates that 'blind mechanical necessity'[18] could not produce the variety of things that exist. The God who is 'eternal and infinite'[19] and who is always and everywhere prevents regression of cause and effect to absurdity. The laws of the universe are still protected from the contradictions produced when they mediate themselves. And in keeping with the idea that in the metaphysical relation one can know that God is, but not what God is, so Newton can know the laws of gravity but does not 'pretend to know'[20] God's work in-itself.

Einstein faces a similar dilemma. Maxwell's work in 1865 in field theory suggests there is a fixed speed of light. If the speed of light is the same for all observers, then it is not relative to the motion of other objects. But implicit in the relativity of position after Galileo and Newton is the relativity of speed. How, then, could this contradiction persist? How could speed be fixed and relative? Einstein resists the temptation to save the appearance of the universe by positing the identity of the ether as that which could mediate speed without itself being relative. Instead, he reasons that when the model of the universe fails to explain itself according to the logic of the model, it is not the universe that is in error but the model and its logic. He realises that there is a second absolute identity upon which the contradiction of fixed and relative motion rests, that of time. He accepts that the contradiction is true and he adjusts the understanding of the universe accordingly, arguing that for the contradiction to be true, time must be relative. The speed of light could be fixed and unmoved by the observer if the time taken by the fixed speed of light was relative to each observer. This is something of a Sherlock Holmes moment for Einstein: when you have eliminated the impossible – that time and the speed of light are both fixed – then whatever remains – the relativity of time (and space) – must be true. Within the special theory of relativity Einstein brings motion into relation with itself. The laws of motion express their relation to themselves in the relativity of time, as they do in the relativity of space. In both cases the natural relation expresses its truth in relation to its truth. Relativity (and relativism) is the law of motion relating to itself as the motion also of law. In sum, Newton and Einstein express the natural relation of motion moved by itself. This is not the Prime Mover, because it is achieved only in relation to the observer. Without the observer, neither time nor space would be the motion of relation.[21]

Einstein famously defended a notion of God and religion within the natural relation of mind and matter. His 'deep religiosity'[22] can be traced to the relation between music, nature and God.[23] Einstein spoke of a 'cosmic religious feeling'[24] which has no anthropomorphism attached to it, and which displays 'the futility of human desires and aims and the sublimity and marvellous order which reveal themselves both in nature and in the world of thought.'[25] The natural relation of mind and matter is expressed as the one religiosity, such that 'everyone who is seriously engaged in the pursuit of science becomes convinced that the laws of nature manifest the existence of a spirit vastly superior to that of men, and one in the face of which we with our modest powers must feel humble.'[26] The natural relation here still falls within the traditional metaphysics of an ineffable mysterious force. It is 'a knowledge of the existence of something we cannot penetrate... [but] it is this knowledge and this emotion that constitutes true religiosity; in this sense, and in this alone, I am a deeply religious man.'[27]

There is a sense in which Newton and Einstein play out the metaphysical relation of Kant and Hegel. Space for Newton and objects for Kant become relative, respectively, to motion and to the motion that is experience. In both cases an ineffable transcendental idea saves the appearance of the universe from the relativity of infinite regression. Time in Einstein and reason in Hegel become relative to the observer and the thinker respectively. What Einstein and Hegel achieve here is that they relieve both nature and thought from the need to be saved from being seen as error within the ancient logic of necessity. As Hegel found truth in the relativity of the mediation of truth by the observer, so Einstein found truth in the relativity of the mediation of time by the observer.[28]

The atom and the end of nature

Motion in the universe is also explained at the atomic level. The early Greek natural philosophers seek the principle of self-animation in elements, primordial substances or atoms. That these serve the purpose of a Prime Mover able to block infinite regression or change without a first cause is evident in that 'atom' means that which is indivisible, non-composite and the most simple element possible. The Milesian philosophers of the sixth century BCE take motion itself to be elemental, whereas the Eleatics prioritise being over becoming, denying the void. Anaxagoras sees the inter-relation of all things ordered by *nus*. Democritus and Leucippus posit a universe of atoms and the void. The void makes movement of atoms possible, and atoms conjoin in infinite varieties to produce an infinity of objects. Epicurus argues for the 'swerve' (*clinamen*) of atoms suggesting a kind of freedom from mechanical determinism.

Hegel argues that the ancient atom is not the modern molecule. It is instead an idea of the One, containing the metaphysical constituents of the in-itself (Parmenides), motion (Heraclitus) and the for-itself (Leucippus). Implicit here is the ancient natural relation of mind and matter in which harmony is motion that is saved from infinite regression. The natural relation of mind and matter becomes explicitly in-and-for-itself when quantum mechanics brings the motion of laws to the laws of motion. Specifically, the laws of motion at the microcosmic level are observed by themselves in Heisenberg's uncertainty principle. It invokes Kant's Copernican revolution in that the mediation of observation means that science 'no longer describes the behaviour of elementary particles but only our knowledge of this behaviour.'[29] The motion created by this mediation, notably by the measuring instrument, means that the atomic scientist has to recognise that science '*cannot simply speak of nature "in itself"*.'[30] The movement of motion imparted by measuring is the for-another of the laws of motion, although, as we will see, not yet also of itself in being for-another. The relativism of Kant's synthetic a priori applies now in the relation between nature and its being observed. We might say here that the conditions of the possibility of nature in-itself are likewise the conditions of the possibility of observing nature, or nature for-another. Here is the spectre of infinite regression where observation undermines all credibility of an objective world, and it undermines science as an objective record of an objective world. If this is the case, then, says Heisenberg, 'the scientific world-view has ceased to be a scientific view in the true sense of the word.'[31]

Heisenberg expresses this shape of the natural relation in his principle of uncertainty. There is uncertainty in a hypothesis that is to be tested; there is uncertainty regarding what happens between two observations; and any certainty of determinism has to be abandoned in the face of Planck's constant. Nor should one describe this uncertainty as unknowable, for that implies that it can be known. Better, says Heisenberg, is to describe the period between observations as undecided. As Richard Feynman said, the mystery of the double-slit experiment encapsulates all of the basic peculiarities of quantum mechanics. It reveals how every experiment can produce only 'incomplete knowledge'[32] of classical reality, an incompleteness held by Bohr's notion of complementarity. If Heisenberg is right that there is no nature in-itself, then nature is at best quantum probability.

Mediation and its accompanying uncertainty is the new natural relation expressing the motion of motion. There is no physical world available to us except via the mediation, or the motion, of motion. The result, as Heisenberg argues, is that it becomes impossible to speak of 'nature' as a fixed identity at all. All nature is relative to the motion of observation, or to culture. Actuality is only ever one outcome of an infinite wave of potentiality prior to its mediation. This extends to anything deemed natural, including identities of race, gender and able-bodied. If there is no essential self-animating substance then, for example, 'gender proves to be performative...always a doing.'[33] For Karen Barad the implications of a quantum logic of necessity, wherein observation moves nature, means the collapse of all anthropomorphism. This post-humanism refuses 'to take the distinction between "human" and "non-human" for granted...[as if each were a] fixed and inherent set of categories.'[34] '*We are,*' says Barad, '*part of that nature that we seek to understand.*'[35] As such, 'quantum physics is inherently [sic] less androcentric, less Eurocentric, more feminine, more post modern, and generally less regressive than the masculinist and imperializing tendencies found in Newtonian physics.'[36] She notes too that the uncomfortable and inseparable properties of Democritus's atoms have offered liberal social theories and scientific theories 'the idea that the world is composed of individuals with separately attributable properties. An entangled web of scientific, social, ethical, and political perspectives...hinges on the various differential instantiations of this presupposition.'[37]

This post-humanism is the death of the identity of human nature. In this death live the possibilities of shaping the body without reference to a blueprint or template – genetics, cyborgs, implants, 'artificial' bodily additions and the combining of body and technology in all manner of ways. Indeed, technology becomes a shape of the new quantum natural relation, a new understanding of what nature is, one defined by the complementarity of material and mediation. No longer is the motion of observation at war with the motion of the material. Now the relation to nature is one where the boundaries between observation and object have broken down.

Modern metaphysics of the modern quantum relation

Heisenberg says that this quantum logic is 'an extension or modification of classical logic.'[38] Classical logic is grounded in the Aristotelian maxim of identity wherein something either is itself or it is not. In the law of the excluded middle – the *tertium non datur* – 'a third possibility does not exist.'[39] But in the quantum logic of complementarity, probability and *potentia* there is a third way between what is and what is not. This logic allows something to be undecided and therefore admits the quantum reality of a particle being in a state that defies the dualism of being or not being itself. This logic 'corresponds precisely to the mathematical formalism of quantum theory.'[40]

However, the modern natural quantum relation has yet to retrieve from within itself the modern metaphysics that is its own self-animation. As before, this involves learning about how uncertainty is its own logic of necessity and has its own truth in learning and education. I offer two brief examples of how, when the necessity of Heisenberg's logic of uncertainty is applied to itself, this uncovers the modern metaphysics of his uncertainty principle, in-itself when for-another, because of-itself and for-itself.

The first example concerns the logic of an objective reality lying behind the necessity of observation. Where Kant reproduces the ancient metaphysical relation by blocking infinite regression by means of ineffable pure reason, Heisenberg believes that the notion of *potentia* expresses a radical incompleteness of actuality. But there are two observations to make of Heisenberg's uncertainty here. The first is that while he shares a metaphysical dilemma with Kant, that two things which oppose each other seem to be unable to coexist (the in-itself and the for-another) nevertheless, with a Kantian ambivalence, he also grants sovereignty to the ancient metaphysical relation in which reality is deemed to need saving from its appearance. In his 1942 manuscript, *Philosophie*,[41] discussing the relation of language to reality, Heisenberg says that language cannot represent reality completely or accurately. Sense can be made of reality in connections between concepts, but 'a complete and exact depiction of reality can never be achieved.'[42] Yet, in the same piece Heisenberg also sees in this view the danger that this implies an objective classical world behind the perceptions. Here the ancient logic of necessity and the modern quantum logic of necessity collide and move each other. The question for us is, what is the significance of the collision of the two logics?

Heisenberg perhaps implicitly accepts that opposites can coexist. For example, when he suggests that knowledge of reality will only ever be incomplete, this does imply that the complete lies somewhere behind, and the appearance is thus saved. But when he says that the incomplete is all there is, due to mediation of observation, subjectivity or language, this could suggest that this necessity is its own truth, its own principle. However, this is never expressed by Heisenberg as an educational necessity.

However, there is somewhat less ambivalence in Heisenberg's *Physics and Philosophy* when he says that mediation by the observer does not mean that nature has become subjective. The observer is a measuring instrument and can only register the transition from 'the "possible" to the "actual." '[43] The Copenhagen interpretation understands that no observations can be made about what really happens in an experiment between observations and that the terms 'really' and 'happens' here refer only to classical physics. They apply only at the point of observation. Since all that can be said of what happens amounts to statistical probability, the actual is 'by its very nature [sic] an incomplete knowledge.'[44] The positing of actuality as incomplete implies the logic of necessity in which the incomplete, or mediation, is error, and not an educational truth in its own right. The appearances are saved here by Heisenberg by describing the world behind incomplete actuality as the totality of 'potentiality.'[45] The error of actuality is redeemed within the infinity of *potentia*, an infinity whose own appearance is now saved from being known, or mediated, or moved, by its own truth, the truth of movement.

Heisenberg overstates what Aristotle means by *potentia*. Aristotle defines the matter of *potentia* by its purpose or end. In the *Metaphysics* the logic here is that nothing 'which is of necessity'[46] can be potential, for the end of all matter is to be actually, not potentially. Priority is given to actuality as, for example in *De anima*, where he states that only 'actual knowledge is identical with its object.'[47] In this sense, Aristotelian *potentia* is unsuitable to replace 'coexistent states' or 'happening' in the time between observations if it is supposed to protect pure movement from its own actuality. Actuality is the condition of the possibility of *potentia* because it is the condition of the possibility of the experience of *potentia*. *Potentia* is not its own possibility. In the *Physics* he confirms that 'the end is the cause of matter, not vice versa'[48] and that nature grows 'not into that from which it comes but into that which it tends,'[49] or, as Zizek would say, retroactively. Aristotelian *potentia* is always already decided; this is its logic and necessity.[50]

Life and death

The most important representation of the natural relation in the history of liberal arts education has been and remains the relation between life and death, where life is posited as self-animation, and death is the absence of such self-movement. Life is what cannot be other than itself, and death is never itself because it is always of an other. Death cannot live its own freedom. As such, life is truth and death is error; life is its own principle and death is only infinite regression. The hope of life after death is the hope of correcting the error of death, the error of its infinite regression into nothing. The soul is granted the microcosmic status of the self-animating Prime Mover, while the body represents death and is only for the soul and unable to animate itself. When the body appears to animate itself, this is a brutish appetite needing to be disciplined by true spiritual movement. An ancient liberal arts education aims to strengthen the soul against any servitude to the body and its appetites and to strengthen the intellect against its becoming servant to the fear and anxiety of the death of the body. In sum, life is to be protected against its being moved or mediated by slavery to the appetites of the body or fear of the death of the body. In Plato, souls are eternal and survive death by leaving the body. In Aristotle, souls seem to need the physical support of the body, although they may contain immortality in the substance of the intellect. In Neoplatonic Christianity the soul will only find eternal peace and harmony by becoming immune to death in and after the death of the body. Aquinas, for example, argued that no man could know the truth of God through anything that was connected to bodily senses. Only those who achieve some kind of spiritual or ecstatic disembodiment can have the divine visions of man.[51] Porphyry says of his teacher Plotinus, that he was ashamed to be living in a body at all.

As truth is assumed always to be free from error, and as the master is assumed to be free from slavery, so life is lived as if it is free from death. Only when we receive bad news does death, temporarily, compromise life. But as Socrates said, for the philosopher who can live in the relation of truth and non-truth, death is that which powerfully moves life to know itself.

Death is not just that which cannot move itself. In appearing as the absence of all motion per se it is the absolute error in relation to that which is all motion, life itself. But life misunderstands death if it believes that death is unable to move or to mediate life. The misunderstanding is grounded in the ancient logic of necessity. Life, as its own principle, is its own harmony, its own self-sufficiency. The collapse of this certainty is rather more obvious in the case of life than it is with truth or, as we will see below, with the independent master. The logic of necessity of life as its own principle is that it cannot be otherwise than it is. The idea of life after death redeems life from the error of death. But the logic of necessity of modern metaphysics offers a different understanding of

UNIVERSITY OF WINCHESTER
LIBRARY

their relationship. Death is where life becomes aware of itself, for it is where life becomes known in relation to another. Death brings motion to the principle of all motion, but a different kind of motion than is found in pure self-animation or life. Death moves or mediates life in a way that life is not accustomed to. It brings a motion that can negate motion. Life posits for itself an identity that can resist this negation, and calls it eternity, or God, or whatever it needs to block the infinite regression, to block the error of reduction to nothingness that death threatens. Within the ancient logic of necessity the struggle of life against death is resolved either by life surviving death or by absorbing death into life's natural and harmonic cyclical totality. In both cases the appearance of the vulnerability of life to negative movement is redeemed. The error that is death is corrected.

Modern metaphysics and its different logic of necessity challenges the presupposition that death is error in relation to the truth of the self-animating principle. Instead of overcoming death, or absorbing it into 'natural' life, it accepts that the contradiction between life and death is true and changes our understanding of the natural relation between life and death in doing so. We learn that the truth of life and death is education. We learn that death teaches life about life, and in such a way that the truth of life now appears as its relation to death. Death is the way life is re-animated to observe or think about itself differently. Without this re-animation life is everything. After this re-animation life is everything and nothing. This contradiction has its own logic of necessity as the education of subjectivity which carries life and death as its own truth. To know this subjectivity as education, and to know this education as subjectivity, is to live in and to live as the relation of opposition carried in life and death. It is to have learned to understand ourselves differently. It is, of course, to have learned how to learn about the biggest question of all: why are we here? We are here because life learning of death is an end in-itself, an educational first principle.

Dante understood this, for the logic of necessity of life and death is the divine comedy in which Dante is able to live death in life as the writer, and life in death as the pilgrim. Writer and pilgrim live the present and the afterlife together. This sets a wonderful challenge for liberal arts education in its attempts to teach of life and death, namely to retrieve precisely this education: of the lived experience of death. To bring them together in the comedy of this collision and complication is to bring life and death into the culture where precisely this kind of learning is freedom's own education within the relation of life and death.

This divine comedy we will explore further below. But the implication of this divine comedy stretches to the meaning and shape of the cosmos itself. As Dante's universe has an educational structure, not just below ground but also in the heavens which embody a hierarchy of liberal arts, philosophy and theology, so, perhaps, the universe has educational substance in the divine comedy of modern metaphysics. The motion of the universe, being moved by the observer, is a universe moving itself by being for the observer. The truth of this is the first principle of movement as education. This raises the difficult and challenging necessity and logic of education as the truth of the universe. This idea has always been behind the questions raised in liberal arts education. In modern liberal arts education the idea forces itself centre-stage. Macrocosm and microcosm are the truth of their motion in being moved by that which they create. This is the logic of Plato's sun, as of the meaning of the journey that Dante's pilgrim takes. But can the truth of the universe really be education? Why not? As Humboldt asks, is it not possible 'that the energy of the universe... at the stage at which we know it, must split itself into multiplicity in order to become meaningful to itself?'[52] Why not a universe whose truth is learning?

7
Social Education

Introduction

To study social relations is to bring freedom to the study of freedom. The metaphysical relation determines the logic of first principles in a modern liberal arts education. The natural relation carries the logic of the necessity of motion in the macrocosm and microcosm. But it is the social relation, because it carries with it the contested idea of freedom, which is perhaps the signature logic and motion of liberal arts education. The idea of freedom in liberal education arises out of the ancient metaphysics of the master of movement, or the free man, and defines the slave as the error that cannot move itself.

This chapter employs a shorthand version of the philosophy of history, one which contains not just movement in the idea of freedom, but also the claim that this movement is freedom as education. It describes how, in the philosophy of Western history, the Western individual is free to the extent that it understands freedom as education. The three different shapes of this movement are (1) freedom is to think – from ancient Stoicism to the Enlightenment, (2) freedom is to think for itself – in modern enlightenment societies and (3) freedom is to learn – a modern re-education of the modern enlightenment concept of freedom and of the sovereign individual. These three phrases are used now as nouns, representing different shapes of subjectivity. We begin with Aristotle who establishes the logic of necessity which defines the master and slave in antiquity.

Aristotle

Aristotle is concerned to establish the harmony of the natural inequalities. He holds a liberal education to be open only to the leisured class of gentlemen-amateurs, distinct from the class of slaves, including slaves to the market who work for the ends of others or have their ends in objects, and whose work was not an end in-itself. Mastery over a slave is *despotike* or that which is in the nature of the master. In the *Politics* Aristotle famously notes that the good life requires the necessities of life to be provided for.[1] This distinguishes leisure (*schole*) and the civilised pursuits of the gentleman (*diagoge*[2]) from the useful skills needed to provide for these necessities of life. The distinction between an end in-itself and a means to an end is the natural and legal definition of master and slave. The slave belongs to his master *tout court* because the slave has his end completely in the master. Thus, 'any human being that by nature belongs not to himself but to another is by nature a slave; and a human being belongs to another whenever, in spite of being *a man*, he is a piece of property, i.e. a tool having a separate existence and meant for action.'[3] Nature designs 'some to rule, some to be ruled.'[4] It is 'nature's purpose to make the bodies of freemen to differ from those of slaves.'[5] But the natural relation, not surprisingly, led to contradictions, and Aristotle distinguishes between natural slavery and forced slavery. With forced slavery a man can become a slave who is undeserving of slavery.[6] A slave can have knowledge that he rightfully teaches to other slaves, for example, in regard to their duties, but this concerns technical knowledge (*techne*) only and not character. Knowledge of how to use a slave is not appropriate to the character of the free man, for it is not leisure or an end in-itself. It is still appropriate to slaves, and hence to pedagogues.[7]

Alongside the view that slaves are born naturally suited to their role, Aristotle also argues that all men, free men and slaves, have a share of excellence or virtue within them. It is nature that distributes virtue differently in the souls of ruler and ruled, explicitly between the rational and irrational parts of the soul. This distribution determines the character of ruler and ruled, which in turn determines their proper and appropriate station in life. Since all men have a share of excellence, it must be possible to distinguish between the character of a master's courage or virtue and that of a slave. A slave requires only so much excellence as is required for him to perform his tasks. 'It is clear then that all men aim at happiness and the good life, but some men have an opportunity to get it, others have not.'[8] The highest virtue that Aristotelian masterfulness or *despotike* can attain is the rule of self-mastery, or leisure, and the rule of free men over slaves, in conformity with nature. .

The roots of the politics of liberal arts education are to be found here. The education of the free man lies in the distinction between *schole* and *techne*. Leisure has to avoid useful tasks that have an end beyond themselves, for such skill is illiberal in its nature.[9] Nothing should be concentrated on in so much detail that one becomes skilled in the mechanics of the task, for this detracts from activities that have their principle in leisure. To be asking constantly what is the use of a particular subject of education 'is unbecoming to those of broad vision and unworthy of free men (*megalopsychos*).'[10] Music is the example that Aristotle rehearses here. Music can be for enjoyment, a stimulus to virtue or a contribution to *diagoge*. The free man will need to avoid becoming skilled in the playing of instruments, for that would involve him becoming merely a mechanic (*banausos*). Rather, he must learn only enough about playing to be able to judge a good performance from a bad one. He should learn only 'up to the point at which the pupil becomes capable of enjoying fine melodies and rhythms.'[11] It is the performer who therein becomes a mechanic, for he performs not for his own virtue but merely to bring pleasure and amusement to others. The paid performer (professional-*tecknikos*) is merely a hireling whose performance can be made more vulgar by the audience that seeks only diversion and amusement. Indeed, Aristotle suggests that the vulgar performers and audiences deserve one another.

Freedom is to think

The logic of non-contradiction first understands itself as freedom in the Stoicism of antiquity. To begin with, there is no distinction between the thought itself and the self of the thought. Thus, 'I am thought' is the free independent being or self that inaugurates the whole conception of Western subjectivity. The first shape that this freedom of the thinking self takes, a freedom from anything and everything that is not itself, is Stoicism.

In Stoicism, freedom is grounded in thinking. Thought is the faculty in which harmony and balance can be understood as a first principle. The Stoic preserves the oneness of the intellect, its harmony and balance, by defending it against becoming unbalanced by desire. Just as the unmoved mover should not be affected by movement heteronomous to it, so, if the mind is to share the tranquillity of truth and be a first principle, it too must not be moved or changed, or unbalanced by anything external. Thus, Stoicism defines freedom as freedom from external disturbance, and the means to achieving freedom is for thought to be moved only by itself. Here, freedom is to think. Epictetus (c. 60–138 CE) is reported in his *Discourses* to have taught that freedom is to think, and slavery is to want. The power of thought is to be used to overcome desires, for desires make one a slave to movement generated externally. Desire makes slaves of free men no matter how noble their background or status. Similarly, a slave can be a free man if he is master over his own desire, for who can have mastery over a man who wants for nothing that is not within his own power.[12] The key to freedom for Epictetus is a stoic state of mind.

Epictetus, himself a former slave, extols Diogenes, who was also taken as a slave, because he understands that freedom is to think oneself free from external disturbances. For Epictetus, Diogenes is free and master of himself, even as a slave, referring not to the spoken word, but to 'the state of mind by which the word is produced.'[13] His science of life is lived as the discipline required for renouncing the desire for anything which can lead one to be slave of another. Since it is evil for anything to be contrary to its nature, it is evil for thought to be in thrall to anything other than itself as its own first principle, its own freedom, its own harmony. If reason is applied, then the evil can be perceived, the disharmony comprehended, and therein 'the desire is stopped, and the ruling faculty of our minds is restored to the original authority.'[14] By placing the objects beyond desire 'you will conquer the appearance'[15] and you will know 'what calm and serenity there is in the ruling faculty.'[16] Precisely here, freedom is to think. All definitions of master and slave in the external world can be overcome by right-thinking in the internal world. The I that thinks is the true reality; the external world is only so much appearance that freedom must liberate itself from with pure thought.[17]

Cicero exemplifies the stoicism of freedom is to think. Whatever is disturbing him is to be realised as an error of reasoning. To think something worth worrying about is to misunderstand the truth and life of the universe. 'A soul empty of these makes men perfectly and completely happy'[18] for 'what in human affairs can seem of consequence to a man who is acquainted with all eternity and the vastness of the universe?'[19] As such Cicero claimed, 'I have so uplifted myself that I bring a free mind [*animus vacuus*] to the writing of difficult things.'[20]

In the philosophy of Western history, Stoicism is the shape of subjectivity which has actual positive significance as the Roman concept of 'the person.' This individual is isolated from the universal because the person is the freedom of each mind. It is not a collective mind of immediate spirit or substance. But freedom is to think is also freedom from everything it thinks about, including other persons. Legal right here is 'personality.' It is positive in the sense that freedom is to think, or the person, can own private property and have its actuality in the world through the property being recognised as 'mine,' and by exporting the error of being unprincipled to the object, including to the slave. But personality is also negative in that it is empty. The thing which it feels to be its freedom is that which has resulted from the universal dissolving into 'the soulless community,'[21] into 'a mere multiplicity of individuals [and] this lifeless Spirit is an equality in which all count as the same, i.e. as persons';[22] and where 'person' here is 'an expression of contempt.'[23]

Contradiction, then, is endemic to this freedom. The object to which the Stoic assigns error, and from which he detaches himself, marks the dependence of this freedom upon the action taken towards the object. The tranquillity of freedom is disturbed by the action taken on behalf of tranquillity. Un-attachment is work. There is no rest for the Stoic in being stoical, and the stoic master contradicts his own tranquillity in the very means he employs to achieve it. The name given to the mind that knows this contradiction of freedom is to think is scepticism. Scepticism knows that when thought actively tries to overcome its activity, it is enmeshed in contradiction. Hence scepticism tries to live in the suspension of all activity and to forestall its accompanying and unavoidable unrest. But even here there is a further education. When freedom is to think learns that all truth, including its own, falls into turbulence, then it comes to know itself as the cause of this turbulence, causing a separation from truth, from the unchangeable, which it can do nothing about. What for Scepticism was a problem for everything else now becomes its own problem. This creates an 'unhappy consciousness,'[24] one unable to escape the contradiction between the in-itself and the for-another, or between truth and thought. These are the subjective shapes taken by freedom is to think. They are at once metaphysical, natural and social relations. Pure independence is the in-itself of the master of self-movement, dependence is the slave who needs movement from another; and their relation is the unhappy consciousness, where movement which ought to be its own truth is only interminable contradiction.

Within this unhappy consciousness there is an education fermenting. Since it knows that it is internally contradictory, it has brought the relation of the in-itself and the for-another into the unhappy consciousness. This means that the contradiction is now for the consciousness that is contradictory and is awaiting its impact as education. This impact is the Reformation and the Enlightenment.

Perhaps the most ignored feature of enlightenment reason is that its ground is essentially negative, or that reason here is groundless. In the Reformation, the doing of good works is seen to be compromised by its necessary machinations. Caesar has colonised even that which is rendered to God, and good works lose their direct line to heavenly reward. This dilemma looks to free itself from Caesar by re-routing the line to heaven via the strength of one's inner faith. Here God deserts the world, leaving a situation where one can be inwardly pious and externally ruthless. This has not resolved the contradictory relationship between fidelity to the unchangeable and its mediation by a changeable inner and outer life. Indeed, it has recognised the absolute dependence of the unchangeable upon the changeable and of self-animation upon the motion of others. The name of the absolute power of this mediation is reason. It resists the infinite regression of such mediation by defining itself within the ancient logic of the necessity of harmony as rational truth in-itself. Because everything must pass through the hands of reason as the changeable, or as mediation, reason takes itself to be the truth of and as the groundlessness of everything else. The modern logic of education and relation will ask reason if it can also be true to its own truth and be the groundlessness of its own infinite regression, its own mediation of itself.

Freedom is to think for itself

Reason takes for itself the identity and subjectivity of self-mediation as that in which freedom is to think for itself. The archetype of this new rationality is found in Kant's famous essay 'What is Enlightenment?' Its opening passage expresses precisely this new truth:

> Enlightenment is man's release from his self-incurred tutelage. Tutelage is man's inability to make use of his understanding without direction from another. Self-incurred is this tutelage when its cause lies not in lack of reason but in lack of resolution and courage to use it without direction from another. *Sapere aude!* [Dare to be wise] 'Have courage to use your own reason!' – that is the motto of the enlightenment.[25]

Each individual here is the freedom to think for itself.

In being for-itself, rational thinking turns mediation – formerly the nemesis of truth in-itself – into the virtue of being its own truth in-itself. Where in metaphysics reason becomes its own logic of the universality of mediation, so in social relations, the dependence of the master upon the slave as his property, as his way of remaining immune from the error of mediation, is made visible and therein collapses. What had been thought to be the inherent weakness of the slave, that it had no truth or freedom of its own, and was always totally defined by being for-another, now becomes its strength. The slave had been for-thought. Now thought is for-itself. The error of the slave – mediation – is taken, in a new way, to be the truth of the master – self-mediation. But, significant though these developments are in the history of Western social relations and beyond, they are still defined according to the ancient logic of identity and necessity of harmony. This unification of the master with himself will again collapse under the weight of the contradiction that it believes it has resolved.

Freedom is to think for itself has remarkable significance in the political world. Because each rational individual is this freedom to think for itself, so – and thinking for the moment only in relation to logic here – slavery contradicts this rationality and is abolished. All are now masters because all enjoy the principle of freedom as self-mediation. This is the condition of the possibility of the Declaration of Human Rights asserting that 'all human beings are born free and equal in dignity and rights.' The Declaration accepts that, because of the principle of freedom as self-animation, 'no one shall be held in slavery or servitude.' It is also the condition of the possibility of equality under law where each self-thinking individual is his or her own rational necessity, self-animation and independence, no longer in tutelage to another.

However, in adhering to the ancient logic of identity and harmony, freedom is to think for itself refuses its mediation of itself by itself. The for-itself is therefore abstracted from the motion, the mediation, that is its truth. Here reason becomes merely instrumental reason, a logic of means and ends separated from the mediation in which it could be an end in-(and for-) itself, and immune from the contradiction in which it could learn of itself as its own educational end or truth. By avoiding the infinite regression of self-mediation, yet still mediating everything else, reason is neither its own substance nor that of its mediation of everything else. Abstraction and nihilism are joined here. Reason becomes merely a method of mediation, lacking truth in-itself because unwilling to risk its own infinite regression. In the social relation method is the legal status of each rational person whose rights are maintained abstractly in law, but not substantially, providing only a legal or formal guarantee of independent identity.

There is an education awaiting this new reflective rational master. As in the metaphysical and natural relations, this master is supreme only by not practising for itself what it preaches for everything else: mediation. When it does mediate itself it moves – negates – the in-itself and is opened up to the doubts, uncertainties and contradictions, once again, of infinite regression. Here, the in-and-for-itself is for-itself ad infinitum, and within the ancient logic of necessity, the modern world here is offered either an unknowable truth over and above rational experience or the scepticism of post-foundationalism. Within this new vulnerability of reason to mediation the modern educational logic of relation retrieves a different notion of truth from within the ancient shape of this contradiction. Within its contradiction there is another education waiting, that of the education of freedom by freedom.

Freedom is to learn

History did not come to an end when the Western mind granted itself the sovereignty of self-determination and of universal individual freedom. Freedom is to think for itself is not the culmination of the education of the self who began life as freedom is to think. Indeed, the arrogance of the idea that this might be the highest point that freedom can attain has been the target of much criticism from Herder onwards. The agendas of the post-men and post-women – the post-foundational philosophers – have been set in opposition to such claims, and much work has been done in trying to expose its fraudulent claims of truth. In particular, its instrumental nature is opposed to humanism, and its taken-for-granted assumptions about subjectivity and truth are seen as cast in the image of white male self-consciousness. Its abstraction from the instability of self-mediation, and its self-preservation as method, is never more powerfully illustrated than in Zygmunt Bauman's thesis that the Shoah is a specifically modern event of methodological means/ends rationality.

Such criticisms open up reason once again to the implications of its self-mediation, similar to what Scepticism did to Stoicism in antiquity. That which asserts itself as a totality – freedom is to think, and now freedom is to think for itself – is undone by its own principle of self-movement. It opens up once again the problem of infinite regression. If freedom is to think, then it too must be thought. Freedom is now freedom to think for itself, but this too must be thought and become for-itself if it is to share in its own truth. What comes next in this regression? What kind of relation is it that is thinking of itself, and then thinking of itself thinking of itself, and then...ad infinitum. Is this not again the madness and the error of infinite regression and the necessity of asserting truth as real but unknowable or as merely dogmatic?

Within modern metaphysics this question takes a different form: what does freedom learn about itself in its modern collapse into infinite regression? What does modern freedom look like when it learns that the fear of the error of infinite regression is in fact the error?

There are two aspects to this modern education in which freedom is to learn. Internally the independent master learns that his self-mediation opposes its own truth just as his dependence upon the slave opposed the master's independence. Externally this contradiction of the self-mediating person is also the contradiction of the mediation of one person by another. Here a person learns that its mediation by the external other is the same collapse to infinite regression as internally. This education regarding freedom, that freedom is to learn of itself by itself, is the same truth of mediation internally and externally, but each can only be experienced as the contradiction in which this education is actual.

The mistake almost invariably made in comprehending these experiences is to judge them according to the ancient logic of necessity. This means that 'the same truth of mediation' is seen as harmony, as the reconciliation of difference and opposition. This presupposes that the contradiction of mediation and infinite regression is somehow overcome. 'Mutual recognition' is a notion that captures this ancient logic. Alternatively, such reconciliation is suspected of overcoming otherness only in favour of the most powerful party in the meeting. Here the ancient logic is employed in demanding that difference be defended against any truth, because all truth is only ever the error of infinite regression, and, logically, that truth must always be deferred.

Education as a modern first principle enacts a different logic here. It finds truth – educational truth – in the relation between master and slave, and of self and other. It comprehends freedom as the relation of the relation(s). As in modern metaphysics, in the experience of experience, and in modern natural education, in the motion of motion, so now in modern social relations freedom relates to itself – mediates itself – as freedom, as the truth of mediation. This freedom of freedom is the freedom that learns of itself and learns that this learning is the freedom of freedom. Here is found a new logic of necessity, one which is not in thrall to saving the appearance of freedom from being the error of non-identity with itself. No longer, here, is freedom to be seen as peace, stability and tranquillity measured according to the ancient logic of necessity. Instead, the freedom of freedom appears in the logic of learning, the drama of the divine comedy where self-movement undermines itself by being the self that moves. It is a first principle of education, grounded in its own difficulty.

This new logic of freedom does not overcome the process of its education; it preserves it in education, and it is precisely the nature of education to be able to preserve differently that which it learns. What it learns is that it does not overcome – and should not pretend to have overcome – the contradictions of self-mediation, for that unstable relation still defines freedom. Moreover, and perhaps even more dramatically, the freedom of freedom, or freedom as a first principle, is the shape of modern Western subjectivity. Not as identity and non-contradiction, but as the non-identity that is infinite regression, where sovereignty expresses itself by undermining itself. This contradiction is the law of the motion, or the freedom, of subjectivity. To learn this is to know thyself. It is to learn of one's logic of necessity as learning. It is to learn that I am freedom is to learn.

Education in 'otherness'

What exactly is 'otherness?' In the ancient logic of necessity the other was defined specifically as error, as the error of the for-another in relation to the in-itself; as the error of death (non-animate) in relation to life (self-animation); and as the error of the slave in relation to the master. 'Other' meant other than a unity in the ancient logic of the necessity of harmony. In the modern logic of necessity 'other' is re-defined according to the first principle of education in which otherness is a condition of the possibility of (educational) truth. Otherness, here, is not error; it is learning.

The stakes involved in the question of the other are obviously high. Article 1 of the Declaration of Human Rights states that human beings should act towards one another 'in a spirit of brotherhood.' This is the recognition that all others, all otherness, constitute a community. But how can individuals live in the truth of their relation to others?

For Kant, the relation to the other is a rational a priori necessity, making itself known in a concept of duty. Unlike in theoretical reason, where the in-itself was known as the necessity of pure reason, but ineffable to the mind from which it is experienced, in practical reason there is no such division. Here the will enjoys the relation in which the willing and the object of the will are the one necessity. The categorical imperative sees this necessity make itself known as the freedom of the will, the self-determining will, and because it is categorical freedom, and not simply the freedom or caprice of the will, its necessity is to express itself universally. Famously for Kant this means learning to act as if 'the maxim of your action were to become through your will a universal law of nature.'[26] Duty is the necessity of being for-another expressed in and as the relation, the logic of the necessity, of the individual will.

But for the post-foundational and post-humanist philosophies of the last 60 years or so, the job has been to try to uncover the ways in which the relation of the self to the other has hidden within it pseudo-universalistic, elitist presuppositions regarding gender, race, sexuality and the continuing legacies of imperialism and colonialism. These universalistic ideologies can be carried in language, in law, in concepts, as well as in inequalities of wealth, opportunity and health. In liberal arts too, this question of the relation between the independent thinker in-and-for-himself and the necessity of being for-another is at the heart of some of its most important and contentious disputes.

In one sense the modern civil society of autonomous persons is the guarantee of individual rights applied equally to all. But there is also a sense in which it resembles the soulless community of separate individual atoms, connected only in the right to be the same as everyone else, where 'same' means only formally the same, with the differences that could sustain a deeper relationship suppressed by these formal relations. Modernity knows the shape of this soulless community only too well, not least in Max Weber's dark analysis of the iron cage of personal asceticism and dehumanised bureaucracy and administration, and in what is called instrumental reason which treats individuals only as a means to achieving ends.

The ancient logic of necessity is ill-equipped to find educational truth in the formal shapes of self and other in modern social relations. The ancient logic of necessity sets itself against the chaos of infinite regression, suppressing it with the logic of the necessity of the identity of movement as the Prime Mover. Enlightenment reason sets itself against the perceived nihilism of an infinite regression of truth, motion and freedom. It sets itself as the guarantor of stability in the face of perceived disorder and chaos, failing to see that it absorbs the principle of chaos within it. This is why reason is the problem, the solution and the problem of the solution ad infinitum. In its formal shape it can only repeat the relation between truth and nihilism as an assertion over and against meaninglessness, or as meaninglessness per se. But there are here the resources to preserve the contradiction of infinite regression by changing how it is to be understood, by changing its meaning. These resources are educational, and they reach into the relation between self and other and re-form the experience of isolated atoms in the soulless formal community.

In the logic of necessity of education, it is possible to preserve an experience of the other as formative, as being a condition of the possibility of freedom moving itself. The free individual owes his understanding of self-animation or freedom to the collapse of mastery into this mediation. To fail to preserve or recollect that experience is to cut each rational master off from the movement that was his education regarding equality and universal human rights. It abolishes the movement without also preserving it (differently). As such, rights remain abstract and fail to do justice to the self-determination of freedom in its divine comedy of self and other. For the ancient logic of necessity this abstraction overcomes the chaos of infinite regression. For the modern educational logic, preserving it differently – in and as learning – is the condition of the possibility of freedom doing justice to its own complex self-determination.

This justice involves not suppressing, or abstracting, or overcoming the contradictory experience of each master being formally free in relation to the other but also dependent upon the education that is 'otherness.' Justice is found in the frailty and vulnerability of the formally free person to its mediation in, by and as freedom is to learn; which means, in the learning that is its own otherness. In freedom is to learn, then, community is re-defined not as the overcoming of the unrest of difference and otherness, but as their expression of their relation. It can only do justice to this experience and relation as a conception of education. This is the key difference between the ancient and modern social relations. The ancient logic of necessity holds truth accountable to overcoming the unrest of difference either by making it an unknowable absolute or absolutely unknowable. The modern logic of necessity preserves them by learning to understand how to do justice to them as the same and different – an ambiguity that is true as education.

Whither the slave? Whither otherness?

We cannot end without commenting on the fate of education in modern global economic and political relations. What happens to the self-mediation or infinite regression of freedom in modern social relations? The master's contradiction does not evaporate, but it does get hidden. This is why universal brotherhood looks like a law which constrains rather than liberates those whose necessity it is. In the abstract freedom of self-interest, then, where has the otherness gone that was such a seminal contribution to the determination of the modern freedom of equality?

The abolition of slavery was a remarkable educational event. Its truth, its necessity, lay in learning that each person could be in-itself only when it was for-itself and not for-another. Thus, the for-another was abolished, and the new Western rational subject was left to try to find social and political ideas and formulas that would somehow reconcile every independent master with the need for cooperative life. If civil society is the realm in which particular interests compete with each other in a relation of abstract persons who have no attachment to each other, other than in the competition of rival needs, then the modern rational state struggles to square the circle of the collective spirit of free, autonomous and private individuals. For each private individual the state is experienced as an external imposition. For Kant, taxes were the litmus test. If a private individual can enjoy paying his taxes, it would be because he recognises it as the mediation and the education of the particular by the public spirit. Against this, taxes, taken from those who have and redistributed to those who have not, are seen by (some) private individuals to be encouraging dependence, which in its own way is encouraging a return to slavery.

The abolition of legal slavery has not ended economic slavery. All individuals are supposed to enjoy the same rights and freedoms that come with modern reason, but one's ability to exercise this freedom is contaminated by one's economic circumstances. One can be a free man and a wage slave. What began as the relation of entrepreneur and worker in one factory, one town or one country has now become the social relation of the global marketplace. The West – the richest nations on earth – can delude itself about its mastery because its chaos, its infinite regression, is transferred, by means of property to the slaves upon whom they depend, but who are now successfully hidden from view. The Western consumer is a master in-itself, and for-itself, but the for-itself loses all educational import if and when the master no longer sees itself also for-another, or dependent upon the suffering of those to whom vulnerability and chaos and infinite regression can be exported, that is, to those who are 'other' than the free master.

The legacy of slavery, of colonialism and of imperialism has all the ambiguities inherent in the social relation. The master has freed former slaves, and given them the opportunity to become independent rational masters. But in broad terms, the master did not also provide the economic resources needed for such a transformation and ensured freedom only in the form of continued dependency. Besides which, the Western version of the free, sovereign rational individual is not always the necessity that drives ideas of freedom for the former slave; Western rational law is not always the first choice of the emancipated. Here the war of modernity is waged militarily, economically and culturally to extend the new mastery, the new freedom, across the world.

This mastery will retrieve its truth in the suffering of others if it can discover how freedom – the relation of master and slave, or of self and other – is to learn. The two have to be held together – independence and dependence, self and other – and the only thing that can hold this together as its own necessity, as its own principle and as its own logic is education. Within the still existing relations of master and slave, at home and across the world, 'we' remain the question of freedom; 'we' are its education; 'we' are its learning. Self-determination is only ever partial and frail. Its strength is to be found in learning to be determined by the necessity that binds vulnerability to itself in its relation to the other: in freedom is to learn.

* * *

I have set out my understanding of how education as a first principle manifests itself in the three relations of metaphysics, nature and politics. I have suggested that all three educational relations have their truth in movement. The ancient logic of necessity grounded itself in the idea of the perfection of the self-mover who was unmoved by anything except itself, and that this self-movement, because it was harmonious with nothing in excess, was the pure movement of peace and tranquillity. The modern logic of necessity is, to all appearances, rather more barbarian than liberal. It is the logic of motion, unrest and instability. But each of these is a first principle that can name itself as the movement which is education. Education is what happens in the experience of experience, in the motion of motion and in the freedom of freedom. In the infinite regression that each threatens is a truth which only now is able to name itself. The truth of infinite regression is learning in-and-for-itself. This truth – education – is the law of motion and the motion of this law. It is now for educators to take up the challenge of being their own time apprehended in and as education.

Part III

The Song That Dialectic Sings

It might seem odd that in promoting the idea of a modern liberal arts education I have not taken the opportunity for a rather more polemical defence of liberal arts against the iron fists of measurable outcomes, vocational training and instrumentalism in university education. This, however, has not been my aim. There are many volumes available which offer just such polemics and critiques.

Nevertheless, I can take this opportunity to say that, in my view, an integrated education does justice to human experience in a way that the division of the world into professionally safeguarded academic subjects cannot. I see that education continues to be clasped by the iron fists of method, subject disciplines, measurable outcomes and economics. I see, with so many others, that university education in general, and liberal arts in particular, have a difficult time swimming against the tide in which education, training and the economy form an almost irresistible current. But it was ever thus. A 'thinking' education has always been opposed by powerful economic forces. My response in this book has been twofold: to argue for liberal arts retrieving its core mission, that is, to giving awe and wonder a home in deep philosophical study of the big questions, and to try to illustrate how it might do this by re-conceptualising the study of first principles for the modern secular and post-metaphysical age.

Having said that, it may be a relief now to emerge from the exploration of logic as educational relation in Part II into what I hope will be areas more familiar to liberal arts students and practitioners in Part III. This final part invites liberal arts to re-consider the role that error (or the barbarian) and the idea of a divine comedy might play in re-configuring a modern liberal arts education. Both can help to re-define what a modern education for its own sake might look like, while both are likely to be uncomfortable to the traditional versions of an education in-itself and its virtuous practitioners.

The character of error

In the past, the liberal arts tradition has made a virtue out of necessity, specifically the logic of the necessity of harmony and proportion. Indeed, not just *a* virtue but the definition of virtue *per se*. The virtue of the character of the liberal gentleman is grounded in the tranquillity that comes from being at one with first principles. This is most identified with the necessity of having nothing in excess in one's character, so that one is measured, self-controlled and disciplined. Such a man, 'whoever he is, who through moderation and constancy is at rest in his soul and at peace with himself, so that he is neither wasted away by troubles, nor broken by fear, nor burns thirsting with desire for something he longs for, nor is he dissipated by exulting in futile joy – he is the wise man whom we seek, he is the blessed man, to whom nothing that happens to humans can seem unbearable to the point of casting down his soul, or so excessively joyful as to carry it away in elation.'[1] Epictetus in the *Discourses* argues that the virtuous individual needs to match his desires to what is possible, because unfulfilled desire brings about 'perturbations, discords, bad fortune, misfortune, sorrows, lamentations and envy.'[2] Learning to desire that which is in harmony with nature is one's education regarding physics; learning one's duties as a human being is an education in ethics; learning only to give assent to the true and not merely to accepting value judgements is an education in metaphysics. In the *Meditations*, Marcus Aurelius sums this up: 'erase fancy; curb impulse; quench desire; let sovereign reason have mastery.'[3]

The modern logic of necessity, or modern metaphysics, looks somewhat barbarian in contrast, bringing struggle, contingency, relation, opposition, vulnerability and even anger to the logic of tranquillity and to the tranquillity of logic. It seems to offer disorder in place of order; disharmony in place of harmony; excess in place of moderation; and error in place of truth. One might ask, is there any idea of virtue anywhere within this modern logic of first principles? If Alasdair MacIntyre is right, then individualism has undermined the *telos* of virtue as a life well-lived, and we are faced with the intriguing question: what is virtue when it is *after virtue*? Is it an empty yearning of that which has exhausted itself?

But it is incorrect to suggest that the uncomfortable logic of relation has not accompanied the ancient logic on its way through Western educational and philosophical history. It has always accompanied the idea of virtue, but as something unwelcome, something barbarian, something that embarrasses the liberal gentleman by contradicting and (re-)animating him. We saw in Chapter 7 that the 'other' is defined according to the ancient logic of necessity as that which is error when compared to the self-animating master, or truth, or motion. The barbarian is also defined in this way, as error when compared to the tranquillity, peace and harmony that defines virtue. Virtue and the master are the one true necessity; the barbarian and the other are the error of contingency and infinite regression. But here we can say that the ancient logic of necessity is itself barbarian, for it suppresses the way its own truth exports the error of infinite regression to the other, to the barbarian, using the ancient logic of metaphysical, natural and social relations to do so. As such, its tranquillity is always a forced relation. The ancient logic of necessity is necessarily barbarian because it has its own history not as truth in-itself, but as the collapse of that truth in its necessary relation to the other. This intrigue is the aspect of the character of virtue that is kept out of sight, so as not to embarrass the guests. It is the part of virtue that is its will-to-power, the part that is cruelty in the ambivalence of *humanitas*, and excess in the ambivalence of self-moderation. It is the illiberal that has always accompanied the liberal gentleman; it is the slave who has always accompanied the master; and it is the struggle with relation that has always accompanied the identity of truth in-itself. If there is to be a re-configured notion of virtue in modern metaphysics, it will be in the ability to do justice to the relations that are the conditions of its possibility, justice, that is, to its own divine comedy.

Modern divine comedy, the comedy of errors

I want to try to do justice to Plato, Dante and Nietzsche in their own attempts to do justice to the barbarian within virtue. Plato, Dante and Nietzsche are exemplary in ensuring that the logic of education informs their projects. Each, in a different way, finds the integrity of a first cause not in its identity in-itself, but in its mediation, or its being moved, by being experienced. They offer comprehensive accounts of the universe and life within it which cannot be told except as education. They are able to do this because they keep the barbarian close: in Plato, in the philosophical struggle of the soul and the city; in Dante, in the struggle of the pilgrim with life and death; and in Nietzsche, in the struggle of the genealogist of morality and immorality.

Each of these struggles is a modern divine comedy. By this I refer not to Dante's Aristotelian definition of a comedy as that which begins in adverse circumstances but whose end is 'fortunate, desirable, and joyful.'[4] Neither do I mean comedy in any sense of raucous humour, joke-telling or mere amusement. Nor do I intend an anachronistic importing of ancient notions of tragedy, comedy and pathos. Instead, I refer to the comedy of modern metaphysics, that is, to a modern educational *comedy of errors*.

This modern educational comedy is different from the comedy, tragedy and pathos that Hegel describes for antiquity. In heroic times, before ethical-spiritual powers (the gods) become objective in state laws or individual moral duties, tragedy and comedy are expressed in the poems which tell of how gods act through human individuals. These powers enact themselves as the pathos of individuals. Any human action is 'at the mercy of complications and collisions.'[5] Collisions disturb unity and tranquillity. They disturb harmony and create 'dissonance and opposition.'[6] The pathos of action is that 'it has to encounter hindrances from other agents and fall into complications and oppositions where both sides struggle for success and control.'[7] In antiquity, this pathos is not calculated or bitter or ironical; it is wholehearted, the whole individual, the whole 'actual human life.'[8] The collisions that enact pathos are tragic if hostile, although ultimately they speak of eternal justice. They are comic if individual actions dissolve into nullity when faced with the substantial. We may laugh at the contradictions in which the folly collapses 'to nought.'[9] But the comedy lies elsewhere. *We laugh when we understand.*[10] Just as tragedy is cathartic regarding the struggles of justice and injustice, so comedy is educative regarding the struggles of truth and folly. Where laughter – and with it derision and scorn – merely register the folly, comedy *educates* us in what is preserved within the collision of opposites *as learning*. It is in this sense of comedy, where opposed elements – logic and subjectivity, truth and error, life and death, master and slave – find the truth of their relation to each other dissolved and preserved in and as education, that I speak of a modern divine comedy.

There is a further difference between the ancient and modern pathos. Pathos in antiquity is a wholehearted and passionate rationality defined in the logic of harmony. The pathos that brings ancient individuals into contact in tragedy is 'without any inner conflict, without any hesitating recognition'[11] of someone else's pathos. The pathos of the comic individual (not the individual at whom one merely laughs) is an 'infinite light-heartedness... [and is] raised altogether above his own inner contradiction and not bitter or miserable in it at all: this is the bliss and ease of a man who, being sure of himself, can bear the frustration of his aims and achievements.'[12] In the age of the death of metaphysics, pathos is no longer wholehearted, but instead turns against itself. As such, tragedy and comedy are both transformed. Judged with the ancient logic of harmony, they speak of the ruin wrought by logic. In modern tragedy, eternal justice becomes merely individual punishment. In modern comedy, light-heartedness is replaced by bitterness at the world. The age of the death of metaphysics acts out religious tragedy as the piety of individual subjective pathos in its collision with an ineffable God, and acts out sceptical comedy as the irony and self-hatred of individual subjective pathos in its collision with the infinite regression of mediation. But this earthly struggle of religion and scepticism, secured in property relations, is tragic and comic: tragic because metaphysics is hostile to itself and comic because metaphysics dissolves in its own contradictions. In divine comedy,

[t]he Divine does not appear here in that tranquil night in which, instead of acting, the unmoved gods remain blessedly sunk in themselves like statuesque figures, but on the contrary it is the Divine here in its community, as substance and aim of human individuality, brought into existence as something concrete, summoned into action and put in movement.[13]

This is true now of the modern divine comedy: a comedy of divine metaphysical errors that defines truth as ineffable and/or impossible, and a metaphysics of modern comedy wherein error mediates itself, dissolves itself and learns of its own first principle in and as this learning.

Wholeheartedness can return (re-defined by a modern logic) if *ressentiment* can learn to know thyself, the task that Nietzsche retrieved for us. This too is passionate rationality, a conscience of method, as Nietzsche calls it. But only in the modern logic of educational necessity can the pathos and *logos* of divine comedy be retrieved, for here the logic judged ruinous is now judged by a different notion of necessity. Now it is seen as *logos* learning of itself in the subjective work in which it seems only to have alienated existence. In the modern comedy of errors – the modern divine comedy – we find the modern educational logic and subjectivity, the subjective substance, of modern metaphysics. Freedom, as we saw, is to learn.

This modern divine comedy threatens to re-define the idea of virtue in liberal arts and beyond. The comedy of errors is its own kind of virtue. This is no longer the ancient vision of the stoic and balanced master. Now it is an individual who is re-invigorated by the educational logic of the struggles which define the aporetic relation between modern subjectivity and the death of substance. Importantly too there is room in this virtue of difficult education for anger at the fate of modern divine comedy in the hands of those who disavow its difficulty.[14] This anger can have its own truth in and as education provided that it mediates itself or does justice also to the anger at being angry.

Holding education now as the first principle of the death of metaphysics, in Chapter 8, I will explore the comedy of the collision of the divine and the human as the pathos and *logos* of the work of 'the moving power in human decisions and actions'[15] in Plato, Dante and Nietzsche. To end, Chapter 9 tries to do justice to the modern metaphysical work, or divine comedy, of the educator. Who, after all, is better placed to do justice to the difficult modern truth of education as modern divine comedy, and modern first principles, than its practitioners, its teachers and students?

8
Divine Comedy of Barbarian Virtue

Plato's divine comedy

Plato's notion of a first principle has its necessity in a logic that is both dialectical and educational. This is illustrated in the short and difficult description of the simile of the sun in the *Republic*. Plato argues that the sun is the cause of sight, by producing light for the eye, but it is not sight in-itself. It makes possible its being seen as the cause of sight, even though it cannot see itself without the eye of the beholder. This is more than just a dialectical truth; the 'independence' or the in-itself of the first cause is negated by what it causes, negated by its own truth, and yet the first cause only learns of itself by means of this negation. The term 'learning' here is what is at stake. In the ancient logic of necessity one learns that first principles are susceptible to mediation, to being composite and to the absurdity of infinite regression, and one learns how to protect them from this barbarism. In the modern logic of necessity one learns that the Forms have educational truth as their first principle, because the experience of the logic of infinite regression is an education and a principle in its own right. Understood in this way, logic here is the divine comedy of knowing the true.

Plato's simile of the sun also explains the metaphysics and the politics of the *Republic*. It is a work of education because it accepts the necessity of dialectical difficulty having its own truth and its own principle as education. When the philosopher-king has learned of this dialectical truth, it has implications for the world soul (*Timaeus*) as for the political harmony of the city. To establish harmony in the *polis* requires the philosophers to design the city in line with the logic of the necessity of their own natural, metaphysical and political education. This notion of harmony is not simply the harmony of equal parts in one overall perfection. It is a harmony of different parts, enacted in a struggle of each against the others. It is, as Plato says, the song that dialectic sings. So, the soul sings the struggle of desire, reason and courage, and the city sings the struggle of markets, rulers and defenders. This is the same song, the same harmony, as in the simile of the sun. As truth has to be known in order to be true, and as the sun has to be seen in order to be known as the first cause of sight, so the truth of the *Republic* has to be lived by those whose lives it makes possible. This song is the sound of harmony being played back to itself by that which is other than itself. It is a harmony of its own disharmony. It is the comedy of the divine lived as political life. It is education in-itself, for-another and-of-and-for-itself. It is the virtuous and barbarian work of education.

Plato's logic of harmony and disharmony is also displayed in his theory of the virtues. In the *Phaedo* Plato argues that the soul can be good or bad, moral or immoral and rational or irrational and that harmony belongs to the first in each of these pairings, and disharmony to the second. The soul is not harmony in-itself, but rather it is the condition of the possibility of the soul understanding itself within the relation of harmony and disharmony, or within the struggle between them. As the sun is not sight in-itself, so the soul is not virtue in-itself.

This logic enables us to see Plato's version of the virtues or harmonies of the soul and the body. The virtues of the soul are the harmony of 'moderation, justice and reason,'[1] while the virtues of the body are the harmony of health and strength. Disharmony is vice in the soul and disease or weakness in the body, while the 'right combination of opposites'[2] will establish the correct balance of virtue and health respectively. In both cases virtue is the symmetry of harmony and balance, which are themselves only examples of 'the universal cosmic law of symmetry.'[3] Vice and virtue, health and disease are opposites that limit the excess of each other, but the pathos of this collision is the struggle between them. Plato here has a different notion from Aristotle as to what harmony consists of. Where *phronesis* and *sophia* are kept apart in Aristotle, Plato defines their harmony in the struggle between them, lived by the philosopher-kings who, in returning to the cave, do justice to the difficulty of harmony, and to the harmony of difficulty. Without the simile of the sun, virtue for Plato is just a balance, a harmony of disharmonies. With the simile of the sun, virtue is also a disharmony of this balance. The work of virtue is not the perfect balance of dialectical opposites, but our learning from their imbalance.

In his discussion in the *Republic* as to why the philosopher-kings need an education in dialectic, Plato states that it is so that they can be tested to see 'which of them can relinquish his eyes and other senses, going on with the help of truth to that which by itself is.'[4] He criticises the prevailing form of dialectic as evil and lawless, because when it opposes traditional law it does so without providing any alternative. This is also Kierkegaard's criticism of Socrates; 'he placed individuals under his dialectical vacuum pump,'[5] sucked out everything that individuals assumed to be true, and then left them standing there. Plato says this is a 'game of contradiction'[6] played by the young which discredits philosophy. The more mature adult world uses dialectic instead to look for the truth. The philosopher-kings will come from this latter group and they will be the ones to return to the city to 'labour in politics and rule for the city's sake, not as if he were doing something fine, but rather as something that has to be done.'[7] This is the model of justice as the necessity of work in the city as in the soul.

But clearly Plato's conception of rulers, duty and justice is not the modern conception of free and equal rational subjectivity and democracy. Judged anachronistically it is at best a system of benevolent dictatorship underpinned by a sense of duty and devotion to work for the good of the people through self-sacrifice and service to others. In the struggle between the individual and the community here, the political character of the philosopher-kings is one of 'service to the community.'[8] Moreover, he or she will 'exchange the only creative work he is permitted in this present world, that of moulding himself for the work of moulding other men's characters.'[9] In this sense, the philosopher-king is a 'demiurge.'[10] At worst, however, it is the rule of self-appointed intellectuals who think they know better than everyone else how everyone ought to live, and who justify their right to lie and deceive the people for their own good.

The *Republic* needs to be seen in its place within the philosophy of history. Plato was witnessing the beginning of the decline of Greek ethical life. His ambition was to check the imbalance of natural inequality by the work of justice. Plato is not setting up the rulers as external wills imposed on a subjected populace. He is setting them up as the struggle that justice for all demands. To the modern mind, with its conception of the equality of sovereign subjectivities, it is hard, if not impossible, to understand how this can mean anything other than a master race of rulers and a subjected population, censored, lied to and patronised. This is exactly how our modern subjectivity has to see it. But it is not how Plato saw it. His solution remained within natural inequality, and not, as he would have seen it, in artificial equality.

This same notion of harmony as disharmony can be found in the *Timaeus*, in Plato's account of the logic of the necessity (or divine comedy) that inheres in creation. Preceding Aristotle, Plato distinguishes between the eternal which has always existed, and is never merely becoming, and the universe which, grasped through sensation, is never fully being in-itself. For Aristotle, this is the fundamental difference between the eternal in-itself and the created which is always for-another. Plato however holds to contradiction and dialectic where Aristotle holds to non-contradiction and identity. The relation between the eternally perfect and the temporally imperfect is the relation of creation, or the demi-urge or craftsman who, in modelling the universe on the perfect harmony of the eternal, can do so only as its mediator. For Aristotle, there is no mediator because there is no relation of creation, only an eternal first cause. The barbarism of error, of work, is allowed to play no part. But for Plato there is a different, more ambiguous logic at play here. The question of creation asked by the creature is a question that registers the metaphysical relation of the creator and created, a relation that is as the relation of harmony and chaos. Creation, then, is the relation of harmony and chaos, and herein the demiurge does justice to the truth of his own condition of possibility as the work that relates them. As with the simile of the sun, it is this relation that is the logic of necessity, for it is the necessity of the 'perfect' being to be experienced 'imperfectly' by his creation. This relation re-defines perfection, no longer an ancient necessity that is ineffable, but a modern necessity in which ineffability is its own educational truth. The eternal is its own principle only in being known by that which it creates. Creation creates that by which it will be understood, and this necessity of disharmony, this element of barbarism, of working to create itself as an object, is its own perfection, its own divine comedy.

Having found a different logic of necessity in both the *Republic* and the *Timaeus*, we are left to ask if Platonic virtue also carries a barbarian disorder within it. Aristotle's notion of virtue belongs to abstract harmony because the virtue of the *phronimos* is abstracted and kept separate from pure *episteme*, preventing both of them from being compromised by the barbarian work of infinite regression. But the logic of the necessity of work is never entirely suppressed by this abstraction. Aristotle is never entirely successful in separating the closed fist of knowledge from the open palm of *phronesis*. But if the two are to coexist in the opposition between the universal and particular, between truth and work, then it requires a logic of necessity that is fit for purpose and that can do justice to the divine comedy of the relation. For Plato virtue is in the individual who allows himself to become true in the logic of necessity of relation, or of education, a truth which can only appear in opposition, in struggle and in contradiction, or with the barbarian rather than without it. The virtue of learning is in the learning of virtue as learning. This struggle and this virtue – this divine comedy – is each of the three Platonic philosophies – the struggle for justice in the soul and the city, the struggle with harmony and disharmony in nature and the struggle with the logic of necessity in metaphysics.

Dante's divine comedy

There is no great difficulty in finding the barbarian in Dante's *Divine Comedy*. The circles of hell contain little else. But it also appears in the relation between the barbarism of eternal death and the virtue of eternal life. The middle of this relation is not Purgatory, for Purgatory is only delayed virtue. Indeed, rather than talking of a middle, the relation of the relation is the contradiction of the pilgrim who experiences life in death, and of Dante who is experiencing death in life. These opposing powers constitute the relation of the relation between the pilgrim and the writer, and it is Dante's genius that he can hold the ambiguity of pilgrim and writer as the one truth of the *Commedia*.[11]

From his earliest days, the young Dante lives in the struggles between rival loves, rival desires, in a 'battle of doubts'[12] fought by means of reason. When the nine-year-old Dante sees the eight-year-old Beatrice the effect is dramatic. His body trembles, and four relations speak to him: here is a God who will reign over him; here is a vision of beatitude for the eyes; here is a power that will for ever disturb him and here is a woman from the heavenly father. The earthly and the divine in relation to each other here are to become the educational logic of the subjectivity that is Dante. This is the subjectivity that later vows to write 'what hath not been written of any woman.'[13]

The ancient logic of necessity appears to Dante a year after Beatrice's death (aged 24 on the 9th June, 1290), in the form of Lady Philosophy. She appears to be offering him tranquillity in place of his suffering at Beatrice's death, by pitying him and allowing him for a while to forget his grief and with it his relation to Beatrice. In the *Convivio* Dante says he was, at this time, like a man who, looking for silver, strikes gold.

Philosophy, here, as the ancient logic of necessity, offers the virtue of tranquillity against the perpetual unrest and disturbance that afflicts Dante. It offers the means not only to console him in his suffering, as it had done for Boethius, but also to enable him to overcome it. Dante here is working with the logic of identity and non-contradiction that characterises Aristotelian necessity. Faced, for the moment, by the choice between resolving the struggle between philosophy and Beatrice or continuing it, Dante turns to philosophy for resolution. He says, 'I who sought to console myself found not only a remedy for my tears but also the words of authors, sciences and books. Pondering these, I quickly determined that philosophy, who was the lady of these authors, sciences, and books, was a great thing.'[14] Nor should one be surprised that, for a time, the remedy for grief means the overcoming of grief. It is of the ancient logic to assert, as Dante does, that 'by nature, one contrary flees another, and the one that flees shows that it flees for lack of strength.'[15]

Yet it is pivotal to the very nature of the *Comedy* that Dante lives with both philosophy/tranquillity and Beatrice/unrest, or, that he sustain and not resolve the difficult relation between them. Dante's pain is soothed by the Lady Philosophy, and his eyes prefer her company to eternal weeping. But this soothing is accompanied by turbulence and unrest. He warns his eyes that to forget crying is to forget Beatrice. Here again is the battle of doubts.[16] Reason suggests that love sent philosophy to Dante as the love of wisdom, but reason also opposes this as a false hope, one designed to replace Beatrice; a third voice says, escape from grief into the condolence of pity, and perhaps the love, of the second woman. Reason here is both the problem and the solution. It knows it can forget Beatrice, and knows that this too is something 'vile.'[17] The Janus face of reason says: seek love by forgetting love. Dante admits here, 'I make myself into two, according as my thoughts were divided one from the other.'[18]

For Dante, then, one heart has two desires; it desires the second lady and would retain the first lady. For a while, it allows love of philosophy to gain mastery over love of Beatrice, but the soul, the counsel of reason, comes to the aid of Beatrice and warns that love of philosophy is driving away all other thoughts. The heart here is the 'adversary of reason,'[19] for it is reason that tries to retain thoughts of Beatrice. Then, following a vision of Beatrice aged nine, a vision that sides with reason, Dante says, 'my heart began painfully to repent of the desire by which it had so busily let itself be possessed during so many days, contrary to the constancy of reason.'[20] Here, now, this 'evil desire'[21] of the heart is rejected, and 'all my thoughts turned again to the excellent Beatrice.'[22] With the strength of reason the tears return to the eyes once again.[23] The logic of the necessity of tranquillity offered by philosophy is rejected in favour of the difficulty of living with both philosophy and Beatrice. Here Dante accepts that his experience of reason as the battle of doubts, as his own thoughts divided against themselves, has its own truth. For a while he treats this opposition as hostile, and tragic, and as self-dissolving and empty, but then, accepting the logic of this necessity and trusting his own experience as affirmative, he comes to see this as an education in divine comedy.[24] The Sonnet 'Beyond the Sphere' reveals this comedy to be an educational journey of philosophical reason through its other, through barbarian disturbance and unrest.[25] This comedy holds oppositions together in a struggle which has its own truth as learning. This learning is the whole journey of the comedy: it is the *Divine Comedy*.[26]

Sometimes overlooked is the way that in the *Convivio* Dante also finds education in the structure of the cosmos and in the motion of the planets.[27] Plato had held to eight spheres or heavens,[28] Ptolemy increased it to nine with the *Primum Mobile* and the scholastics of the Middle Ages contested a tenth or Empyrean sphere.[29] For Dante, each sphere or heaven is governed by an intelligence (or Angel) which moves it and the planet within it. But Dante finds in this geocentric version of the universe an allegory of human and divine education. The ancient logic of necessity confirms that heaven and science share three similarities: each turns around itself, presupposing itself, and turning on its own centre; each illuminates things, the heavens illuminate visible things and the sciences illuminate intelligible things; and each seeks to enact perfection in those things which are able to do so by their own natures. Each of the first seven spheres is also one of the seven liberal arts, sharing as they do certain characteristics. The moon is grammar, for light and reason are not exhausted in them and enjoy variation of forms. Mercury is dialectics; it is the smallest star in heaven and is more concealed than any other; their truths must remain hidden. Venus is rhetoric; they are the sweetest and appear in the morning and the evening.[30] The sun is arithmetic, for anything that is requires number, and as the eye cannot look upon the sun, nor can the mind look upon the number which is infinite. Mars is music, the beauty of the middle of relation and of the appeal to the spirit. Jupiter is geometry, moving between opposites, and is pure white, without error. Finally, Saturn is astrology, both moving slowly, taking longest to master, and being the noblest and the highest.

Above the first seven spheres is the eighth heaven, the fixed stars, which are compared to physics and to metaphysics. The starry heaven displays the multitude of stars and the galaxy; it displays one pole but hides the other; and it reveals movement from East to West but not West to East. This is played out in physics which knows the movement of the stars, and in metaphysics which understands the effects of unseen stars to be the galaxy; physics treats of visible things where metaphysics treats of the invisible; and physics knows the observable characteristics of corruptible nature on its cycles, while metaphysics treats of the incorruptible things, created by God and which have no end.

The ninth sphere is the Crystalline Heaven, or the Prime Mover. It resembles moral philosophy in that both govern the movement of the other spheres/sciences, and without which there would be disorder in the universe and no happiness in social life.[31] The tenth and highest heaven is the Empyrean. By its peace it 'resembles the divine science [theology] which is full of peace and suffers no diversity of opinion or sophistical reasoning because of the supreme certainty of its subject, which is God.'[32]

Here, at the conclusion of the *Comedy*, the ancient logic of necessity arrives at truth as harmony, tranquillity and blissful peace. This final triumph is explained in Aristotelian terms by Dante in his letter to Can Grande della Scala. Reason tells us, says Dante, that everything that exists has its being from itself or from something else. Only that which is its own principle, its own necessity and cause has its being from itself and this belongs alone to the one, the first or the beginning which is the cause of all else. The virtue of all objects also comes from the cause of all virtue, which is in itself only in the one. Since the one is in all things, virtue shines everywhere in the universe. In the *Vita Nuova* Dante makes the same point in regard to the 'knowledge' of the one that lies at the end of the education of the pilgrim. Here 'thought rises into the quality of her [Beatrice] in a degree that my intellect cannot comprehend, seeing that our intellect is, towards those blessed souls, like our eye weak against the sun.'[33] This is the ancient metaphysics which says that, in relation to truth, human finite thinking will always be in error.

Yet while this is the literal end of the *Divine Comedy* it is not the actual end, for Dante is still alive, still writing and living this impossible journey as his own earthly and divine education. Even in the peace of the Empyrean Dante remains in the 'drama of salvation'[34] or in 'the drama of the soul's choice.'[35] Hell is passed through in the literal action of the *Comedy*. But it is not overcome by the pilgrim who will become the writer, and who is already Dante the writer. The writer remains in relation to Hell, as to Purgatory and Heaven, even though the pilgrim is able to move through them. The barbarism of hell is not just a warning of what might happen. It is a sociological description of what is happening, to Dante as to everyone else. With Sayers here, the Inferno is 'something actual and contemporary, something one can see by looking into one's self, or into the pages of tomorrow's newspaper.'[36] The barbarism is not overcome at the end of the *Comedy* for the drama continues. The barbarism is preserved in the continuing unrest and the work of the writer.

In addition, the notion of justice that Dante defends in the *Comedy* demands that heaven, earth and reason be held together, in tension, remaining true to the limits they have been granted. To exceed these limits is injustice. The truth of the identity of each, judged according to the ancient logic of necessity, rules out the justice that can only be found in the educational logic of their relation, that is, in each learning of themselves and their limits in relation to the learning of the limits of the other. This is a sophisticated model of earthly, rational and divine justice, having its principle in education mediating itself.

Dante, then, is able to work with two logics of necessity, one the tranquillity of identity and non-contradiction, and one the struggle and disturbance of tranquillity – the barbarism and illiberalism – of education. The logic of education, claiming to hold contraries together and apart, and having the truth of this impossibility known as learning, seems to do the impossible. Yet Dante achieves the impossible. Sayers, speaking of the relation between the allegorical and the literal, reminds the reader that their paths travel in the same direction but do not cross each other. 'The *whole work*, in its literal acceptation, is about "the state of souls after death;" the *whole work*, taken allegorically, is about man's rendering himself liable to the awards of justice by the exercise of his free will – its exercise, that is to say, in this world.'[37] Here Dante brings life and death together as a living of death. This ambiguity expresses itself on the journey consistently in the mystery that is the pilgrim's shadow. It is one of the most comedic aspects of the *Comedy* that life and death, polar opposites, can coexist in the comedy of their shadow. But, as well as the shadow, the relation has its own truth in the comedy of life and death, of God and man and of man and man. The whole comedy is education – its natural universe, its metaphysics and its social relations all exist as a comedy that is divine and human education.

Nietzsche's divine comedy

Against the tradition of virtue being the highest state of humanity in tranquillity, Nietzsche proclaims 'one is fruitful only at the cost of being rich in contradictions; one remains young only on condition the soul does not relax, does not long for peace.'[38] Here one can find in Nietzsche a championing of the barbarian over the *gebildeten*, a barbarian who, in

Nietzsche's revaluation of all values, will be the new master, the over-man. Bruford interprets Nietzsche as suggesting that 'the church and the liberal humanists have overreached themselves in their efforts to raise man above the animal.'[39] It is in the animal, in the barbarian, that Nietzsche finds the antidote to modern cultural and religious ressen-timent. The slave morality has turned the creative deed of the master inwards to attack itself. Of the barbarian races one sees 'the beast of prey, the splendid *blonde beast* prowling about avidly in search of spoil and victory.'[40] The core of this barbarian needs to erupt at times and 'go back to the wilderness: the Roman, Arabian, Germanic, Japanese nobil-ity, the Homeric heroes, the Scandinavian Vikings – they all shared this need.'[41] It is the instrument of culture (*Kultur*) that has domesticated the barbarian.

Nietzsche's view of the will to power is well known.

> To demand of strength that it should not express itself as strength, that it should not be a desire to overcome, a desire to throw down, a desire to become master, a thirst for enemies and resistances and triumphs, is just as absurd as the demand of weakness that it should express itself as strength.[42]

In 1884 Nietzsche spoke of his satisfaction regarding the end of peace in Europe, and the return again to the virtue of the body. 'Pallid hypocrisy... is over. The barbarian in each of us is affirmed.'[43]

For Nietzsche, Christianity internalises the master/slave relation, such that the master, unable to attain his energies outwardly, turns them upon himself in a spirit of self-hatred. Here is the genealogy of Christian morality, that one must punish oneself, and encourage others to do the same. Internally, morality is the ressentiment of the slave preventing the master from acting externally on his own impulses. The slave parades his triumph over the master as piety, humility and asceticism, all of which for Nietzsche are the war of self-hatred. Zarathustra was intended to be Nietzsche's version of the next phase of human being, no longer fighting a war against himself, but reborn and no longer disfigured by religion and morality.

For Bruford, here, Nietzsche is neglecting 'the social and intellectual inheritance of man, the fact accepted by the vast majority of mod-ern historians and philosophers that human evolution now takes place almost entirely in the domain of thought, and of social action result-ing from thought and foresight.'[44] But the 'land of culture' (*Bildung*) in Part Two of Zarathustra is the land of men that Zarathustra cannot endure. 'With the characters of the past written all over you'[45] these men hide from life. They are 'half-open gates at which the gravediggers wait.'[46] Through this critique of the *gebildeten* Nietzsche carves the history of humanity in two: before Nietzsche and Zarathustra, and after them. For Bruford, 'this is the culmination ... of a tendency to megalomania ... foreshadowed in the excessively self-confident tone of even his earliest writings.'[47]

Alternatively, Peter Levine defends humanism as 'the study of history, literature, and of the arts, intended for moral purposes,'[48] and defends Nietzsche against the idea that he sought simply to undermine them. Disagreeing with Nietzsche that culture reduced itself to relativism, and to the nihilism of the 'last man,' Levine finds in the last man someone who can belong to many cultures without the need to assign universal superiority to any of them. Unlike Nietzsche's portrayal of the last man, Levine's pluralist last men are cultural without being condemned to 'passive nihilism,'[49] and even though they believe 'that all of their customs and beliefs are contingent ... [they] can still feel profound attachment toward their cultural traditions.'[50] Thus, the 'labour of humanistic scholarship epitomizes the virtues that are required for life in a pluralist democracy ... The humanist wishes not to explain, but to describe culture. That is all that is required to broaden our horizons and make us better moral agents.'[51]

I think that while Bruford rejects Nietzsche's barbarism, Levine domesticates it. Rejecting both of these interpretations, one can ask whether Nietzsche's barbarism is a divine comedy, and if so, whether it is one that can play a part in the modern metaphysics of a modern liberal arts education? I want to answer this question in a slightly unusual way, and one which gives me perhaps my most difficult and most uncomfortable expression of the divine comedy of educational logic. In defining the divine comedy in the Introduction to Part III, I noted the individual who fails to do justice to his anger at being angry, and who represses this anger as ressentiment. Perhaps now, relating ressentiment to anger, anger about the suppression of the barbarian aspects of virtue in liberal arts education, and at times anger in and at the divine comedy of trying to overcome both the barbarian and the anger at it, will affirm the fire in the belly of modern liberal arts education. So here it goes.[52]

The concept of modern metaphysics is angry at the continuing refusal of the ancient logic of first principles, and of its liberal gentlemen representatives, to take seriously the struggles that the contradictions of first principles demand. The cost of settling for the virtues of peace and tranquillity is the barbarian repression of barbarian repression. The barbarian meets such virtue with a sense of outrage. From Aristotle onwards, this is the virtue that comes from being generous while powerful, benevolent while despotic, courageous while safe, humble while self-important and dutiful while privileged. The barbarian lives in the contradictions which are glided across with such calm and tranquillity by the masters. This barbarian is faced with either the necessity and freedom of the *telos* to know thyself or to turn down this self-necessity in favour of a career with all of the fawning of the masters and the gatekeepers that such pathways often demand. Nietzsche of course withdrew from such a career. The barbarian can choose the difficult path of battling to give the contradictions a voice, that they might make themselves known both against the virtuous and within them. He will likely be an uncouth embarrassment, railing against the illusions of tranquillity and virtue. His anger is a modern barbarism. But his education comes in the truth of his relation to this anger, a relation that is absolutely necessary if he is not to luxuriate in this anger and see it turn inwards as ressentiment. The barbarian can be angry and learn to hold this anger to account for itself within freedom is to learn.

How personal should I make this? I am a barbarian because I have not resolved the ambivalence of my humanity, and I don't consider myself virtuous. My freedom rests on the slavery of others; my humanity survives only by its own inhumanity; my subjectivity is an inequality of the world's resources; my entitlements are grounded in theft; of course I am angry. I spend my life trying to understand how the structural features of human organisation define me, my whole being, in this way. I try to create educational spaces in which the truth of education can have a voice against so much else in the educational world which suppresses it. I educate for education; nothing more, nothing less. The work is the anger. I am not so angry at the history of liberal arts education that I believe it must not be taught, for such censorship would only mediate in advance the anger and the education of others. But I am angry that justice in the world is so difficult, and made more so by the gentlemen who traduce the truth of education into tranquillity. I am angry at education which preserves injustice, sometimes not knowingly, sometimes in full ironical, cynical awareness, and sometimes parading itself as virtue, as *humanitas*, as the highest and best that humanity can be.

As Plato says that anger will be part of reason, so here anger will be part of the divine comedy of reason, and not allied to the abstract reason that (resentfully) eschews its contradictions for tranquillity. The barbarian learns from anger without overcoming it. The tranquil master exports anger as his other, assigns it to the barbarian as mere property and fails to see how this diminishes both master and slave. But modern metaphysics, aware of the anger within the divine comedy of truth in which reason opposes itself at every turn, also educates anger to know itself differently, to find the truth of the modern barbarian: that is, that the anger has its *telos* not just in freedom, but in the discipline of freedom is to learn. So, can a modern liberal arts education be barbarian, can it be angry, can it oppose the tradition that is its own subjectivity? Can it bite the hand – its own hand – that feeds it? Of course. Modern liberal arts education climbs inside the ancient foundation of privilege by reforming the nature of first principles which have served the masters for so long. Modern liberal arts education is self-opposition. It is a self that may not be welcome. But it is a self that was ever present in the work of the slave of which the master's liberal character was a parody. 'I am slave to duty' said the master. 'You are slave only to your own privilege,' said the slave.

The slave will not go away, for he or she was the truth of the master all along. But now this contradiction demands a different kind of character; it demands the barbarian for whom truth is the burden of necessity as self-education, and for whom, anger, in mediating itself, does not become a new tyranny, for it is angry even at that. This same individual will find comedy in his or her anger. This anger will struggle with its own integrity, and this will form part of the pathos and *logos* of his or her divine comedy.

9
The Work of Education

I have argued that a modern notion of education for its own sake is to be found in the discomfort of the ancient logic of identity. This education unsettles perfection and tranquillity and harmony. The work of education is just this unsettling, and is, in this sense, barbarian and illiberal. But I relate leisure to the barbarian not from any ideological stance. Far from it. Modern metaphysics does not advocate that work overcomes leisure. The very idea of overcoming is merely the logic of mastery, another propertied relation in which the victor establishes himself as his own principle, casting out the vanquished as other and as error.

This same point is relevant to contemporary issues in liberal arts education about the canon that reflects the mastery mostly of dead white male philosophers and writers. The aim of 'overcoming' this canon rebounds on itself because overcoming simply installs new masters, new victors. The furniture is shuffled around the room, but such change is very much the status quo in terms of learning and education. To seek to overcome the mastery of imperialism, colonialism, racism, sexism and elitism, whether in the canon or more broadly, is in effect to employ a thief to catch a thief. The logic of overcoming, here, resists the logic of education that can be retrieved from the infinite regression of mastery overcoming mastery.

In retrieving the idea of education for its own sake, I am also distinguishing it from the logic of leisure. The modern logic of education for its own sake holds within it a joy and a depth very different from ancient tranquillity or virtue. But if education is a truth in-and-for-itself, how are we to work with the truth of education? This question returns us to the beginning of our study and to two central tensions in liberal arts education – the relation between philosophy and rhetoric and the relation between discipline and freedom. If, in my version of modern liberal arts education, rhetoric seems to have been displaced once again by metaphysics, now in this final chapter, philosophy will be challenged to find a way of speaking its own difficult truth.

Speaking of education

If education has a voice and can speak of itself as something in its own right, we have heard it divide itself into the opposing camps of philosophy and rhetoric, discipline and freedom, the closed fist and the open palm, the *vita contemplativa* and the *vita activa*; and heard it experiencing itself in the ambivalence of *paideia*, humanism and *Bildung*. But it can also be heard in the contradictions of the teacher of *humanitas*. Teachers might punish some for the benefit of the whole class; they might teach freedom of expression yet demand students remain quiet; they might teach the duties of active life, yet insist on passivity in learning; they might teach freedom of thought through the discipline of a prescribed curriculum; they might teach the equality of human beings yet do so from their position of power and authority over the student; they might encourage individuality by means of conformity; they might, in short, use methods to achieve their universal aims and goals which oppose and contradict those goals. In this sense teachers might perfectly embody the ambivalence and pathos of the divine comedy of *humanitas*.

Education speaks of itself in the logic of these troubling contradictions. When education is judged according to the ancient logic of necessity, it is found wanting, for it is unable to achieve the peace and tranquillity that this logic holds to as its truth. It is unable to overcome its finite, subjective and temporal mediation of the infinite, objective and eternal truth. As such, education here is always error in relation to truth, always its other. The problem is compounded because within this logic of necessity education is judged according to its ability to overcome contradiction, ambiguity and inconsistency. But all attempts to overcome the error of mediation only repeat the mediation they seek to overcome. The most fundamental model of this education is where enlightenment claims to overcome ignorance but where, instead, the answer to the question only becomes another question needing to be answered. Sometimes called the dialectic of enlightenment, this is where education falls into infinite regression. The subjectivity of this infinite regression is the distraught teacher who might feel she must resign herself to the ultimate meaninglessness of education in this eternal return of the divine comedy. Her resignation can become a cynical nihilism, an ironic game-playing or an intrigue which hides power behind piety and ruthlessness behind duty. It appears, within this logic of necessity, that education cannot have meaning in-itself.

Yet education can do justice to the conditions of its possibility, if it takes responsibility for its difficulties rather than trying to avoid them or become cynical about them. It can speak its truth as these difficulties. It can accept that the barbarian is present in the virtue of teaching; that the nature of education is concerned to disrupt, to unsettle, to move the stationary mind and to make things harder, not more peaceful. (This is sometimes expressed by teachers who feel they are corrupting their students by encouraging self-enquiry through philosophical questioning, and who make life more difficult for their students.) It can understand too, that if the barbarian in education is the turbulence of mediation *contra* tranquillity, then denying the barbarian in education is itself a mediation, a forced tranquillity, and a forced tranquillity is turbulent, or a repetition of the barbarian. Understanding complicity in the barbarian is a step towards the modern logic of education as a first principle.

This ambivalence of education is liberal and barbarian, master and slave, freedom and discipline, and repose and revel. It has always accompanied virtue and *humanitas* in liberal arts and beyond it. If there is to be a modern first principle of the *humanitas* of education, then we should remember the roots of the term *umanista* in the Renaissance as referring to the teacher and student. The modern first principle of *humanitas*, today, is to be found in the discomfort of the oppositions experienced in teaching, not in avoiding them, or in simply resigning from the work, becoming cynical regarding it, or, the ancient response, separating the population into those who can understand first principles and universality, and those who can't.

Philosophy and rhetoric

In Part I we saw Kimball present the history of the *artes liberales* as the debate between philosophers and orators. We can re-assess this relationship now in the challenge of education speaking of itself. The vocation of sophistic education is to give voice to the ancient conception of human being that emerged out of tradition and into Greek political culture. The vocation of this culture is rhetoric, that is to speak for itself and as itself. The orators knew the importance of knowledge gained from philosophical study if a speech is to be eloquent and logical. It is less clear that the philosophers thought rhetoric essential for the understanding of truth. In the separation of theory and practice, or of *episteme* and *phronesis*, philosophy could inform the structure and content of speech, but only rhetoric could enact the true and the beautiful as the good. In this communication of the truth of human culture to itself, by itself, this human culture is its own truth as education. The oratorical tradition tries to capture this educational truth, demanding that its practitioners enact the logic of necessity of harmony by being a model of virtue that others might emulate. The philosophical tradition has its educational truth enacted in the Socratic dialogue or *elenchus* of question and answer. But in the rhetorical tradition the speech is deemed creative even though it can be a set piece, while the *elenchus* is deemed formulaic by its restriction to a preconceived method. Rhetoric surpasses the logical through its embellishment in the affective. A virtuous oratorical education is not based on logic alone, but as well on the power of persuasion.

In trying to comprehend the relationship between philosophy and oratory, it would be easy to claim that their opposition can be reconciled in a relation of mutual dependence. In Kantian terms one might say rhetoric without philosophy is verbosity, while philosophy without rhetoric is idle. They appear to need each other; rhetoric needs contemplation and contemplation needs to practice.[1] This idea of mutual dependence is one of the most powerful interventions that the ancient logic of necessity makes on its own behalf. It represents itself as the logic of identity by being a block to infinite regression, without appearing to posit the truth of a relationship in an illegitimate sphere of the beyond. This is the attraction of all middles, of all ideas of intersubjectivity. But mutual dependence still carries the presupposition of the ancient logic of necessity. What it is prejudiced against is the idea that infinite regression can be a relation with a subjective substance – an experienced truth – of its own. Mutual dependence and intersubjectivity mend the error of infinite regression, denying it its own educational truth.

The relation of unrest between philosophy and rhetoric is just such an educational truth in modern educational logic, and here one does not have to choose between philosophy and rhetoric, or suppress their educative relation by means of mutual dependence. Instead, each invites re-education about their relation from within the opposition of the relation. A modern liberal arts programme does not aim to train abstract thinkers any more than it does verbose speakers. It aims at a different voice from either of these. The voice of the modern logic of education cannot do justice to itself unless it mediates thought and speech by their truth in and as education. This mediation re-defines both the notion of a philosopher and an orator. I will illustrate this now with the examples of the modern educational logic of the student voice and of the work of teaching. Both are examples of education speaking of itself.

The student voice

The two logics have two very different notions of philosophy and rhetoric. As such, they also create very different kinds of educational programmes and aim for different kinds of student voice. The programme grounded in ancient logic will reward the rigorous cleansing of contradiction, ambiguity and opposition within the student essay or presentation. The voice will seek to win over its audience by the consistency of its argument and in the way it overcomes criticisms by revealing inconsistencies and contradictions in an opponent's position. Indeed, the ancient logic of necessity lends itself to the idea of the student defending his or her 'position.' Even though all positions are finite and therefore compound, nevertheless prizes are on offer for those positions which are best at avoiding or masking this contingency, and appearing able to stand on their own two feet. At its worst, the logic of the 'position' sees education as the battle between abstract positions each seeking to overcome the other.

A programme of modern liberal arts education, grounded in modern metaphysics, works with the relation between philosophy and rhetoric differently. It rewards the mediation of that abstract voice in the student essay or presentation which can work with, and find meaning in, contradictions, ambiguities and unresolved oppositions. The work will mediate its own abstractions, encouraging the reader or the audience away from positions and into tensions. The student voice which mediates itself will be heard not as a position but as learning. It will attend to the educational voice that lies suppressed within the abstract voice. It will illustrate that abstractions are as if shot from a pistol, and it will put itself in harms way. On a modern liberal arts programme the student may lose the abstract voice altogether on the pathway of doubt and its apparent infinite regression, and believe he or she has nothing to say. But the modern liberal arts programme also plans for its return. The silence, for a while, speaks as the self-mediating educational voice.

I paraphrase Rowan Williams here,[2] who observes that in speaking, and in continuing to speak, one is perhaps also rejecting the idea of a 'descriptive closure' that is somehow adequate to reality. What is interesting is precisely those things which unsettle such closure, for these are likely to be the mysteries, perhaps the awe and wonder, that lead one to ask the big questions. Faced with these questions, 'what is lacking is not more evidence, more facts, more knowledge, in the usual sense of the word.' Indeed, one needs to yield to what is known and learn that 'what confronts us is still interrogating us.' He says,

> What I'm talking about is less a matter of a tight conceptual agreement being unfolded, than a matter of a particular kind of practice of speaking and asking... a rhetoric, a verbal practice of asking about the world until it hits the buffers; at which point you don't look for an explanation, some bit of it you haven't yet explained; you ask is there another way of talking about this?

Or, in modern metaphysics, is there another logic by which the limits of the descriptive and explanatory logic of necessity might make sense or have significance in themselves?

The voice of modern liberal arts education and its philosophical rhetoric think to the edge of what the ancient logic makes possible, and, 'if there is not going to be an answer, you have to break through into something that is not an answer but is nonetheless a real mode of consciousness which itself eludes precise characterization' in the ancient logic. The aim of modern liberal arts education, then, would be for its students' voices to recognise 'the way that language puts questions to itself and destabilizes our expectations that we can settle or complete our thinking of the world we inhabit.' Here I think 'complete' would mean an end to infinite regression by means of the logic of an ancient first principle, and 'settle' would mean to accept that there can be no absolute truth per se. Williams also speaks the voice of difficulty that is the subject and substance of modern logic, stating that in the difficulty of struggling for words that can speak of itself, speak of the difficulty, perhaps this 'most clearly underlines what language as freedom means.' The modern metaphysics of the student voice speaks this difficulty of language that Williams is describing. It is the way in which modern metaphysics, the voice of education as a first principle, can speak of itself and for itself. This is the rhetoric of the philosophy and the philosophy of the rhetoric of a modern liberal arts education. In the student voice that returns from the loss of voice is the educational necessity that does justice to the loss and finds a way to express this justice in the voice and as the voice.

What does all this mean for the more usual sense of rhetoric? Let us raise the stakes again. Oratory's proud history is that it is the practice of nation-building, of moving hearts and minds towards the good, the virtuous and the principled. To mediate this voice in any way would surely reduce its effectiveness, depress its power to enact the good and weaken its ability to bring about change. But if the mediation of oratory by education does this, then education is doing its job. It cannot let oratory be unjust to the very foundations that it claims to stand upon. Education fights for rhetoric to do justice to education. This could be as little as to see the speaker raise doubts and concerns about her own power, about the case she is making and mediate the power that she knows her voice can command. But, one may respond, would even this not dampen the passion and conviction with which she holds and presents her case? Would this mark the transition of the conviction politician to the doubtful politician? In reply, if it does, would this not be a welcome addition to the political landscape? Would this not admit to the relation of virtue and the barbarian in the authority of the nation-builder? Would politics suffer if an educational voice were to mediate the power of political rhetoric? Or, rather, would it be challenged to find meaning in the expression of its limits? Education as a first principle does not seek the resolution of the relationship between philosophy and oratory; it asks only that they honestly express its difficulty and express the difficulty of this honesty. This is the modern metaphysical student voice available to all masters who speak the truth of learning.

The work of education – the teacher

How does the modern logic of necessity, the work of education, appear as pedagogy? This is to ask, if the truth of modern education for its own sake is difficulty, then how should the teacher's pedagogy relate to this? An example of the problem is provided by an allegory told to me many years ago by a student about teachers on her programme.

The student said, there are three kinds of teachers on the programme. There is K. She knows that the goal of education is to get the student across the water to the island. So, pursuing this outcome, she comes with you to the waters edge, she helps to chop down trees and build a raft, she joins you on the raft and sails with you across the water to the island. Then there is O. He takes you to the water, helps you to chop down trees and build the raft, but then when the raft is complete, he gently pushes you onto the water and lets you row to the island yourself. Then there is E. He just gives you an axe.

The allegory touches upon a fundamental truth of education, expressed by the philosopher Hegel, that 'no man can think for another any more than he can eat or drink for him.'[3] Given this, the dilemma arises that the more effectively one teaches, potentially the more damage one does to students learning from difficulty for themselves.[4] What, then, is the teacher to do? If the teacher is reading Plato's *Republic* or Augustine's *Confessions*, just how much work should she do for the students and how much should she resist doing? One can say that one learns from difficulty – and this is a truth that underpins my vision of modern liberal arts education – but how is one to keep difficulty alive so that it can be an educational experience? How does one build a programme of studies around a philosophy of education as difficulty?

Hegel relates something of a similar story in his *Aesthetics* with regard to the three styles of art: the severe style, the pleasing style and the ideal style. The severe style grants priority to the content and refuses to mediate its difficulty for the audience. The pleasing style compromises the content in order to flatter the audience into liking the art and finding it attractive. The ideal style somehow straddles the severe and the pleasing and holds the difficulty of art and the experience of the audience together. Hegel says of this style that it has grace.

It is not difficult here to translate styles of art into pedagogy. Pedagogy or style is always already authority, an authority which is the necessary pre-condition of the possibility of education. The severe teacher protects the in-itself of curriculum content and offers no help to students with the materials. No attempts are made to make it easier for them to understand the content. The content is never mediated by being for-the-students, for example, by the teacher putting on an entertaining performance or reducing the content to simplistic and easily accessible formulas. Lectures here would be hard work and judged not only as severe but probably cold, impersonal, and in the absence of any connection with the material, boring. This is the scenario in which the student often says 'he knows his stuff but he can't teach it.' Alternatively, the severe teacher says, if students are bored in her lecture, tough! They are not working hard enough. She believes she is doing justice to the difficulty of the content by ensuring the students experience this difficulty. However, in holding to difficulty purely in-itself she is abstracting it from its educational truth in being mediated or being for-another.

Alternatively, the pleasing teacher is prepared to sacrifice the material and its difficulty in a performance that will entertain, engage and command. The teacher flatters the audience in order to be the centre of attention. She ensures that the material is completely for-another and does not worry about compromising the (difficulty of the) material in-itself. When contrasted with each other, the severe teacher believes education to be completely in-itself as the content, and the pleasing teacher believes education to be the sacrifice of the content or to be completely for-another. The ideal teacher, from Hegel's description of the ideal style, is seemingly in the middle, hovering gracefully between content and performance. But the ideal teacher collapses into complicity with the two extremes of severe and pleasing whenever she reflects upon her effectiveness, or whenever her pedagogy, her style, becomes for-itself. The ideal performer prioritises the difficulty of effect while ideal severity prioritises the effect of difficulty. In the collapse of the ideal style (and its grace) all teachers, by virtue of being teachers, find themselves complicit in mediating the relation between student and content.

This makes uncomfortable reading because teaching is intervention and intervention is power. The question here is whether this intervention is carried out according to the logic of education as overcoming, or as the work of education. Practised as the logic of overcoming, teaching is merely power. Realised as this power the teacher can oppose it and try to overcome it, but the unavoidable infinite regression of mastery overcoming mastery leads to cynicism or irony. The ironic teacher will become the court jester. But more seriously still, the disillusionment of the teacher at the impossible reconciliation of the content and the student can be the birth of the intriguer. He is now the courtier at the baroque palace of education, a tranquil demon having the inner discipline of resentment and the outer freedom of unscrupulous action.

The collapse of the ideal style into the separation of severity in-itself and performance for-another looks very different when viewed according to modern educational logic. Here the relation between the content and the student or between the in-itself and the for-another is the subjectivity of the teacher. In the teacher, and speaking in logical terms, the in-itself which is also for-another becomes of-itself and for-itself. Or, more directly, she is the difficulty of the relation speaking itself as education. She holds their relation to each other as her own learning. She is the relation of difficulty to itself. The temptation here is to say that this teacher is a middle. But this is precisely what she is not. There is no middle, no resting point, no resolution of the relation of difficulty to itself, there is only education; and the teacher is this education. Relation requires educational work; the teacher is not a fixed point who can hold the difficulties in tension. She is the tension, and she is the difficulty of the tension. As such, she is the content and the experience of education as a first principle. Her subjectivity is this education and her goal is that her students become their own difficulty.

This is not the 'facilitator.' The teacher is not neutral in the work of education. She is complicit in all its difficulties. She lives the complicity as her subjectivity because her subjectivity and her substance are found in the work of education. She is, for example, the work of education between a racist text and its critique, just as she is also the work of education between the critique of the racist text and the critique of the critique of the racist text. The 'facilitator' is grounded in the two fears of error that characterise the ancient logic: the fear of being the closure of open enquiry and the fear that the work of openness leads only to the error of infinite regression. The divine comedy of the facilitator here sees the fear of power and the fear of no power collide into an opposition that is itself suppressed, and never made its own educational content or choice. The modern liberal arts teacher, who understands the work of education, knows that fear of being the error of closure or openness is the real error. She is not afraid to be complicit in teaching and knows that complicity in education is a truth in-of-and-for-itself.

It sounds counter-intuitive but, to paraphrase Hegel, teachers find the truth of education in the work wherein they seemed to have only an alienated existence.[5] Within the ancient logic, separation is only opposition. Within the modern logic separation is its own version of truth. The opposition has an educational significance and meaning – a substance – of its own. The teacher and student are brought together and kept apart by the content of what is to be taught and learned. In this difficult relation there is always another content speaking itself (the kind of content which Williams draws attention to above). This content is education and can become the content of a whole education programme as we will see in a moment. This content is the educational truth of the teacher/student relation, both when they are separate individuals, and when one individual is learning to know thyself as this relation.

But the significance of this work goes outside the classroom. It is also the content of Western humanity learning to know thyself in relation to its 'other(s).' Culture, as we saw above, is actual in its relation to nature. Education is the truth of this relation, and teaching and learning are the philosophy and rhetoric of this human culture, for it is the practice in which human cultures speak to themselves of themselves. Teaching in this sense is the closest profession there is to the truth of *humanitas*, for it is the necessity, the *logos*, of human culture. The teacher who is also student is humanity knowing and doing itself by speaking itself. Politically this means that the teacher who is open to learning of human culture in all its difficult shapes, who is open to learning about *humanitas* from the oppositions in which it makes itself known, is the teacher who lets education speak. The humanity of the teacher is precisely in the difficulties that make teaching a singularly human activity. The humanity of the teacher lies in doing this human work. As this opens her up to an educational relation to the student, so it opens up Western culture to an educational relation to others and otherness. Humanity is in this work of education. Is it too hard to imagine human education speaking of itself in the relation between the I and the We, between self and other, between man and nature, between truth and contingency and between universal and particular? Is it too hard to imagine that nation speak unto nation in the voice of education?

The work of education – the curriculum

But what is perhaps most challenging for educators about the modern logic of education is that it can become its own content not only within parts of an education programme but as the whole programme, its structure, rationale, pedagogy and assessment. This is the challenge now for a modern liberal arts education, to retrieve its vocation to work with first principles and to make the modern difficulty of doing so the subjectivity and the substance of whole programmes. We have seen how different the concept of student voice and identity of the teacher become within this logic. To end, I want to look briefly at how different the idea of the curriculum becomes when it practises the modern first principle of the work of education. The example here is the 'Great Books.'

At a general level the Great Books curriculum attracts the criticism that it has decided in advance the repository of all that is finest and best in Western intellectual history. It is seen by many to be the unacceptable face not only of Western power and privilege across the world, but of white male power and privilege within the West. The critique of the Great Books takes many forms, including replacing them with a more pleasing curriculum of books that are easier because more contemporary, or more local to the experiences of the students, or indeed easier and more pleasing because they criticise in simple ways the imperialism of the Great Books tradition. The pleasing style is also found when secondary texts or even textbooks are employed which simplify the content and enable the students to believe they are arriving at their own opinions of the tradition. One severe response is to refuse to put the Great Books on the curriculum at all because they are racist, sexist, imperialist, colonialist and so on. This is severe because it refuses to allow the students to mediate the tradition for themselves. The severity lies in asserting that, because the tutors know how insidious the Great Books are, there is no need for the students to read them for themselves. This removes from the work of education the essential pedagogical truth that the identities which claim truth as in-itself have to become for-another if the work of education is to become of-and-for-itself. If the teacher, either tyrannically or benevolently, intervenes to ensure that the in-itself of the Great Books is mediated by her and not by the students, then the work of education can never be their own.

The modern liberal arts programme understands that the Great Books must be read by the students and that the difficulties of these readings must also be those of the students. The teacher holds the tension between student and curriculum as her own work, her own subjective substance of education. She does not arrogate that work to herself. Her truth is to be the tension between content and student until such time as the student becomes the tension of-and-for-itself. This is not just to teach the content of the Great Books; it is also to teach the work of education as the experience of their content. This experience then seeks its own philosophical voice recognised in the curriculum, and, more boldly, recognised as the curriculum.

Adorno has a very interesting take on how texts are to be read in this regard. He warns against knowing too much of the text in advance, in favour of pursuing the logic of the matter at hand, and he notes too that it is through the contradictions found in texts that education begins to speak. Just as Hegel says in the *Logic* that the principles of contradiction and identity contain more than is meant by them, so Adorno says that what we should be concerned with is what a text 'objectively expresses'[6] and that this will be found in the 'immanent tension'[7] in the text. Rather than accept 'the idiotic choice of either embracing a philosophy that is unacceptable ... or else of seizing the opportunity to gloat over its defects, [one can] appreciate its truth content as one that contains its own untruth.'[8] This means letting educational necessity speak freely for itself in the text, and not merely judging an argument inconsistent where such necessities are found. It means too that the tension expresses more than is found on the page. In this phenomenological method of reading, students will already be dealing with the shapes of the in-itself and the for-itself and will be rehearsing the shapes in which modern first principles appear, not fearing them as errors, but working with their own integrity.[9]

This integrity in the work of education is not so visible in many post-metaphysical and post-colonial criticisms of the canon. The problem here is that they tend to suppress the culture (the work of education) of such critique. This suppression takes many forms, but primary among them currently is the identity of the for-another as difference. This is an example of the power of illusion in enlightenment reason. Difference is not the truth (or non-truth) of mediation or contingency or scepticism. Nor is it their a priori condition of possibility. It is, instead, one of the shapes that modern enlightenment reason takes in first trying to understand and then to fix its own instability. Difference is only a particular shape of the relation that reason in-itself has to reason for-itself. Its dogma is that it is not part of the metaphysics of the in-itself and the for-itself. This dogma in effect fetishizes the new universality of the for-another by casting it adrift from the social conditions which produce it, including the property relation. Here, bluntly, is where post-foundational thinking loses the work of humanity. It makes 'difference' different from the totality of the phenomenological experience of difference. The challenge of the modern liberal arts degree to post-foundational theorists is this. If they use the idea of culture to express only the for-another, then they refuse the challenge of the culture of culture, and suppress how it is reformed in expressing itself. Here, within the culture of liberal arts education in general, and debates over the canon in particular, the opportunity already exists to experience this culture as the work of education.

Finally, then, to the question of how the teacher can bring education as its own first principle into the curriculum of a modern liberal arts education. As we saw above, it is by making subjectivity not only its own substance but also the substance of the curriculum. Both students and teachers will experience education as the struggle with the difficulty of thought which looks at face value to be thinking of separate subjects and objects. But in fact it thinks in relations and is itself a relation – the relation of the relation. The curriculum that is prepared to make difficulty not just its experience but also its content is the curriculum that allows education to be its own programme of studies. This requires the teacher and student being able to study difficulty and to do justice to its substance. This will be not just to talk about education but also to allow education to do itself. And it will be done for no other reason than it is its own truth.

Liberal arts education has a significant role to play here. Since part of its history has been to defend the principle of education as its own truth, and as its own end, so now, the opportunity to express the modern form of this principle can be embraced by a modern liberal arts education. The experience of the Great Books in particular lends itself to just such an education, for the experience of its ambivalence can be studied as the logic and content of the three relations which have always characterised liberal arts education – the metaphysical, social and natural relations. In this way I offer part II as above one contribution towards finding the new liberal arts curriculum in the difficulties of the old liberal arts curriculum.

But a word of caution here. The modern metaphysics of learning for its own sake and of education as an end in-itself is not a freedom from content or discipline or rigour. It is not a licence to teach whatever we want, however we want, believing that each individual will take from such an education whatever he or she chooses to. Such a laissez-faire approach to education precisely fails to do justice to the idea that education and learning are substance in their own right. It is this substance that needs to be taught if one is to do justice to education as a first principle. It is to take education more seriously as something existing in its own right than perhaps it has ever been taken before. Education has ends of its own, and these demand a tougher and more difficult education than any of the subordinate ends imposed upon it. The most difficult educational work is the work of education in-of-and-for-itself when it is also for-another. This is because, if learning is the truth of all movement, then it is the truth of all aspects of life, including who we are and what we do. To work in a modern liberal arts degree with education as its first principle is to bring everything within the realm of learning.

But there is an added significance here, for it brings to the truth of learning the three most important relations: truth and thought, life and death, and master and slave. To learn in this way is to know all relation as learning; that thought is in truth, that death is in life and that the slave is in the master. Taking life-and-death specifically for a moment here, this is to say that, whatever the content one is learning about, in a modern liberal arts education one is always living with death in life. For education as a first principle to demand that we live a life of learning, a life where death is part of every educational experience, is incredibly demanding, and probably too demanding, most of us cannot live life like this. But, as noted above, education is relentless and unforgiving. One can shut oneself off from learning and return to the industries of distraction, but education reminds us that we are deceiving ourselves, and death once again returns to life.

I would add from experience that a programme of learning in which thought, death, and the slave are part of the explanation of everything risks being a very powerful education. It can drive students and tutors to their limits, in order to learn the truth of those limits, or of relation. Perhaps such a programme is simply too educational, too hard, too difficult and too profound to be coped with by students and their tutors. All I can say is that whatever the dangers and difficulties, to teach education as a first principle is above all to trust the process as its own truth, and to do one's best to live with its joyful and profound difficulties.

Notes

Preface

1. R.M. Hutchins, *The Higher Education in America* (New Haven, Yale University Press, 1967), p. 96.
2. Hutchins, *Higher Education*, p. 105.
3. See S. Kierkegaard, *The Concept of Irony* (Princeton, Princeton University Press, 1989), p. 272.

Introduction

1. Dante, *Convivio*, trans. Elizabeth Price Sayer (London, George Routledge & Sons, 1887), Chapter XII, Book IV, p. 210.
2. Aristotle, *Metaphysics*, 982b 16–17, in *The Complete Works of Aristotle, vol. 2*, ed. Jonathan Barnes (Princeton, Princeton University Press, 1984).
3. Aristotle, *Metaphysics*, 981b 29.
4. Aristotle, *Physics*, 242a 54–5, in *The Complete Works of Aristotle, vol. 1*, ed. Jonathan Barnes (Princeton, Princeton University Press, 1984).
5. R. Descartes, *Meditations on First Philosophy* in *The Philosophical Writings of Descartes vol. 2*, trans. J. Cottingham, R. Stoothoff & D. Murdoch (Cambridge, Cambridge University Press, 1984), p. 29.
6. G.W.F. Hegel, *Aesthetics vol. 2* (Oxford, Oxford University Press, 1975), p. 497.
7. Plato, *Republic*, 432, in Plato, *The Complete Works*, ed. John M. Cooper (Indianapolis, Hackett Publishing Co., 1997).
8. Aristotle, *Nicomachean Ethics*, 1106a 28, in *The Complete Works of Aristotle, vol. 2*, ed. Jonathan Barnes (Princeton, Princeton University Press, 1984).
9. Aristotle, *Nicomachean Ethics*, 1124a 14–16.
10. J.H. Newman, *The Idea of a University* (London, Longmans, Green and Co., 1931), p. 137.
11. Newman, *University*, p. 101.

Part I: Introduction

1. B. Kimball, *Orators and Philosophers* (New York & London, Teachers College Press, 1986), p. 2. This argument can be found elsewhere, for example in Kristeller, who argues that 'since the rhetorician offers to speak about everything, and the philosopher tries to think about everything, they have always been rivals in their claim to provide a universal training of the mind' (P.O. Kristeller, *Renaissance Thought, The Classic, Scholastic, and Humanist Strains* (New York, Harper Torchbooks, 1961), p. 12). This rivalry

> appeared in Plato's polemic against the Sophists; it continued throughout the later centuries of Greek antiquity in the competing schools of the

philosophers and rhetoricians; it was largely forgotten among the Romans and their successors in the early Middle Ages, for the simple reason that it had a strong rhetorical, but no philosophical, tradition; it reappeared in various ways in the high Middle Ages with the rise of philosophical studies, and again in the Renaissance when humanistic learning began to compete with the Scholastic tradition of Aristotelian philosophy.

(p. 12)

In a comment that opens up the nature of the relation of these opposing traditions to each other, Kristeller notes that 'the rhetoricians ever since Isocrates have been concerned with morals and have liked to call themselves philosophers, whereas the philosophers ever since Aristotle have tended to offer their own version of rhetoric as part of philosophy' (p. 12). Also, Gadamer notes that 'rhetoric was always in conflict with philosophy and, as against the idle speculation of the sophists, claimed to teach true wisdom' (H.G. Gadamer, *Truth and Method* (London, Sheed & Ward, 1979), p. 20).

2. Kimball, *Orators*, p. 26.
3. Kimball, *Orators*, p. 17.
4. Kimball, *Orators*, p. 17.
5. Kimball, *Orators*, p. 26.
6. Kimball, *Orators*, p. 26.
7. Kimball, *Orators*, p. 11.

1 Antiquity: Finding Virtue in Necessity

1. The Pythagorean *Division of the Canon* states 'All things put together are related to one another by numerical ratio' (Andre Barbera, *The Euclidean Division of the Canon* (Lincoln and London, University of Nebraska Press, 1991), pp. 115–17).
2. W. Jaeger, *Paideia, The Ideals of Greek Culture vol. 1* (New York, Oxford University Press, 1965), p. xxii.
3. T. Davidson, *Aristotle and Ancient Educational Ideals* (New York, Charles Scribner's Sons, 1892), p. 4; see also Diogenes Laertius, *Lives of Eminent Philosophers* (Loeb Classical Library, 2006) V. I. 6–8, p. 451.
4. *Ne quid nimis*; Diogenes Laertius, *Lives*, I.2, p. 63.
5. Diogenes Laertius, *Lives*, I.1, p. 41.
6. Davidson, *Aristotle*, p. 56.
7. Aristotle, *Metaphysics*, in *The Complete Works of Aristotle, vol. 2*, ed. J. Barnes (New Jersey, Princeton, 1984), 986a1.
8. Jaeger, *Paideia, vol. 1*, p. xxii.
9. See Davidson, *Aristotle*, p. 239.
10. On the relationship between Pythagorean number and Platonic ideas, see W. Burkert, *Lore and Science in Ancient Pythagoreanism* (Harvard University Press, 1972), Chapter 1, and on number and the cosmos, see Burkert, *Lore*, IV. 4.
11. This may not be credible; see Burkert, *Lore*, pp. 375–6.
12. Jaeger, *Paideia, vol. 1*, p. xxiii.
13. Jaeger, *Paideia, vol. 1*, p. xxiv.
14. Jaeger, *Paideia, vol. 1*, p. 287.

15. Jaeger, *Paideia, vol. 1*, p. 290.
16. Jaeger, *Paideia, vol. 1*, p. 300.
17. Jaeger, *Paideia, vol. 1*, p. 300.
18. Jaeger, *Paideia, vol. 1*, p. 301.
19. Jaeger, *Paideia, vol. 1*, p. 314.
20. Jaeger, *Paideia, vol. 1*, p. 314.
21. Jaeger, *Paideia, vol. 1*, p. 314.
22. Jaeger, *Paideia, vol. 1*, p. 302.
23. Jaeger, *Paideia, vol. 1*, p. 303.
24. As I will show, it is the precondition of the development of the West's philosophy of history as freedom is to think, freedom is to think for oneself, and freedom is to learn.
25. Jaeger, *Paideia, vol. 1*, p. 306.
26. Jaeger, *Paideia, vol. 1*, p. 304.
27. Jaeger, *Paideia, vol. 1*, p. 304.
28. Jaeger, *Paideia, vol. 1*, p. 304.
29. G.W.F. Hegel, *Lectures on the History of Philosophy, vol. II*, trans. Haldane and Simson (New York, Humanities Press, 1974), p. 48; G.W.F. Hegel, *Werke 19, Vorlesungen über die Geschichte der Philosophie II* (Frankfurt, Suhrkamp Verlag, 1970), p. 61. The relation of dialectics to metaphysics is determined by the degree to which dialectics is seen as an abstract method – in which case it is employed by metaphysics for demonstrating truths – or, rather, where dialectics is not separated from the truth it demonstrates and is employed, somehow, as metaphysics, that is, as form and content of truth. This relationship is central to the presentation of modern metaphysics and to the conception of modern liberal arts education.
30. Hegel, *History of Philosophy, vol. 2*, p. 48 (*Werke 19, Geschichte der Philosophie II*, p. 61). Hegel notes too that Diogenes Laertius recorded a division of the three philosophies, in that the Ionians philosophised only in physics, then Socrates introduced ethics, and Plato dialectics (Diogenes Laertius, *Lives*, III.56, p. 327). Plato incorporates Pythagorean number into the scientific education of the philosopher-kings (in arithmetic, geometry and astronomy) up to the age of 30, as a preparation for the song that dialectic sings. Only by the age of 50 were the students ready to lead the truth of the contemplative life by serving the education of others in order to make life better for them.
31. W. Jaeger, *Paideia, The Ideals of Greek Culture*, vol. 2 (New York, Oxford University Press, 1986), p. 277.
32. Jaeger, *Paideia, vol. 2*, p. 277.
33. Jaeger, *Paideia, vol. 2*, p. 278.
34. Plato, *Republic*, in *Plato The Complete Works*, ed. John M. Cooper (Indianapolis, Hackett Publishing Co., 1997), 435b.
35. Plato, *Phaedrus*, 238.
36. Plato, *Phaedrus*, 246.
37. Plato, *Republic*, 525d.
38. Plato distinguishes between plane geometry and solid geometry, *Republic* 528b.
39. Plato, *Republic*, 532.
40. From Cicero's account, in *Academic Questions and Tusculan Disputations*, trans. C.D. Yonge (London, George Bell and Sons, 1880), book 2, XLVII, p. 91.

41. See Diogenes Laertius, *Lives*, VII, 42, p. 153.
42. Cassiodorus, *An Introduction to Divine and Human Readings*, trans. L.W. Jones (New York, Norton, 1969), p. 159. See also Isidore, *Etymologies*, trans. Priscilla Throop (Charlotte, Vermont, Medieval MS, 2005), II, 23, pp. 1–2.
43. Cassiodorus, *Introduction*, p. 159.
44. A.A. Longe, *Stoic Studies* (Cambridge, Cambridge University Press, 1996), p. 87.
45. B. Kimball, *Orators and Philosophers*, p. 14.
46. Plato, *Gorgias*, 502e.
47. Isocrates, *Against the Sophists*, trans. G. Norlin (London, Heinemann, 1929), iv., p. 165.
48. Isocrates, *Against the Sophists*, i., p. 163.
49. W. Jaeger, *Paideia, The Ideals of Greek Culture* vol. 3 (New York, Oxford University Press, 1986), p. 69.
50. Jaeger, *Paideia, vol. 3*, pp. 51–2.
51. Jaeger, *Paideia, vol. 3*, p. 52.
52. See Jaeger, *Paideia, vol. 3*, Chapter 1.
53. Jaeger, *Paideia, vol. 3*, p. 61.
54. Jaeger, *Paideia, vol. 3*, p. 61.
55. Isocrates, *Antidosis*, trans. G. Norlin (London, Heinemann, 1929), pp. 245–7, 327.
56. Isocrates, *Antidosis*, 257, p. 329. ' "Talking well" (*eu legein*) has always had two meanings; it is not merely a rhetorical ideal. It also means saying the right thing, i.e. the truth, and is not just the art of speaking' (Gadamer, *Truth and Method*, p. 19).
57. Jaeger, *Paideia, vol. 3*, p. 62.
58. Kimball, *Orators*, p. 19, 20n.
59. Jaeger, *Paideia vol. 3*, p. 89; see Isocrates, *Nicocles*, 9, in Isocrates, *vol I*, ed. G. Norlin (Loeb Classical Library No. 209, 1928).
60. Jaeger, *Paideia, vol. 3*, p. 309n. Isocrates allied his own rhetorical outlook to *philosophia* in the *Panegyricus*, for he saw his work as aiming at the universal culture, with the Platonists restricting themselves to one particular method. 'Thus, in the opposing claims made by both sides to ownership of the title "philosophy", and in the widely differing meanings given to the word by the opponents, there is symbolised the rivalry of rhetoric and science for leadership in the realm of education and culture' (Jaeger, *Paideia, vol. 3*, p. 49). Remember, too, that Isocrates saw the difference between the human and the beast to be the gift of speech, or the logos, which is 'the one quality which truly gives man his humanity' (Jaeger, *Paideia, vol. 3*, p. 89). The nature and effects of speech are 'simply glorifications of an entity personified as a god... [as] Logos, the creator of all culture' (Jaeger, *Paideia, vol. 3*, p. 89).
61. Jaeger, *Paideia, vol. 3*, p. 46.
62. Jaeger, *Paideia, vol. 3*, p. 46.
63. Jaeger, *Paideia, vol. 3*, p. 46.
64. Jaeger, *Paideia, vol. 3*, p. 46.
65. Jaeger, *Paideia, vol. 3*, p. 46.
66. Jaeger, *Paideia, vol. 3*, p. 47.
67. Jaeger, *Paideia, vol. 3*, p. 47.
68. Jaeger, *Paideia, vol. 3*, p. 47.

69. Jaeger, *Paideia, vol. 3,* p. 300.
70. Aristotle, *Topics,* 145a 15–17, in *The Complete Works of Aristotle, vol. 1,* ed. J. Barnes (New Jersey, Princeton, 1984), p. 244.
71. Aristotle, *Metaphysics,* 982a 2, in *The Complete Works of Aristotle, vol. 2,* ed. J. Barnes (New Jersey, Princeton, 1984), p. 1555.
72. I am presenting Aristotle here as if he did not recognise the *aporia* of his own reasoning, which at times explicitly he did. See E. Booth, *Aristotelian Aporetic Ontology in Islamic and Christian Thinkers* (Cambridge, Cambridge University Press, 1983) and N. Tubbs, *History of Western Philosophy* (Basingstoke, Palgrave Macmillan, 2009), Chapter 1.
73. See, for example, Jo Dunne, *Back to the Rough Ground* (Indiana, University of Notre Dame Press, 1997).
74. For Aristotle, the science of first principles – philosophy, or metaphysics – stands in relation to all the other branches of philosophy, and 'there are as many parts of philosophy as there are kinds of substance' (Aristotle, *Metaphysics,* 1004a 2–3). It falls to the science of first principles, then, 'to examine not only substances but also their attributes' (*Metaphysics,* 1005a 15–16). Natural science, for example, is also a kind of wisdom, but it is not the first kind (*Metaphysics,* 1005b 1–2).
75. Aristotle, *Metaphysics,* 1005b 12, p. 1587.
76. Aristotle, *Metaphysics,* 1005b 24–8, p. 1588.
77. Aristotle, *Metaphysics,* 1005b 34, p. 1588.
78. Aristotle, *Metaphysics,* 1006a 9, p. 1588.
79. Aristotle, *Metaphysics,* 1064a 16–18, p. 1681.
80. Aristotle, *Physics,* 192b 9–10, in *The Complete Works of Aristotle, vol. 1,* ed. J. Barnes (New Jersey, Princeton, 1984), p. 329.
81. Aristotle, *Metaphysics,* 1026a 8, p. 1620.
82. Aristotle, *Metaphysics,* 1026a 15–16, p. 1620; W. Jaeger, *Aristotle* (Oxford, Oxford University Press, 1962), pp. 216–17.
83. Aristotle, *Metaphysics,* 1026a 27–30, p. 1620.
84. Aristotle, *Metaphysics,* 1064a 38, p. 1681.
85. Aristotle, *Metaphysics,* 1064b 1–5, p. 1681. The Medievals will take up this threefold classification of the speculative sciences. But in many ways this 'theology' reflects the earliest version of Aristotelian metaphysics, where the transcendental religious notion of platonic forms still enjoyed an independent existence. Book XII (Λ) especially is seen as the theology of Aristotle, being perhaps a piece written independently from the rest of the *Metaphysics;* see Jaeger, *Aristotle,* Chapter VIII.
86. Jaeger, *Aristotle,* p. 83.

2 The Seven Liberal Arts: Varro's Secret Path

1. H. Parker, 'The Seven Liberal Arts,' *The English Historical Review* no. XIX, July, 1890, p. 432 (hereafter *LA*). Varro's work seems to have been extant, in part, as late as the beginning of the ninth century (Parker, *LA,* p. 451). Parker says that Varro had a reputation as 'an exceedingly dry and tedious author' (p. 433). He is of the view that Varro's nine disciplines

made up an encyclopaedia on which the author had bestowed much time and labour. The existence of such an encyclopaedia was afterwards forgotten, or almost forgotten, because each article in it was a complete treatise in itself, and not because as a whole it was an elementary school-book, which contained no valuable matter.

(p. 452)

2. *Astrologia*; see Parker, *LA*, pp. 417–61, 427.
3. Parker, *LA*, p. 448. Kimball notes philosophy, medicine and architecture, plus six of the later seven liberal arts.
4. Parker, *LA*, p. 432.
5. Davidson notes here that there is no distinction between liberal and illiberal arts; T. Davidson, *Aristotle and Ancient Educational Ideals* (New York, Charles Scribner's Sons, 1892), p. 241.
6. Letter 88, in Seneca, *Letters from a Stoic* (London, Penguin, 2004), pp. 151–5.
7. 'Rome never coined any phrase which precisely represented the *enk[u]klios paideia*' (Parker, *LA*, p. 423). Vitruvius uses the term *enkuklios paideia* but meant by this 'studies which might conceivably be useful to an architect, not some list which was a necessary qualification for a well-educated citizen' (Parker, *LA*, p. 426).
8. Neither in Virtuvius nor Seneca 'is there a vestige of the theory that there must be a definite list of seven' (Parker, *LA*, p. 426). Kimball adds that Vitruvius (First century BCE) offered 11 liberal arts for architects, Galen eight for doctors (Kimball, *Orators and Philosophers* (New York & London, Teachers College Press, 1986), p. 30).
9. W. Jaeger, *Paideia, The Ideals of Greek Culture vol. 1* (New York, Oxford University Press, 1965), p. 316. Jaeger argues that the addition of the *trivium* to the mathematics of the Pythagoreans 'was really the work of the sophists' (p. 361).
10. Parker, *LA*, p. 424.
11. In letter 88 he says he would not include painters, sculptors, wrestlers, cooks and various others into a list of liberal arts. Plutarch, Vitruvius and Quintilian also saw the definition of such general education as an 'open question' (Parker, *LA*, p. 427).
12. Parker, *LA*, p. 418.
13. Cicero, *De Oratore*, trans. EW Sutton and H Rackham (Cambridge, MA, Harvard University Press, 1948).
14. Cicero, *De Oratore,* trans. H Rackham (Cambridge, MA, Harvard University Press, 1942), III, xvi, pp. 60–1.
15. Here I draw on Richard Bauman, *Human Rights in Ancient Rome* (New York, Routledge, 2000).
16. Bauman, *Human Rights*, p. 1.
17. Diogenes Laertius, *Lives of Eminent Philosophers* (Loeb Classical Library, 2006), III. 98, p. 363.
18. Plato, *The Laws* (London, Penguin, 1970), 713e.
19. Plato, *The Laws*, 714a.
20. Hesiod describes the race of men created by Cronos as of gold, thereafter silver, bronze, then the heroic race, and finally the race made of iron, describing a fall into misery and toil the further from the *philanthropia* of the gods

mankind became (Hesiod, *Works and Days* (Oxford, Oxford University Press, 2008), pp. 109–204).

21. Cicero defended *humanitas* as the cruel and the humane in *On Duties* [I.88, I.35], the former being justified if it was in the interests of the state. Cicero also demanded that *humanitas* extend beyond customary behaviour and spare all enemies who surrender, including those who did so after they were attacked (*On Duties*, MT Griffin and EM Atkins (eds.) (Cambridge, Cambridge University Press, 1991), p. 15n).

22. Bauman is citing the case put by Wolfgang Schadewaldt here: see Bauman, *Human Rights*, pp. 21–7. Schadewaldt argues that the term *humanitas* was coined within this circle by Aemilianus, who drew on ideas from Panaetius of Rome who, in response to Carneades, wrote a work called *On Duties*. Here he offered an ethical justification of the Roman Empire by arguing for the benevolence of the ruler over the ruled. Those born to be led benefited from their masters, but their masters, in turn, had a duty of care. 'In this way severity and morality were reconciled' (Bauman, *Human Rights*, p. 25).

23. Terence, *Heauton Timorumenos*, 77. Terence may have frequented Aemilianus' circle (Bauman, *Human Rights*, p. 27).

24. Bauman, *Human Rights*, p. 26; he also finds similar sentiments in 390 BCE in the idea of universal legal rules or *ius gentium*, p. 29.

25. Bauman, *Human Rights*, p. 36.

26. Bauman, *Human Rights*, p. 37. His earliest reference to *humanitas* is in a speech on behalf of Quinctus in 81 BCE.

27. Bauman, *Human Rights*, p. 38.

28. Bauman, *Human Rights*, p. 39.

29. Cicero, *On Duties*, I.88, p. 35.

30. Cicero, *On Duties*, I.35, p. 15.

31. Bauman, *Human Rights*, p. 40.

32. Other names which are to be found on this path might be Macrobius, who presents 'in readily accessible form the classical liberal arts' (William Harris Stahl, *Macrobius: Commentary on the Dream of Scipio* (New York, Columbia Press, 1990), p. 9); Alcuin (730–804) of whom it was said by the monk Notker that his teaching 'was so fruitful that the modern Gauls, or Frenchmen, became the equals of the Ancients of Rome and Athens' (E. Gilson, *History of Christian Philosophy in the Middle Ages* (London, Sheed and Ward, 1980), p. 111); Maurus Hrabanus; Erigena; St Bonaventure, and perhaps most notably, Hugh of St Victor (c. 1096–1141) whose *Didascalion* finds 21 arts within the categories of theoretical, practical, mechanical and logical. Of his own liberal arts education Hugh writes that in his youth he would experiment with the truths and facts of the *trivium* and *quadrivium* (*The Didascalion of Hugh of Saint Victor*, trans. J Taylor (New York, Columbia Press, 1991) VI. 3). And of the liberal arts, he argues that the ancients 'selected seven to be mastered by those who were to be educated' (III. 3), seven in which 'the foundation of all learning is to be found' (III. 4); these seven were the *trivium* and *quadrivium*. Hugh's 'ambivalence' (Kimball, *Orators*, p. 60) Kimball sees as indicative of the changing nature of the definitions of liberal arts and philosophy in the 12th century.

33. A.F. West, *The Seven Liberal Arts* http://classicalsubjects.com/resources/TheSevenLiberalArts.com/ p. 7 (accessed May 2013); originally published

in A.F. West, *Alcuin and the Rise of the Christian Schools* (New York, Charles Scribner's Sons, 1903), p. 7.

34. Parker, *LA*, p. 458.
35. See A. Grafton and L. Jardine, *From Humanism to the Humanities* (Cambridge, MA, Harvard University Press, 1986), Chapter 2.
36. See O. von Simson, *The Gothic Cathedral* (New York, Princeton University Press, 1988).
37. J. A. Weisheipl, *Nature and Motion in the Middle Ages* (Washington, The Catholic University of America Press, 1985), p. 213.
38. Parker, *LA*, p. 432.
39. Parker, *LA*, p. 439.
40. Parker, *LA*, p. 438. Weisheipl agrees that while Capella's book 'was of no doctrinal value it was instrumental in establishing the accepted enumeration of the seven liberal arts in the Middle Ages' (Weisheipl, *Nature*, p. 206). Capella's book was known as the *Satyricon*. This is a medieval construction noting that *Satura* is the oracle in the text.
41. See West, *The Seven Liberal Arts*, p. 5, and Parker, *LA*, p. 447.
42. Martianus Capella, *The Marriage of Philology and Mercury*, ed. W.H. Stahl and E.L. Burge (New York, Columbia University Press, 1977), p. 346.
43. Capella, *The Marriage*, p. 381.
44. For a discussion of the relation of liberal arts to pansophy or polymathy, see R. McKeon, 'The Transformation of the Liberal Arts in the Renaissance,' in B.S. Levy, *Developments in the Early Renaissance* (Albany, SUNY, 1972).
45. Parker, *LA*, p. 451.
46. 'Among all the men of ancient authority who, following the lead of Pythagoras, have flourished in the pure reasoning of the mind, it is clearly obvious that hardly anyone has been able to reach the highest perfection of the discipline of philosophy unless the nobility of such wisdom was investigated by him in a certain four-part study, the *quadrivium*'; M. Masi, *Boethian Number Theory, A Translation of De institutione arithmetica* (New York, Rodopi, 2006), p. 71.
47. West, *The Seven Liberal Arts*, p. 5.
48. Weisheipl, *Nature*, p. 207. He translated the four works of Aristotle's *Organon* (Masi, *Boethian Number Theory*, p. 64) and 'established the foundation of the scholastic method and offered the only direct contact with Aristotle's thought before the 12th century' (Weisheipl, *Nature*, p. 207).
49. Kimball, *Orators*, p. 47.
50. Masi, *Boethian Number Theory*, p. 71. Another image of roads meeting is the so-called Pythagorean letter ϒ (upsilon). Isidore says that the letter symbolised a moment in one's life when one faced two paths: to the right a difficult one to happiness, or to the left and easier one to ruin and destruction (Isidore, *Etymologies, vol. 1*, trans. Priscilla Throop (Vermont, MedievalMS, 2005), 1.3.7). Petrarch retells his choosing the left path in *Secretum* (book 3) where Petrarch imagines himself questioned by St Augustine. Kimball notes that the term *trivium*, used 'for the three language arts, came into use in Alcuin's circle of scholars' (*Orators*, p. 51) in the late eighth century at York. West suggested the term *trivium* may go back to the time of Boethius (*Alcuin and the Rise of the Christian Schools*, p. 23). It degenerated into 'trivial' studies when it became the petty instruction in grammar in the grammar schools

of the 16th century. Jaeger suggests that the subjects of the *trivium* were first invented by the sophists (*Paideia, vol. 1*, p. 314).

51. Masi, *Boethian Number Theory*, p. 13.
52. Masi, *Boethian Number Theory*, p. 14.
53. Gilson, *Christian Philosophy*, p. 97.
54. Each part has its own method of reasoning: the method of natural science is scientific reasoning (rationaliter), the method of mathematics is disciplinary (disciplinaliter) and the method of theology is intuitive or intellectual (intellectualiter); see Weisheipl, *Nature*, p. 209.
55. Weisheipl, *Nature*, p. 209.
56. Gilson, *Christian Philosophy*, p. 98.
57. Weisheipl, *Nature*, p. 210.
58. Cassiodorus, *An Introduction to Divine and Human Readings*, trans. L.W. Jones (New York, Norton, 1969).
59. James O'Donnell, *Cassiodorus*, Chapter 5, at http://www9.georgetown.edu/faculty/jod/texts/cassbook/chap5.html.
60. O'Donnell, *Cassiodorus*, Chapter 5.
61. This is Cassiodorus's *De artibus ac disciplinus liberalium Litterarum*, 'On The Liberal Arts'; see Cassiodorus, *Introduction*, p. 52; and J.E. Sandys, *A History of Classical Scholarship*, vol. 1 (Cambridge, Cambridge University Press, 1903/2010), p. 253.
62. See *Etymologies*, II, 24, pp. 3–5.
63. See *Etymologies*, II, 24, pp. 9–16.
64. In this attempt at a *Disciplinarum libri*, Augustine had access to the similarly titles work of Varro; see West, *The Seven Liberal Arts*, p. 7, and A. Fitzgerald and J.C. Cavadini (eds.) *Augustine Through the Ages: An Encyclopedia* (William B. Eerdmans Publishing Co., 1999), p. 863.
65. The controversy regarding Augustine as the source of the seven liberal arts arises in translating *de quinque aliis disciplinis* either as *the* five other (liberal arts) disciplines, or rather as just five other disciplines (Parker, *LA*, p. 427; West, *The Seven Liberal* Arts, p. 4). Ritschl holds to the former view, arguing that Augustine thus defined *the* seven liberal arts (*Opuscula Philological III. 354* from *West, The Seven Liberal Arts*, p. 7).
66. Augustine, *Confessions* (Oxford, Oxford University Press, 1998), IV. xvi. 30, p. 70.
67. P.O. Kristeller, *Renaissance Thought* (New York, Harper Torchbooks, 1961), p. 83.
68. Augustine, *City of God*, trans. H. Bettenson (London, Penguin, 1972), p. 392.
69. Augustine, *The Retractions*, trans. Sister M.I. Bogan (Washington, The Catholic University of America Press, 1968), 1. 1.2, p. 8.
70. Augustine, *Against the Academicians*, trans. Sister M. P. Garvey (Milwaukee, Marquette University Press, 1957), pp. 12, 27.
71. *The Retractions*, 1.1.4, p. 10.
72. Augustine, *On Christian Doctrine*, trans. J.F. Shaw (New York, Dover Publications, 2009), Book II, Chapter 36, p. 71.
73. Augustine, *On Christian Doctrine*, II. 39, p. 74.
74. Augustine, *On Christian Doctrine*, IV. 2, p. 123. Kimball sees this as elevating 'the sophistic *artes liberales* of late antiquity closer to the oratorical model advanced by Cicero and received from Isocatean Hellenistic civilization'

(*Orators*, p. 41). McKeon notes that Augustine knew, 'as we tend to forget, that *doctrina* means both teaching and what is taught' (McKeon, 'Transformation,' p. 169).
75. Augustine, *On Christian Doctrine*, II. 40 (60), p. 75.
76. Augustine, *On Christian Doctrine*, II. 40 (60), p. 75. This ambivalence is found in a letter (Letter 101, AD 409) where Augustine writes

> to men who, though they are unjust and impious, imagine that they are well educated in the liberal arts, what else ought we to say than what we read in those writings which truly merit the name of liberal –'if the Son shall make you free, you shall be free indeed' [John, 8. 36]. For it is through Him that men come to know, even in those studies which are termed liberal by those who have not been called to this true liberty, anything in them which deserves the name.

77. Augustine, *On the Trinity*, trans. S. MacKenna (Cambridge, Cambridge University Press, 2002), Book 8, Chapter 5. 8, p. 12. Elsewhere Augustine writes *crede, ut intelligas*, meaning 'believe in order to understand' (Sermon 43, 7 & 9). Anselm preferred *credo ut intelligam*, 'I believe so that I may understand.' It is often accompanied by its corollary, *intellego ut credo*, 'I think/understand so that I may believe,' and by Anslem's other famous phrase, *fides quaerens intellectum*, 'faith seeking understanding.' See F. Copleston, *A History of Philosophy*, *Vol. 2, Part 1* (Image Books, 1962), p. 64.
78. Augustine, *Confessions*, VII. xx. 26, p. 130.
79. Augustine, *De ordine* (New York, Cosmopolitan Science and Art Service Co. Inc. 1942), 1.1, p. 7.
80. Augustine, *Confessions*, VII. xxi. 27, p. 131.
81. Augustine, *On the Trinity*, 13. 7. 10, p. 115.
82. Augustine, *Confessions*, VII. xxi. 27, p. 131. Copleston says here, Augustine 'found in Platonism doctrines which he considered admirably adapted for the exposition of a fundamentally Christian philosophy of life' (*History of Philosophy*, vol. 2, part 1, p. 74).
83. Augustine, *City of God*, VIII. 4, p. 303.
84. Augustine, *City of God*, VIII. 6, p. 307.
85. Augustine, *City of God*, VIII. 6, p. 307.
86. Augustine, *City of God*, VIII. 5, p. 304.

3   Renaissance Humanism

1. B. Kimball, *Orators and Philosophers* (New York & London, Teachers College Press, 1986), p. 57.
2. Kimball, *Orators*, p. 61.
3. Kimball, *Orators*, p. 61.
4. Dominicans supported the new methods, Franciscans held to the more spiritual resources. Dante treats them with equal respect in the *Paradiso* (XI).
5. Kimball, *Orators*, p. 31.
6. P.O. Kristeller, *Renaissance Thought* (New York, Harper Torchbooks, 1961), p. 29.
7. Kristeller, *Renaissance Thought*, p. 30.

8. L.J. Paetow, *Introduction*, H. d'Andeli, *The Battle of the Seven Liberal Arts* (Berkeley, University of California Press, 1914), p. 20.
9. Paetow, *Introduction*, d'Andeli, *The Battle*, p. 19.
10. Paetow, *Introduction*, d'Andeli, *The Battle*, p. 20.
11. Kimball, *Orators*, p. 73.
12. Henry d'Andeli, *The Battle of the Seven Arts* (Nabu Press, 2012).
13. C.H. Haskins, *The Rise of the Universities* (Ithaca & London, Cornell University Press, 1957), p. 42. For John of Salisbury on the need for grammar and for history and literature, see J.B. Ross and M.M. McLaughlin (eds.) *The Portable Medieval Reader* (London, Penguin, 1977), pp. 598–602.
14. Kristeller, *Renaissance Thought*, p. 31.
15. Kristeller, *Renaissance Thought*, p. 31.
16. Gordon Leff, 'The Trivium and the Three Philosophies,' in W. Ruegg, *A History of the University in Europe*, vol. 1 (Cambridge, Cambridge University Press, 2003), p. 319.
17. Aristotle, *On the Parts of the Animals*, 645a, in *The Complete Works of Aristotle*, vol. *1*, ed. J. Barnes (New Jersey, Princeton, 1984), p. 1004.
18. There were condemnations in 1210, 1215 and 1231. Paris extended its arts curriculum in 1255 to include Aristotelian natural philosophy and metaphysics, and Oxford did similar in 1268 -see Leff, *Trivium*, p. 322. Commentaries became one of the main ways in which the new material was incorporated into the arts curriculum.
19. Leff, *Trivium*, p. 325. For example, the Oxford Calculators at Merton developed a specialism in a mathematical science of mechanics.
20. Leff, *Trivium*, p. 331.
21. Edward Grant argues that natural science was 'the most significant part of the arts curriculum of every medieval university'; E. Grant, 'Science and the Medieval University,' in James. M. Kittleson and Pamela J. Transue, *Birth, Reform and Resilience, Universities in Transition 1300–1700* (Columbus, Ohio State University, 1984), p. 71. It was taught mainly by *questiones disputate*. However, Robert Rait says, 'the quadrivium was of comparatively little importance'; R. S. Rait, *Life in the Medieval University* (Bibliobazaar, 2007/1912), p. 91. For a discussion of the texts making up the university *quadrivium*, see Grant, 'Science' and James A. Weisheipl, 'Curriculum of the Faculty of Arts at Oxford in the Early Fourteenth Century,' *Medieval Studies*, 26, 1964.
22. E. Gilson, *History of Christian Philosophy in the Middle Ages* (London, Sheed and Ward, 1980), p. 248.
23. Gilson, *Christian Philosophy*, p. 312.
24. Gilson, *Christian Philosophy*, p. 318.
25. J. A. Weisheipl, *Nature and Motion in the Middle Ages* (Washington, the Catholic University of America Press, 1985), p. 251.
26. Gilson, *Christian Philosophy*, p. 364.
27. Gilson, *Christian Philosophy*, p. 364.
28. Gilson, *Christian Philosophy*, p. 381.
29. Interestingly, Ballard's solution to this is 'the unity of method' of the liberal arts (E.G. Ballard, *Philosophy and the Liberal Arts* (Dordrecht, Kluwer, 1989) p. 281); specifically he seeks to unify humanities (concerned with values and the good) and science (concerned with the true) around a shared

liberal arts method of language construction and analogy. The language of the quadrivium sees mathematics/geometry as grammar, music as rhetoric and astronomy as dialectic.

30. R. McKeon, 'The Transformation of the Liberal Arts in the Renaissance,' in B.S. Levy, *Developments in the Early Renaissance* (Albany, SUNY, 1972), p. 168.
31. McKeon, 'Transformation,' p. 184.
32. McKeon, 'Transformation,' p. 169.
33. McKeon, 'Transformation,' p. 169.
34. Campana, quoting Vittorio Rossi, in A. Campana, 'The Origin of the Word "Humanist",' *Journal of the Warburg and Courtauld Institutes*, vol. 9 (1946), pp. 60–1.
35. The English use of the term 'humanist' repeats this association with schools – see Campana, 'Origin,' p. 71.
36. Dante, *Monarchy* (Cambridge, Cambridge University Press, 2010), p. 8, I.iv.1–3.
37. Dante, *Monarchy*, p. 13, I.8.4–5.
38. Dante, *Monarchy*, p. 19, I.12.1.
39. Dante, *Paradiso*, trans. M. Musa (London, Penguin, 1986), V.19–24.
40. Dante, *Monarchy*, p. 20, I.12.8.
41. Dante, *Monarchy*, pp. 20–1, I.12.9.
42. Dante, *Convivio*, A.S. Kline trans., http://www.poetryintranslation.com/klineasconvivio.htm, 2008, pp. 137–8.
43. Dante, *Monarchy*, p. 21, I.12.12–13.
44. E. Gilson, *Dante and Philosophy* (New York, Harper Torchbook, 1963), p. 79.
45. Gilson, *Dante*, p. 179.
46. Kristeller, *Renaissance Thought*, p. 11.
47. Kristeller, *Renaissance Thought*, p. 18.
48. Hanna Holborn Gray, *Searching for Utopia, Universities and their Histories* (Berkeley, University of California Press, 2012), p. 36.
49. Gray, *Utopia*, p. 35.
50. Petrarch, *Letters on Familiar Matters* IX–XVI (New York, Italica Press, 2005), letter XVI, 14, p. 326.
51. Petrarch, *Letters*, letter X, 5, p. 77.
52. Gray, *Utopia*, p. 36.
53. Kimball, *Orators*, p. 77.
54. Kimball, *Orators*, p. 78.
55. Kimball, *Orators*, p. 78.
56. Kimball, *Orators*, p. 96.
57. Kimball, *Orators*, p. 97.
58. Ruegg in W. Ruegg (ed.) *A History of the University in Europe*, vol. II (Cambridge University Press, 1996), p. 7.
59. Note that in Thomas More's *Utopia* (1516) the humanistic curriculum was not tied to an institution.
60. Goethe, in N. Copernicus, *On the Revolutions of the Heavenly Spheres*, ed. S. Hawking (Philadelphia, Running Press, 2002), p. xvi.
61. Kristeller, *Renaissance Thought*, p. 19.
62. Kristeller, *Renaissance Thought*, p. 113.
63. Kristeller, *Renaissance Thought*, p. 117.
64. Kristeller, *Renaissance Thought*, p. 92.

65. Seneca, *Epistle VIII*, from *Moral Epistles*, trans. RM Gummere (London, Heinemann, 1917), pp. 39–41.
66. Kristeller, *Renaissance Thought*, p. 132.
67. M. Ficino, *Meditations on the Soul* (Rochester, Inner Traditions, 1997), p. 26.
68. Ficino, *Meditations*, p. 26.
69. Pico della Mirandola, *On The Dignity Of Man*, trans. C.G. Wallis, P.J.W. Miller & D. Carmichael (Indianapolis, Hackett, 1998), p. 5.
70. Kristeller, *Renaissance Thought*, p. 138.
71. R. Proctor, *Defining the Humanities*, 2nd edition (Bloomington, Indiana University Press, 1998), p. 12.
72. Proctor, *Humanities*, p. 12. See also Jacob Burckhardt's book *The Civilization of the Renaissance in Italy* (London, Phaidon Press, 1944) and for a critique, see Nauert who argues that while Burckhardt's thesis dominates views of the Renaissance well into the 20th century, 'it has only one major flaw: both in its general thrust and in virtually every detail, it is untrue' (C.G. Nauert, *Humanism and the Culture of Renaissance Europe* (Cambridge, Cambridge University Press, 2006), p. 2).
73. P.O. Kristeller, *Renaissance Thought and the Arts* (Princeton, Princeton University Press, 1990), p. 50.
74. Kristeller, *Renaissance Thought and the Arts*, p. 65.
75. Kristeller, *Renaissance Thought and the Arts*, p. 28. Kristeller notes that at the same time the Renaissance has a dubious reputation for crimes of violence and passion and cruelty.
76. See Ruegg, 'The Rise of Humanism,' in Ruegg, *A History of the University in Europe*, vol. 1 (Cambridge, Cambridge University Press, 2003), pp. 442–68. Ruegg notes that the term 'humanism' was first used in 1808 by Niethammer in Bavaria, specifically against the philanthropinism of the practical training at the Philanthropinum in Dessau, which Niethammer saw as lacking the tradition of the liberal arts and therein lacking *humanitas*, or the *studia humanitatis* of Cicero. The entire period of the Renaissance was, says Ruegg, only described as humanist after 1869 (p. 443).
77. Nauert, *Humanism*, p. 19. Against Petrarch's view, Theodore Mommsen notes that 'the notion of the mediaeval period as the "Dark Ages" is now destined to pass away for good.' T. Mommsen, 'Petrarch's Conception of the "Dark Ages," ' *Speculum*, vol. 17, no. 2 (April 1942), pp. 226–7.
78. Mommsen, 'Petrarch's Conception,' p. 240, from Petrarch, *Africa* IX, 451–7.
79. Petrarch, *Books on Matters to be Remembered*, in J.H. Robinson, *Petrarch* (New York, Haskell House Publishers, 1970), p. 26; *Rerum memorandum* i, 2.
80. J Hankins, *Introduction*, in L. Bruni, *History of the Florentine People*, vol. 1 (Cambridge, MA, I Tatti Renaissance Library, 2001), p. xvii.
81. G. Vasari, *The Lives of the Artists* (Oxford, Oxford University Press, 1998).
82. J. Bodin, *Method for the Easy Comprehension of History* (London, Norton, 1969), p. 15.
83. Bodin, *Method*, pp. 15–16.
84. Bodin, *Method*, p. 16.
85. On Melanchthon's contribution to the University of Marburg, see L.W. Spitz, 'The Importance of the Reformation for Universities,' in J.M. Kittleson and

P.J. Transue, *Birth, Reform and Resilience* (Columbus, Ohio State University, 1984).
86. P. Melanchthon, *Orations on Philosophy and Education*, ed. Sachiko Kusukawa (Cambridge, Cambridge University Press, 1999), p. 93.
87. Melanchthon approved of astrology as 'the art of things that do not fail' *Orations*, p. 121.
88. Melanchthon, *Orations*, p. 81.
89. Melanchthon, *Orations*, p. 24.
90. Melanchthon, *Orations*, p. 33.
91. Melanchthon, *Orations*, p. 34.
92. Melanchthon, *Orations*, p. 44.
93. Melanchthon, *Orations*, p. 81.
94. Melanchthon, *Orations*, p. 36.
95. Kimball, *Orators*, p. 78.

4 *Bildung* and the New Age

1. W.H. Bruford, *The German Tradition of Self-Cultivation* (Cambridge University Press, 1975), p. vii. Perhaps the source of the term 'culture' moving from horticulture to the human mind is Cicero who, in the *Tusculan Disputations*, talks of *cultura animi* as the cultivation of the mind, in stating that *cultura autem animi philosophia est* (philosophy is the culture of the mind) (*Academic Questions and Tusculan Disputations*, trans. C.D. Yonge (London, George Bell and Sons, 1880)), II.5 (and see also III.3, III. 13, IV. 58, and V.2). Petrarch spoke of *cultus anima* in *De remediis* (II.17); Francis Bacon spoke of the culture or cultivation of the mind in *The Advancement of Learning* (book 2, XX.3). Montaigne spoke of *culture de l'ame*, cultivation of the mind or soul, in *On Presumption* (2.17); Montaigne's meaning is Ciceronian, similar to the meaning of *humanitas*: 'ethical-urbane refinement, in contrast to raw power' (H. Friedrich, *Montaigne* (Berkeley, University of California Press, 1991)), pp. 377–8. Note too that Plotinus, in the *Enneads* (I.6) having advised the soul to 'withdraw into your self and look,' says that if one does not find oneself beautiful in doing so, then 'act as does the creator of a statue... He cuts away here, he smooths there... until a lovely face has grown upon his work. So do you also: cut away all that is excessive, straighten all that is crooked... And never cease chiselling your own statue until there shall shine out on you from it the godlike splendour of virtue' (I.6.9). Bruford says of Humboldt that *Bildung* meant 'the weeding of his mental and emotional garden,' echoing ideas of cultivation (Bruford, *The German Tradition* p. 14).
2. 'Theory of *Bildung*,' fragment 1793–4, in I. Westbury, S. Hopman and K. Riquarts, *Teaching as Reflective Practice* (New Jersey, Lawrence Erlbaum, 2000), p. 58.
3. For a discussion of the etymology and various meanings of *Bildung*, see S.E. Nordenko, '*Bildung* and the thinking of *Bildung*,' *Educating Humanity*, Lovlie, Mortensen and Nordenko (eds.) (Oxford, Blackwell, 2003), pp. 25–35.
4. W. von Humboldt, *Limits of State Action* (Indianapolis, Liberty Fund, 1993), p. 22. Even as a child Humboldt practised self-control and the discipline of a stoic. But during his acquaintance with a predominantly female group

of intellectuals this stoic self-control was led towards experience, desire and enjoyment; see Bruford, *The German Tradition*; Humboldt, *Limits*, p. 31.

5. J.W. Burrow, in Humboldt, *Limits*, p. xxiv.
6. Burrow, in Humboldt, *Limits*, p. xxix.
7. Humboldt, *Limits*, p. 31.
8. Humboldt in M. Cowan, *Humanist Without Portfolio* (Detroit, Wayne State University Press, 1963), pp. 143–4.
9. Humboldt in M. Cowan, *Humanist*, p. 58. 'Resolved' here is *Zusammenfliessen* (see Humboldt, *Ideen zu einem Versuch die Grenzen der Wirkamkeit des Staats zu bestimmen* (Brieslau, Verlag von E Trewendt, 1851), p. 68).
10. Humboldt, *Limits*, p. 80.
11. Humboldt in M. Cowan, *Humanist*, p. 144.
12. 'For there is an imprint with which all great things that emanate from man are of necessity stamped, because it is the imprint of great humanity itself' (Humboldt in M. Cowan, *Humanist Without Portfolio*, p. 149).
13. Humboldt in Cowan, *Humanist*, p. 149.
14. Humboldt in Cowan, *Humanist*, p. 155.
15. Humboldt in Cowan, *Humanist*, p. 155.
16. Humboldt in Cowan, *Humanist*, p. 155.
17. Humboldt in Cowan, *Humanist*, p. 125.
18. Humboldt in Cowan, *Humanist*, p. 399.
19. Humboldt in Cowan, *Humanist*, p. 144.
20. Humboldt, *Limits*, p. 50.
21. Humboldt, *Limits*, p. 51. Rousseau had noted that 'true happiness consists in decreasing the difference between our desires and our powers, in establishing a perfect equilibrium between the power and the will' – J.J. Rousseau, *Emile* (London, Everyman, 1974: 44; 1993: 52). Ficino noted that 'only he has all he desires who desires all he has' (M. Ficino, *Meditations on the Soul* (Rochester, Inner Traditions, 1997), p. 27).
22. Humboldt, *Limits*, p. 56; 1851: 65.
23. Humboldt, *Limits*, p. 57.
24. D. Sorkin, 'Wilhelm von Humboldt: The Theory and Practice of Self-Formation (*Bildung*) 1791–1810,' *Journal of the History of Ideas*, vol. 44, no. 1, (January–March 1983), p. 63.
25. Barrow describes the tension in Humboldt as that between his restless inner Faustianism and his Hellenistic obedience to reason and of the moral law.
26. A. Flexner, *Universities* (New York, Oxford University Press, 1930), p. 275.
27. J.G. Herder, *Philosophical Writings* (Cambridge University Press, 2002), p. 23. I have removed italics in Herder's quotations for ease of style.
28. Herder, *Philosophical Writings*, p. 23.
29. Herder, *Philosophical Writings*, p. 24.
30. Herder, *Philosophical Writings*, p. 26.
31. R. Horlacher, '*Bildung* – a construction of a History of Philosophy of Education,' *Studies in Philosophy and Education*, vol. 23 (2004), p. 420.
32. See J.H. Zammito, *Kant, Herder and the Birth of Anthropology* (Chicago, University of Chicago Press, 2002), p. 313.
33. Zammito, *Kant, Herder*, p. 313; see Chapter 8.
34. Horlacher, '*Bildung*,' p. 421.
35. Herder, *Philosophical Writings*, p. 321.

36. Herder, *Philosophical Writings*, p. 319.
37. Herder, *Philosophical Writings*, p. 324.
38. Herder, *Philosophical Writings*, p. 324.
39. Herder, *Philosophical Writings*, p. 319.
40. Herder, *Philosophical Writings*, p. 322.
41. Herder, *Philosophical Writings*, p. 332.
42. Herder, *Philosophical Writings*, p. 322.
43. Herder, *Philosophical Writings*, p. 355.
44. Herder, *Philosophical Writings*, p. 355.
45. Herder, *Philosophical Writings*, p. 355.
46. Herder, *Philosophical Writings*, p. 355.
47. Herder, *Philosophical Writings*, p. 343.
48. Herder, *Philosophical Writings*, p. 344.
49. Herder, *Philosophical Writings*, p. 346.
50. Herder, *Philosophical Writings*, p. 346.
51. Herder, *Philosophical Writings*, p. 346.
52. Herder, *Philosophical Writings*, p. 347.
53. Herder, *Philosophical Writings*, p. 347.
54. I. Kant, 'Lectures on Pedagogy,' *Anthropology, History, and Education*, trans. R.B. Lowden (Cambridge, Cambridge University Press, 2007), p. 448.
55. Kant, 'Lectures on Pedagogy,' p. 449.
56. Kant, 'Lectures on Pedagogy,' p. 445.
57. In *Purpose of Higher Education*, also translated as *Some Lectures Concerning the Scholar's Vocation* (*Einige Vorlesungen über die Bestimmung des Gelehrten*, 1794), Fichte speaks of *Kultur*, not *Bildung*.
58. J.G. Fichte, *The Purpose of Higher Education* (Maryland, Nightsun Books, 1988), p. 58.
59. Fichte, *Higher Education*, p. 58.
60. Fichte, *Higher Education*, p. 23.
61. Fichte, *Higher Education*, p. 24.
62. Fichte, *Higher Education*, p. 24.
63. Fichte, *Higher Education*, p. 25.
64. Fichte, *Higher Education*, p. 25.
65. Fichte, *Higher Education*, p. 26.
66. Gadamer notes, from Schaarschmidt, the origin of the term *Bildung* in mediaeval mysticism, 'its continuance in the mysticism of the baroque, its religious spiritualisation in Klopstock's *Messiah*... And finally Herder's basic definition as "reaching up to humanity"' (H.G. Gadamer, *Truth and Method* (London, Sheed & Ward, 1979), p. 11).
67. Gadamer, *Truth and Method*, p. 15.
68. Gadamer, *Truth and Method*, p. 24.
69. Gadamer, *Truth and Method*, p. 29.
70. Gadamer, *Truth and Method*, pp. 318–19.
71. Gadamer, *Truth and Method*, p. 320.
72. Gadamer, *Truth and Method*, p. 319.
73. Gadamer, *Truth and Method*, p. 319.
74. Gadamer, *Truth and Method*, p. 319.
75. Gadamer, *Truth and Method*, p. 320.

76. G.W.F. Hegel, *Philosophy of Right*, trans. T.M. Knox (Oxford, Oxford University Press, 1967), and §296.
77. Knox says in his notes that *Bildung* 'is used especially of education in the humanities' (Hegel, *Philosophy of Right*, p. 315, n58) and that the phrase *gebildeter Mensch* 'originates at the Renaissance and means a man of literary attainments, a scholar, not a scientist' (Hegel, *Philosophy of Right*, p. 315, n58). This is one of the occasions in Hegel where he appears to approve of the logic of necessity of harmony, found here in the demeanour of the civil servant. Another example seen in Chapter 8 is the tranquillity of the man who transcends the dichotomy of individual and particular in (the divine) comedy.
78. See Hegel, *Philosophy of Right*, §187 (*zusatz*).
79. See Hegel's, *Introduction to the Lectures on the History of Philosophy*, trans. T.M. Knox and A.V. Miller (Oxford, Clarendon Press, 1985), p. 50.
80. H.S. Harris, *Hegel's Ladder, The Odyssey of Spirit* (Indianapolis, Hackett Publishers, 1997), p. 258.
81. See G.W.F. Hegel, *The Philosophy of History*, trans. J. Sibree (New York: Dover Publications, 1956), p. 417; *(Werke 12 Vorlesungen über die Philosophie der Geschichte*, Frankfurt, Suhrkamp Verlag, 1970), p. 496.
82. Hanna Holborn Gray, *Searching for Utopia, Universities and their Histories* (Berkeley, University of California Press, 2012), p. 43.
83. Gray, *Utopia*, p. 43.
84. F. Paulsen and E.D. Perry, *The German Universities: Their Character and Historical Development* (London, Macmillan and Co., 1895), p. 54.
85. W. Schmidt-Biggemann, 'New Structures of Knowledge,' in W. Ruegg (ed.) *A History of the University in Europe*, vol. 2 (Cambridge, Cambridge University Press, 1996), p. 517.
86. Gray, *Utopia*, p. 43.
87. Gray, *Utopia*, p. 43.
88. B. Kimball, *Orators and Philosophers* (New York & London, Teachers College Press, 1986), p. 165.
89. Gray, *Utopia*, p. 42.
90. F. Rudolph, *Curriculum* (San Francisco, Jossey-Bass, 1977), p. 196.
91. Rudolph, *Curriculum*, p. 214.
92. Rudolph, *Curriculum*, p. 215. Oakley argues that 'the old collegiate values not only survived into the late-twentieth century but recovered much of their vitality'; F. Oakley, *Community of Learning* (New York, Oxford University Press, 1992), p. 29.
93. A. O'Hear and M. Sidwell, *The School of Freedom* (Exeter, Imprint Academic, 2009), p. 174.
94. Kimball, *Orators*, p. 141. This is part of what Sheldon Rothblatt refers to as the shift from eternal and abiding truth to 'contingent truth' in *Tradition and Change in English Liberal Education* (London, Faber and Faber, 1976), p. 196.

Conclusion to Part I

1. M. Heidegger, 'Letter on Humanism,' in *Basic Writings*, ed. D. Krell (London, Routledge, 1993), p. 225.

2. Heidegger, 'Letter on Humanism,' p. 220.
3. There is no space to undertake a critique of Heidegger's position here, but see Tubbs, *Philosophy's Higher Education* (Dordrecht, Kluwer, 2004); Tubbs, *Philosophy of the Teacher* (Oxford, Blackwell, 2005); and Tubbs, 'Existentialism and Humanism: Humanity – Know Thyself,' *Studies in Philosophy and Education*, September, 2013, vol. 32, no. 5, pp. 477–90.
4. P.O. Kristeller, *Renaissance Thought and the Arts* (Princeton, Princeton University Press, 1990), p. 31.
5. F. Fanon, *The Wretched of the Earth* (London, Penguin, 2001), p. 251.
6. Fanon, *The Wretched*, p. 251.
7. Sartre, 'Preface' to Fanon, *The Wretched*, p. 7.
8. Sartre, 'Preface' to Fanon, *The Wretched*, p. 21.
9. J.P. Sartre, *Existentialism and Humanism* (London, Methuen, 2007), p. 38.
10. Sartre, *Existentialism*, p. 54.
11. Sartre, *Existentialism*, p. 55.
12. Sartre, *Existentialism*, p. 65.
13. Karen Barad, *Meeting the Universe Halfway* (Durham, Duke University Press, 2007), p. 134.
14. Gilles Deleuze, *Difference and Repetition* (London, Continuum, 2001), p. xix.
15. Deleuze, *Difference*, p. xix.
16. Deleuze, *Difference*, p. xix.
17. Deleuze, *Difference*, p. xxi.
18. Emmanuel Levinas, *Difficult Freedom* (London, Athlone Press, 1990), p. 170.
19. I. Kant, 'Idea for a Universal History with a Cosmopolitan Intent,' in *Perpetual Peace and Other Essays* (Indianapolis, Hackett Publishing, 1983), p. 29.
20. Kant, 'Idea for a Universal History,' p. 32.
21. R. Bernasconi, 'Kant as an Unfamiliar Source of Racism,' in J.K. Ward and T.L. Lott (eds.) *Philosophers on Race* (Oxford, Blackwell, 2002), p. 147.
22. Bernasconi, 'Kant as an Unfamiliar Source,' pp. 147–8.
23. Bernasconi, 'Kant as an Unfamiliar Source,' p. 150.
24. G.W.F. Hegel, *Philosophy of Mind*, trans. W. Wallace & AV Miller (Oxford, Clarendon Press, 1990), p. 42.
25. Hegel, *Philosophy of Mind*, p. 43. To say that Kant and Hegel are merely expressing the common sense truths of their time is undermined somewhat for example by Herder who promotes women, rejects the concept of race, denounces slavery and colonialism and argues for 'equal respect for all peoples' (in M.N. Forster, *Herder, Philosophical Writings* (Cambridge, Cambridge University Press, 2002), p. xxxiii). Herder says, for example, that in the arrogance of the view that modernity stands 'high over the Earth' (p. 325) it is the case that 'when a storm shakes two small twigs in Europe how the world quakes and bleeds... When have more power and mechanism been possessed for shaking whole nations to the core with one press, with one movement of a finger?' (325).
26. Kant, 'Determination of the Concept of a Human Race,' in *Anthropology, History, and Education*, G. Zoller and R.B. Louden (eds.) (Cambridge, Cambridge University Press, 2007), p. 153.
27. G.W.F. Hegel, *Philosophy of Mind*, trans. W. Wallace (Oxford, Clarendon Press, 1990), p. 41.

28. I argue that we think dualisms as relations all the time. It is the idea that thinking is not a relation which is in fact the illusion. To describe metaphysics, for example, as Kimball does, as 'a sort of Hegelian cloud' (B. Kimball, *Orators and Philosophers* (New York & London, Teachers College Press, 1986), p. 37) is to miss the way that metaphysics only exists in the relation of thought and truth, or in the relation of subjectivity and education.
29. Kimball, *Orators*, p. 239.
30. Kimball, *Orators*, p. 239.
31. Kimball, *Orators*, p. 240.
32. Kimball, *Orators*, p. 223.
33. Kimball, *Orators*, p. 224.
34. Hanna Holborn Gray, *Searching for Utopia, Universities and their Histories* (Berkeley, University of California Press, 2012), p. 17. Rudolph describes this as grounded in a 'neo-Thomist metaphysics' (F. Rudolph, *Curriculum* (San Francisco, Jossey-Bass, 1977), p. 279).
35. Gray, *Utopia*, p. 17.
36. Gray, *Utopia*, p. 17.
37. In *The Great Conversation* Hutchins says that the dogma of individual differences is one of the basic dogmas of American education.

    > It runs like this: all men are different; therefore, all men require a different education; therefore, anybody who suggests that their education should be in any respect the same has ignored the fact that all men are different; therefore, nobody should suggest that everybody should read some of the same books; some people should read some books, some should read others

    (Accessed at http://www.britannica.com/blogs/2008/12/the-great-conversation-robert-hutchinss-essay-for-the-great-books/, 14.05.13.)
38. Hutchins says his own liberal education in the *trivium* only began at law school (in *Education for Freedom* (Louisiana, Louisiana State University Press, 1943), pp. 7–8).
39. Regarding the Great Books, Hutchins notes that 'when no adequate translation of a great book could be found or made, it was excluded from the list' (*The Great Conversation*).
40. Hutchins, *Education for Freedom*, p. 14.
41. Hutchins says 'the West needs an education that draws out our common humanity rather than our individuality. Individual differences can be taken into account in the methods that are employed and in the opportunities for specialisation that may come later' (*The Great Conversation*).
42. Hutchins, *The Great Conversation*.
43. Hutchins, *The Great Conversation*.
44. Hutchins, *The Great Conversation*.
45. Hutchins, *The Higher Learning in America* (New Haven, Yale University Press, 1936), p. 105.
46. Thomas Aquinas, *Summa Theologica*, vol. 8, trans. by the Fathers of the English Dominican Province (London: Burns Oats and Washbourne Ltd, 1920), Part II, 94.4, p. 47.
47. Hutchins, *The Higher Learning*, p. 66.

48. Hutchins, *The Higher Learning*, p. 96.
49. Hutchins, *The Higher Learning*, p. 96.
50. Hutchins, *The Higher Learning*, p. 97.
51. Hutchins, *The Higher Learning*, p. 99.
52. Kimball, *Orators*, p. 180.
53. Kimball, *Orators*, p. 180.
54. Hutchins, *The Higher Learning*, pp. 102–3.
55. Hutchins, *The Higher Learning*, p. 105.
56. Hutchins, *The Higher Learning*, p. 105.

Part II: Introduction

1. Aristotle, *Physics*, in *The Complete Works of Aristotle*, vol. 2, ed. J. Barnes (New Jersey, Princeton, 1984), 256a 28.
2. See also Chapter 5, first section.
3. R.M. Hutchins, *The Higher Learning in America* (New Haven, Yale University Press, 1936), p. 105.
4. Hutchins, *The Higher Learning*, p. 105.

5   Metaphysical Education

1. W. Jaeger, *Aristotle* (Oxford, Oxford University Press, 1962), p. 83.
2. Jaeger, *Aristotle*, p. 83. See Jaeger's discussion pp. 81–6.
3. Jaeger, *Aristotle*, p. 82.
4. Jaeger, *Aristotle*, p. 83.
5. See N. Tubbs, *History of Western Philosophy* (Basingstoke, Palgrave, 2009).
6. Aristotle, *Metaphysics*, 993b, pp. 24–9; *The Complete Works of Aristotle*, vol. 2, ed. J. Barnes (New Jersey, Princeton University Press, 1984), p. 1570.
7. Aristotle, *Metaphysics*, 994a 19, p. 1570.
8. Aristotle, *Physics*, 256a, p. 29, in *The Complete Works of Aristotle*, vol. 1, ed. Jonathan Barnes (Princeton, Princeton University Press, 1984).
9. Plato had made this observation in the *Phaedrus* with regard to the soul. The soul is immortal because it is always in motion, and moves itself;

> this self-mover is also the source and spring of motion in everything else that moves; and a source has no beginning. That is because anything that has a beginning comes from some source, but there is no source for this, since a source that got its start from something else would no longer be the source.

> (*Phaedrus* 245 c–d; *Plato The Complete Works*, ed. John M. Cooper (Indianapolis, Hackett Publishing Co., 1997), p. 524.)

10. See below, Chapter 8.
11. Aristotle, *Topics*, 145a, pp. 15–17; *The Complete Works of Aristotle, vol. 1*, ed. J. Barnes (New Jersey, Princeton, 1984).
12. Aristotle, *Nicomachean Ethics*, VI. 3, in *The Complete Works of Aristotle, vol. 2*, ed. J. Barnes (New Jersey, Princeton University Press, 1984).
13. I have described these in Tubbs, *History of Western Philosophy*, and do so only briefly here.

14. G. Leff, 'The Trivium and the Three Philosophies,' in Ruegg (ed.) *A History of the University in Europe*, vol. 1 (Cambridge, Cambridge University Press, 1992), p. 315. Plato's *Republic* was only translated into Latin by Manuel Chrysolorus between 1400–03; see T. Boter, *The Textual Tradition of Plato's Republic* (Leiden, E.J. Brill, revised edition, 1989), p. 261. Henricus Aristippus first translated Plato's *Meno* and *Phaedo* into Latin in the 12th century. See also C.H. Haskins, *The Rise of the Universities* (Ithaca and London, Cornell University Press, 1957).
15. See Tubbs, *History of Western Philosophy*, Part II.
16. See H. Corbin, *History of Islamic Philosophy* (London, Kegan Paul, 2006), p. 249.
17. I. Kant, *Critique of Pure Reason* (London, Macmillan, 1968), A63/B88.
18. Kant, *Critique of Pure Reason*, Bxxx.
19. In Introduction, Part II.

6   Natural Education

1. The *Division of the Canon* begins 'If there were stillness and non-motion, there would be silence' (Andre Barbera, *The Euclidean Division of the Canon* (Lincoln and London, University of Nebraska Press, 1991), p. 115).
2. Georges Bataille, *Theory of Religion* (New York, Zone Books, 1992), p. 19.
3. Plato, *The Laws* (London, Penguin, 1975), p. 424, §894.
4. Plato, *Laws*, p. 425, §895.
5. Aristotle, *Metaphysics*, 982b, *The Complete Works of Aristotle*, vol. 2, ed. J. Barnes (New Jersey, Princeton University Press, 1984), pp. 24–5.
6. M.R. Wright, in *Cosmology in Antiquity* (New York, Routledge, 1995, p. 3), notes *kosmos* in Homer's *Iliad* referring to the order of soldiers and their equipment (*Iliad* 10.472) and the absence of *kosmos* referring to the rout of an army (*Iliad* 2.214), and in the *Odyssey* to the order of rowers in a boat (*Odyssey* 13.77). It also referred to the order and beauty of the adornment of objects and people, hence 'cosmetics.'
7. Diogenes Laertius, *Lives of Eminent Philosophers* (Cambridge, MA, Loeb Classical Library, 2006), 8.48, p. 365.
8. Twenty seven if you count the fixed stars.
9. Plato names ether the fifth element (*Timaeus* 55c) which God uses for the whole universe. The *Timaeus* illustrates how the universe contains the *logos* by means of the intellect of the world-soul, copying the *logos* of the intellectual creator and first principle. Aristotle assigns the rationality and order of the stars and planets to the ether, in contrast to the four elements which are changeable.
10. Having argued for the unity and oneness of the Prime Mover in *Metaphysics* XII, and particularly in Chapter 7, in the next chapter Aristotle immediately issues a revision, prompting speculation that this represents a much later and less Platonic stage of Aristotle's thinking (*Metaphysics*, 1074a 11).
11. E. Cassirer, P.O. Kristeller, J.H. Randall Jr, *The Renaissance Philosophy of Man* (Chicago, University of Chicago Press, 1948), p. 74.
12. Cassirer, *Renaissance*, p. 58n.

13. This aids the development of the experimental method and empirical science, alongside Leonardo's case for the fine arts to be included within the liberal arts.
14. Leonardo da Vinci, *Notebooks* (Oxford, Oxford University Press, 2008), p. 190.
15. Leonardo, *Notebooks*, p. 190.
16. Leonardo, *Notebooks*, p. 211.
17. I. Newton, *Newton's Philosophy of Nature* (Mineola, NY, Dover publications, 2005), letter to Richard Bentley, 1692, pp. 47.
18. I. Newton, *The Principia*, trans. A. Motte (New York, Prometheus Books, 1995), p. 442.
19. Newton, *Principia*, p. 442.
20. Newton, *Philosophy*, p. 53.
21. As long as the speed of light is fixed, the motion of laws of time and motion will be relative. If and when something faster than the speed of light is discovered, this will demand that the laws of motion and the motion of laws learn of a different logic of necessity. Who can say what this will be? My own question will be, is this still the logic of necessity of learning and education, of the motion of motion, or will it realise something as yet unimaginable to our education, something like the breakdown of necessity *per se*, something that is not education?
22. M. Jammer, *Einstein and Religion* (Princeton, Princeton University Press, 2002), p. 19.
23. Jammer, *Einstein*, p. 18.
24. A. Einstein, 'Religion and Science,' in *New York Times Magazine*, 4th November, 1930, pp. 1–4, www.sacred-texts.com/aor/einstein/einsci.htm; Jammer, *Einstein*, p. 52.
25. Einstein, 'Religion and Science'; and Jammer, p. 52.
26. Einstein, letter to P. Wright, 1936; Jammer, *Einstein*, p. 93.
27. Jammer, *Einstein*, p. 73.
28. Einstein's general theory of relativity required a similar overturning of the presupposition of saving appearances. He argued that if gravity and relativity could not be reconciled, this was not an error requiring to be redeemed. The error lay in supposing the redemption to be necessary. This time the error was the presupposition of Euclidean geometry (as for Hegel it had been Aristotle's definition of truth that it could not be otherwise than it is, and assuming that what it is was simple and unmediated). Einstein saw that straight line geometry was the natural relation that was holding back the necessity of the natural relation of (the opposition between) mass and energy in relation to objects. If gravity did not conform to the new understanding of relativity, it might not be because gravity was conceived incorrectly, but rather because the universe in which it operated was conceived incorrectly. Perhaps gravity could not operate instantaneously in a straight-lined and flat Euclidean universe because, after all, the universe was not Euclidean.
29. W. Heisenberg, *The Physicist's Conception of Nature* (London, The Scientific Book Guild, 1962), p. 15.
30. Heisenberg, *Nature*, p. 15.
31. Heisenberg, *Nature*, p. 29.
32. W. Heisenberg, *Physics and Philosophy* (London, Penguin, 1958), p. 95.

33. J. Butler, *Gender Trouble* (New York, Routledge, 2006), p. 34.
34. K. Barad, *Meeting the Universe Halfway* (Durham, Duke University Press, 2007), p. 32.
35. Barad, *Universe*, p. 67.
36. Barad, *Universe*, p. 67. However, Barad is clear that she is not putting any argument 'to the effect that the quantum theory of the micro-world is analogous to situations that interest us in the macro-world' (p. 70).
37. Barad, *Universe*, p. 138.
38. Heisenberg, *Physics and Philosophy*, p. 124.
39. Heisenberg, *Physics and Philosophy*, p. 124.
40. Heisenberg, *Physics and Philosophy*, p. 126. But Heisenberg is also clear that quantum physics is still dependent upon the classical model. How could physics do away with observation? It is part of the paradox of the Copenhagen interpretation (1926) that it must employ classical concepts which nevertheless it knows in advance 'do not fit nature accurately' (Heisenberg, *Physics and Philosophy*, p. 23).
41. W Heisenberg, *Philosophie – la manuscript de 1942*, translated from German to French by C. Chevalley, Seuil, Paris, 1998. German original edition: *Ordnung der Wirklichkeit*, Munich, R. Piper GmbH and Co KG, 1989. English version available at www.werner-heisenberg.unh.edu/ trans. M.B. Rumscheidt and N. Lukens.
42. Heisenberg, *Philosophie*.
43. Heisenberg, *Physics and Philosophy*, p. 89.
44. Heisenberg, *Physics and Philosophy*, p. 95.
45. Heisenberg, *Physics and Philosophy*, p. 127.
46. Aristotle, *Metaphysics*, IX 8 1050b 18.
47. Aristotle, *De anima*, III. 7. 431a 1, *The Complete Works of Aristotle, vol. 1*, ed. J. Barnes (New Jersey, Princeton, 1984).
48. Aristotle, *Physics*, II. 9. 200a 3–4, *The Complete Works of Aristotle, vol. 1*, ed. J. Barnes (New Jersey, Princeton, 1984).
49. Aristotle, *Physics*, II. 1. 193b 17–18.
50. What is interesting here is that the relation between actual and potential is Aristotle's most modern moment. His logic is still one of identity, where the actual is what it must be, that is itself. Nevertheless, in the ambiguity of its relation to itself via *potentia*, it is as the simile of the sun in Plato: the actual is both cause and effect of its own conditions of possibility.
51. See, for example, Aquinas, *Summa Theologica*, Second Part, Part II, 180.5.
52. Humboldt in M. Cowan, *Humanist Without Portfolio* (Detroit, Wayne State University Press, 1963), p. 331.

7 Social Education

1. Aristotle, *Politics*, trans. T. A Sinclair and T. J. Saunders (London, Penguin, 1981), I. iv.
2. But also including the pastimes of children, see *Politics* VIII. xvii, 1336a 40.
3. Aristotle, *Politics*, I iv. 1254a, pp. 15–18.
4. Aristotle, *Politics*, I. v. 1254a, pp. 23–4.

5. Aristotle, *Politics*, I. v. 1254b, pp. 25–6.
6. To avoid this, and in line with the ambiguity of a natural slave, the term 'slave' was often reserved for foreigners or non-Greeks.
7. It is interesting to note that Aristotle also detests something technical and made only for use trying to turn itself into its own end. His example here is the charging of interest, 'for the gain arises out of currency itself, not as a product of that for which currency was provided' (*Politics*, I. x. 1258b 3–4). Currency was intended only as a means of exchange, not as something that should reproduce itself, and therefore of all the ways that exist for accruing wealth, usury 'is the most unnatural' (*Politics*, I. x. 1258b 7) in that it makes the means an end in-itself. There can be no money-lenders who are also free.
8. Aristotle, *Politics*, VII. xiii, 1331b, p. 39.
9. When Kimball says that in Aristotle 'leisure means by definition that one has no end in view' (B. Kimball, *Orators and Philosophers* (New York & London, Teachers College Press, 1986), p. 231) this is not quite accurate. Leisure means one has only one end in view, the end in-itself that is in harmony with itself. It has no other end in view, but it is exactly and crucially for freedom, its own end.
10. Aristotle, *Politics*, VIII. iii. 1338b, p. 2.
11. Aristotle, *Politics*, VIII. vi. 1341a, pp. 13–14.
12. Seventeen hundred years later, Rousseau would make this the principle of education in *Emile*: 'true happiness consists in decreasing the difference between our desires and our powers, in establishing a perfect equilibrium between the power and the will' (J.J. Rousseau, *Emile* (London, Dent, 1993), p. 52).
13. Epictetus, *Discourses*, in *Great Books of the Western World*, vol. 11 (Chicago, Encyclopedia Britannica, 1990), p. 207. It is worth remembering that dialectic is a virtue for the Stoics (Diogenes Laertius, *Lives of Eminent Philosophers* (Cambridge, MA, Loeb Classical Library, 2006), VII, 46).
14. Epictetus, *Discourses*, p. 152.
15. Epictetus, *Discourses*, p. 152.
16. Epictetus, *Discourses*, p. 153.
17. Edwyn Bevan argued that Stoicism offered control over the only thing that could be brought under control, namely the will, by the rational judgements opened to the trained thinker. Stoicism offered protection against the chaos of the external world (Bevan, *Stoics and Sceptics* (Oxford, Clarendon Press, 1913)).
18. Cicero, *Academic Questions and Tusculan Disputations*, trans. C. D. Yonge (London, George Bell and Sons, 1880), 17, 38; R. Proctor, *Defining the Humanities*, 2nd edition (Bloomington, Indiana University Press, 1998), p. 64.
19. Cicero, *Tusc. Disp.* 17, 37; Proctor, *Humanities*, p. 66.
20. Cicero, *Atticus* 279:1; Proctor, *Humanities*, p. 64.
21. Hegel, *Phenomenology of Spirit* (Oxford, Oxford University Press, 1977), p. 290, §477.
22. Hegel, *Phenomenology*, p. 290, §477.
23. Hegel, *Phenomenology*, p. 292, §480.
24. I am following Hegel in his *Phenomenology of Spirit* here.

25. I. Kant, *Foundations of the Metaphysics of Morals*, 2nd edition, trans. L. W. Beck (New York, Macmillan, 1990), p. 83.
26. I. Kant, *Foundations of the Metaphysics of Morals*, p. 38, §421.

Part III: The Song That Dialectic Sings

1. Cicero, *Academic Questions and Tusculan Disputations*, trans. C.D. Yonge (London: George Bell and Sons, 1880), IV, 17, 37, in R. Proctor, *Defining the Humanities*, 2nd edition (Bloomington, Indiana University Press, 1998), p. 200. He then offers the aging figure of Alfred North Whitehead as a modern exemplar of *humanitas*.
2. Epictetus, *Discourses*, III. 2. *Great Books of the Western World, vol. 11* (Chicago, Encyclopaedia Britannica, Inc., 1990), p. 167.
3. Marcus Aurelius, *Meditations*, trans. M. Staniforth (London, Penguin, 1964), p. 139.
4. Dante, *A Translation of Dante's Eleven Letters*, trans. C.S. Latham (Boston & New York, Houghton Mifflin Co., 1891), p. 197.
5. G.W.F. Hegel, *Aesthetics*, vol. 2. trans. T.M. Knox (Oxford, Clarendon Press, 1998), p. 1160.
6. G.W.F. Hegel, *Aesthetics*, vol. 1. trans. T.M. Knox (Oxford, Clarendon Press, 1998), p. 205.
7. Hegel, *Aesthetics*, vol. 2, p. 1162.
8. Hegel, *Aesthetics*, vol. 2, p. 1210.
9. Hegel, *Aesthetics*, vol. 2, p. 1221.
10. I owe this sentence to Adriana Bontea. When I heard her say this, I laughed, because I understood.
11. Hegel, *Aesthetics*, vol. 2, p. 1209.
12. Hegel, *Aesthetics*, vol. 2, p. 1200. Gillian Rose rightly here asks whether this serenity is to be achieved by work or grace? (G. Rose, *Mourning Becomes the Law* (Cambridge, Cambridge University Press, 1996), p. 64).
13. Hegel, *Aesthetics*, vol. 2, p. 1162.
14. I am interpreting anger (*thumos*) here to be an example of pathos; see Barbara Koziak, *Retrieving Political Emotion: Thumos, Aristotle and Gender* (Pennsylvania State University Press, 1999).
15. G.W.F. Hegel, *Aesthetics*, vol. 1. trans. T.M. Knox (Oxford, Clarendon Press, 1998), p. 497.

8 Divine Comedy of Barbarian Virtue

1. Plato, *Republic*, in *Plato The Complete Works*, ed. John M. Cooper (Indianapolis, Hackett Publishing Co., 1997), IX. 591b.
2. Plato, *Philebus* in *Plato The Complete Works*, ed. John M. Cooper (Indianapolis, Hackett Publishing Co., 1997), 25e.
3. W. Jaeger, *Aristotle* (Oxford, Oxford University Press, 1962), p. 43.
4. Plato, *Republic*, 537d.
5. S Kierkegaard, *The Concept of Irony* (New Jersey, Princeton University Press, 1989), p. 178.
6. Plato, *Republic*, 539b.

7. Plato, *Republic*, 540b.
8. W. Jaeger, *Paideia, The Ideals of Greek Culture*, vol. 1 (New York, Oxford University Press, 1965), p. xxvi.
9. W. Jaeger, *Paideia, The Ideals of Greek Culture*, vol. 2 (New York, Oxford University Press, 1986), p. 277.
10. Jaeger, *Paideia, vol. 2*, p. 277.
11. This ambiguity is also found in the debates concerning whether or not Beatrice is a real living person, and whether thereafter Dante's struggles are earthly or divine.
12. Dante, *The New Life (Vita Nuova)*, trans. G Rossetti (New York, New York Review of Books, 2002), p. 78, ch. 38.
13. Dante, *The New Life*, pp. 86–7, ch. 42.
14. Dante, *Convivio*, A.S Kline trans., http://www.poetryintranslation.com/klineasconvivio.htm, 2008, pp. 137–8, 2.12.
15. Dante, *Convivio*, 2.7.
16. Dante, *The New Life*, p. 78, ch. 38.
17. Dante, *The New Life*, p. 78, ch. 38.
18. Dante, *The New Life*, p. 79, ch. 38.
19. Dante, *The New Life*, p. 80, ch. 39.
20. Dante, *The New Life*, p. 81, ch. 39.
21. Dante, *The New Life*, p. 81, ch. 39.
22. Dante, *The New Life*, p. 81, ch. 39.
23. Gilson says here that 'Never will Dante assume that one love must exclude the other – not even in the *Divine Comedy*' (E. Gilson, *Dante and Philosophy*) (New York, Harper Torchbook, 1963), p. 97n.
24. See also Dorothy L. Sayers' essay 'The Comedy of Dante' in which she finds 'a diffused spirit of high comedy' and Dante's own 'self-mockery' throughout the poem (D.L. Sayers, *Introductory Papers on Dante* (Eugene, Oregon, Wipf & Stock, 1954), pp. 154–5).
25. Christopher Ryan notes that the inferno is really stasis, for movement in hell is repetitive and goes nowhere (C. Ryan, 'The Theology of Dante,' in *The Cambridge Dante* (Cambridge, Cambridge University Press, 1993)).
26. Dante, *The New Life*, pp. 86–7, ch. 42. The originality of the *Comedy* as a whole is not as clear as it might once have been assumed, when certain Arabic texts are compared with it. Enrico Cerulli (1898–988) in *Il Libro della Scala' e la questione della forti arabspagnole della Divina Commedia* (1949) asked whether Dante had been influenced by *The Book of Muhammad's Ladder*, telling the story of Muhammed's ascent to the heavens. Another suggestion is that the *Commedia* has similarities to the *Resalat Al-Ghufran* or *Epistle of Forgiveness* by Abu l-'Ala' al-Ma'arri, a tale again based around a visit to Paradise. This has recently appeared in two volumes: *The Epistles of Forgiveness, vols 1 & 2*, 2013 (New York University Press), edited and translated by Geert Jan Van Gelder and Gregor Schoeler. The *Liber Scala* is available in English in R. Hyatte, *The Prophet of Islam in Old French* (Leiden, Brill, 1997). Copleston in his *History of Philosophy* has noted that Dante is sympathetic enough to Avicenna and Averroes to place them in Limbo where they suffer no pain, but without the hope of ever seeing God. They have not sinned but nor have they been baptised (*Inferno*, IV), whereas Dante places the Prophet in Hell. Copleston asks whether Dante owed to Al-Farabi, Avicenna, Al-Ghazali

and Averroes 'the light-doctrine of God, the theory of the Intelligences, the influence of the celestial spheres, the idea that only the intellectual part of the soul is directly and properly created, the need of illumination for intellection, etc' (*History of Philosophy* (New York, Image Books, 1962), vol. 2, part 1, p. 225) and suggests that even though some of these ideas were found in the Augustinian tradition, nevertheless Dante 'owed a considerable debt to the Muslims and to Averroes in particular' (*History of Philosophy*, 2.1, p. 226). The Latin Averroes, Siger of Brabant, is placed in Heaven by Dante. See also Copleston, *History of Philosophy*, vol. II, part 2, pp. 160–1; Francesco Gabrielli, 'New Light on Dante and Islam,' in *Diogenes*, 2nd March, 1954, pp. 61–73; Bruno Nardi, 'Intorno al tornismo di Dante e alla quistione di Sigieri,' in *Giornale Dantesco*, XXII, 5; Asin Palacios, *Islam and the Divine Comedy* (New Delhi, Goodword Books, 2008); and Gilson, *Dante and Philosophy*.

27. Gilson (in *Dante and Philosophy*) describes the *Convivio* as 'a work of learning for the masses' (p. 85) written so that worldly folk could have access to the science of philosophy 'without which they cannot attain the temporal themes which are their prerogative' (p. 86).

28. Aristotle at one stage speculated on 55 spheres.

29. Gilson says that only Basil, Strabo and Bede in fact confirmed the existence of the 10th sphere. Aquinas accepts it on grounds of expediency (Gilson, *Dante and Philosophy*, p. 113).

30. Rhetoric in the evening is the Writer; 2.13. I am using the translation by Richard Lansing (1998) found at http://dante.ilt.columbia.edu/books/convivi/convivio.html. The paragraph numbering differs slightly from the translation by Elizabeth Price Sayer, 1887.

31. Gilson says placing ethics above metaphysics 'is quite extraordinary for the Middle Ages' (*Dante and Philosophy*, p. 105) and could not find authority in either Aristotle or Aquinas. He does so because, if metaphysics is divine, it lies beyond. Therefore, the greatest source of consolation available on Earth is the most human of the sciences – ethics. Dante's only immediate environment and his impending exile make this turn from the speculative to the practical eminently understandable (*Dante and Philosophy*, p. 109).

32. Dante, *Convivio*, 2.14.

33. Dante, *The New Life*, p. 85, ch. 41.

34. Musa, *Paradiso*, Introduction, p. x.

35. D. L. Sayers, *The Divine Comedy: Hell* (London, Penguin, 1949), p. 11.

36. D. L. Sayers, *Introductory Papers*, p. 128.

37. D. L. Sayers, *Introductory Papers*, p. 106.

38. F. Nietzsche, *Twilight of the Idols/The Anti-Christ*, trans. R. J. Hollingdale (London, Penguin, 1968), p. 44.

39. W.H. Bruford, *The German Tradition of Self-Cultivation* (Cambridge, Cambridge University Press, 1975), p. 176.

40. F. Nietzsche, *Genealogy of Morals*, in *Basic Writings*, ed. W. Kaufmann (New York, The Modern Library, 1968), pp. 476–7; *Genealogy* I.11.

41. Nietzsche, *Genealogy*, p. 477; I.11.

42. Nietzsche, *Genealogy*, p. 481; I.13.

43. F. Nietzsche, *The Will To Power*, ed. W. Kaufmann (New York, Vintage Books, 1968), p. 78, §127.

44. Bruford, *The German Tradition*, p. 177.
45. F. Nietzsche, *Thus Spoke Zarathustra* in *The Portable Nietzsche*, trans. W. Kaufmann (New York, Penguin, 1982), p. 231; Book 2, chapter 14.
46. Nietzsche, *Thus Spoke Zarathustra*, p. 232.
47. Bruford, *The German Tradition*, pp. 183–4. Bruford argues that the idea of *Bildung* was one of Nietzsche's 'principal preoccupations at all stages of his life' (*The German Tradition*, p. 164), covering his early work on German education, on Schopenhauer as educator, and his other untimely meditations which are critical of *Bildung* as superficial and shallow and against nature. However, Bruford notes too that even today Nietzsche could be described as 'a secular humanist, and as fully conscious of his spiritual descent from the enlightenment and from Goethe's Germany' (*The German Tradition*, p. 171). Nevertheless Nietzsche's sense of intellectual superiority in the herd was replacing any 'humanitarian sense of the wonders of mankind' (*The German Tradition*, p. 171) and leaving him vulnerable to the 'absurdity of intolerance and fanaticism' (*The German Tradition*, p. 171). Still, 'while constantly throwing doubt on the traditional notions of humane culture, Nietzsche continued for a long time, though not consistently, to express his belief in a man's power to change his own character' (*The German Tradition*, p. 1750). As Goethe and Schleiermacher had said: become the man you are, so, Nietzsche's genealogy asks how one becomes what one is.
48. P. Levine, *Nietzsche and the Modern Crisis of the Humanities* (Albany, SUNY, 1995), p. xii.
49. Levine, *Nietzsche*, p. 199.
50. Levine, *Nietzsche*, p. 199.
51. Levine, *Nietzsche*, p. 207.
52. Plato finds anger (*thumos*) to be a third part of the soul, alongside reason and appetite (*Republic* 439–41). See also Aquinas here, on the idea that anger is also judgement (*Summa Theologica*, II. II. Q. 158, art. 2 & 8).

9   The Work of Education

1. Kant, arguing that concept and intuition need each other, understands this relation to be the art of judgement, bringing concept and intuition together under one common representation. But judgement in Kant itself falls apart into the closed fist of determinative judgements and the open palm of reflective judgements. How one understands this duality or this relation now depends on the logic of necessity one brings to the table. The ancient logic of the necessity of identity keeps them separate; determinative judgements defy infinite regression, while reflective judgements defy objective pre-determination. But the point here is that their separation is the result of one logical necessity, that something either is and cannot be otherwise or that it can only be otherwise than it is. I hope I have illustrated above how the experience of this logic draws out a second logic, the logic of their relation known as education. The *aporia* of this relation Kant expresses by stating the synthetic a priori; 'the conditions of the *possibility of experience* in general are likewise conditions of the *possibility of the objects of experience*' (Kant, *Critique of Pure Reason* (London, Macmillan, 1968), A158/B197). In the logic of

the necessity of education this difficult relationship is not resolved. It is that which we learn to live with.

2. These quotations which follow are from Rowan Williams' first Gifford Lecture, 'Representing Reality' (4th November, 2013, University of Edinburgh). He is enquiring into a different kind of natural theology and perhaps I might say, a different logic for natural theology. I have not had access to the text and have transcribed the quotations from the lecture at http://www.youtube.com/watch?v=_ib-HOy3vtA&list=SPEA9467 E8E8D991AE. Any inaccuracies are my own.

3. G.W.F. Hegel, *Hegel's Logic* (Oxford, Oxford University Press, 1975), p. 36, §23.

4. This same thought came to the educator Carl Rogers, who declared that nothing of any real importance could be taught by one person to another, and moreover the more effective one's teaching became, the more damage it did to the student (see D. Schön, *Educating the Reflective Practitioner* (San Francisco, Jossey-Bass 1987), pp. 82–95).

5. See G.W.F. Hegel, *Phenomenology of Spirit*, trans. A. V. Miller (Oxford, Oxford University Press, 1977), p. 119, §196.

6. T.W. Adorno, *Kant's Critique of Pure Reason* (Cambridge, Polity Press, 2001), p. 78.

7. Adorno, *Kant's Critique of Pure Reason*, p. 79.

8. Adorno, *Kant's Critique of Pure Reason*, p. 137.

9. See also Walter Kaufmann, *The Future of the Humanities* (New Brunswick, Transaction Publishers, 1995), Chapter 2.

Bibliography

Adorno, T.W., *Kant's Critique of Pure Reason* (Cambridge, Polity Press, 2001).

Aquinas, T. *Summa Theologica 22 volumes*, trans. the Fathers of the English Dominican Province (London: Burns Oats and Washbourne Ltd, 1920).

Aristotle, *Politics*, trans. T.A. Sinclair and T.J. Saunders (London, Penguin, 1981).

Aristotle, *The Complete Works of Aristotle, vol. 1*, ed. J. Barnes (New Jersey, Princeton, 1984).

Aristotle, *The Complete Works of Aristotle, vol. 2*, ed. J. Barnes (New Jersey, Princeton, Princeton University Press, 1984).

Augustine, *De ordine* (New York, Cosmopolitan Science and Art Service Co. Inc. 1942).

Augustine, *Against the Academicians*, trans. Sister M. P. Garvey (Milwaukee, Marquette University Press, 1957).

Augustine, *City of God*, trans. H. Bettenson (London, Penguin, 1972).

Augustine, *Confessions* (Oxford, Oxford University Press, 1998).

Augustine, *On the Trinity*, trans. S. MacKenna (Cambridge, Cambridge University Press, 2002).

Augustine, *On Christian Doctrine*, trans. J.F. Shaw (New York, Dover Publications, 2009).

Augustine, *The Retractions*, trans. Sister M.I. Bogan (Washington, The Catholic University of America Press, 1968).

Aurelius, M., *Meditations*, trans. M. Staniforth (London, Penguin, 1964).

Ballard, E.G., *Philosophy and the Liberal Arts* (Dordrecht, Kluwer, 1989).

Barad, K., *Meeting the Universe Halfway* (Durham, Duke University Press, 2007).

Barbera, A., *The Euclidean Division of the Canon*, Lincoln and London (University of Nebraska Press, 1991).

Bataille, G., *Theory of Religion* (New York, Zone Books, 1992).

Bauman, R., *Human Rights in Ancient Rome* (New York, Routledge, 2000).

Bernasconi, R., 'Kant as an Unfamiliar Source of Racism,' in J.K. Ward and T.L. Lott (eds.) *Philosophers on Race* (Oxford, Blackwell, 2002).

Bevan, E., *Stoics and Sceptics* (Oxford, Clarendon Press, 1913).

Bodin, J., *Method for the Easy Comprehension of History* (London, Norton, 1969).

Booth, E., *Aristotelian Aporetic Ontology in Islamic and Christian Thinkers* (Cambridge, Cambridge University Press, 1983).

Boter, T., *The Textual Tradition of Plato's Republic* (Leiden, E.J. Brill, revised edition, 1989).

Bruford, W.H., *The German Tradition of Self-Cultivation* (Cambridge University Press, 1975).

Burckhardt, J., *The Civilization of the Renaissance in Italy* (London, Phaidon Press, 1944).

Burkert, W., *Lore and Science in Ancient Pythagoreanism* (Harvard University Press, 1972).

Butler, J., *Gender Trouble* (New York, Routledge, 2006).

Campana, A., 'The Origin of the Word "Humanist",' *Journal of the Warburg and Courtauld Institutes*, vol. 9 (1946).

Cassiodorus, *An Introduction to Divine and Human Readings*, trans. L.W. Jones (New York, Norton, 1969).

Cassirer, E., Kristeller, P.O., Randall, J.H. Jr, *The Renaissance Philosophy of Man* (Chicago, University of Chicago Press, 1948).

Cicero, *Academic Questions and Tusculan Disputations*, trans. C.D. Yonge (London, George Bell and Sons, 1880).

Cicero, *De Oratore*, trans. H. Rackham (Cambridge Mass., Harvard University Press, 1942).

Cicero, *De Oratore*, trans. E.W. Sutton and H. Rackham (Cambridge Mass., Harvard University Press, 1948).

Cicero, *On Duties*, eds. M.T. Griffin and E.M. Atkins (Cambridge, Cambridge University Press, 1991).

Copernicus, N., *On the Revolutions of the Heavenly Spheres*, ed. S. Hawking (Philadelphia, Running Press, 2002).

Copleston, F., *History of Philosophy, vol. 2, part 1* (New York, Image Books, 1962).

Corbin, H., *History of Islamic Philosophy* (London, Kegan Paul, 2006).

d'Andeli, H., *The Battle of the Seven Arts* (Carolina Charleston, Nabu Press, 2012).

da Vinci, L., *Notebooks* (Oxford, Oxford University Press, 2008).

Copleston, F., *A History of Philosophy, vol 2, part 1* (New York, Image Books, 1962).

Cowan, M., *Humanist Without Portfolio* (Detroit, Wayne State University Press, 1963).

Dante Alighieri, *A Translation of Dante's Eleven Letters*, trans. C.S. Latham (Boston & New York, Houghton Mifflin Co., 1891).

Dante Alighieri, *Convivio*, A.S. Kline trans., http://www.poetryintranslation.com/klineasconvivio.htm (2008).

Dante Alighieri, *Convivio*, trans. Elizabeth Price Sayer (London, George Routledge & Sons, 1887).

Dante Alighieri, *Monarchy* (Cambridge, Cambridge University Press, 2010).

Dante Alighieri, *Paradiso*, trans. M. Musa (London, Penguin, 1986).

Dante Alighieri, *The New Life (Vita Nuova)* trans. G Rossetti (New York, New York Review of Books, 2002).

Davidson, T., *Aristotle and Ancient Educational Ideals* (New York, Charles Scribner's Sons, 1892).

Deleuze, G., *Difference and Repetition* (London, Continuum, 2001).

Descartes, R., *Meditations on First Philosophy* in *The Philosophical Writings of Descartes, vol. 2*, trans. J. Cottingham, R. Stoothoff & D. Murdoch (Cambridge, Cambridge University Press, 1984).

Diogenes Laertius, *Lives of Eminent Philosophers* (Loeb Classical Library, 2006).

Du Bois, W.E.B., *The Education of Black People* (New York, Monthly Review Press, 2001).

Dunne, J., *Back to the Rough Ground* (Indiana, University of Notre Dame Press, 1997).

Einstein, A., 'Religion and Science,' *New York Times Magazine*, 4th November, 1930, pp. 1–4, www.sacred-texts.com/aor/einstein/einsci.htm.

Epictetus, *Discourses*, in *Great Books of the Western World, vol. 11* (Chicago, Encyclopedia Britannica, 1990).

Fanon, F., *The Wretched of the Earth* (London, Penguin, 2001).

Fichte, J.G., *The Purpose of Higher Education* (Maryland, Nightsun Books, 1988).

Ficino, M., *Meditations on the Soul* (Rochester, Inner Traditions, 1997).

Fitzgerald, A. and Cavadini, J.C. (eds.) *Augustine Through the Ages: An Encyclopedia* (William B Eerdmans Publishing Co., 1999).

Flexner, A., *Universities: American, English, German* (New York, Oxford University Press, 1930),

Friedrich, H., *Montaigne* (Berkeley, University of California Press, 1991).

Gadamer, H.G., *Truth and Method* (London, Sheed & Ward, 1979).

Gilson, E., *Dante and Philosophy* (New York, Harper Torchbook, 1963).

Gilson, E., *History of Christian Philosophy in the Middle Ages* (London, Sheed and Ward, 1980).

Grafton, A. and Jardine, L., *From Humanism to the Humanities* (Cambridge, Mass., Harvard University Press, 1986).

Grant, E., 'Science and the Medieval University,' in eds. James. M. Kittleson and Pamela J. Transue, *Birth, Reform and Resilience, Universities in Transition 1300–1700* (Columbus, Ohio State University, 1984).

Gray, H.H., *Searching for Utopia, Universities and their Histories* (Berkeley, University of California Press, 2012).

Hankins, J., *Introduction*, in ed L. Bruni, *History of the Florentine People*, vol. 1 (Cambridge Mass., I Tatti Renaissance Library, 2001).

Harris, H.S., *Hegel's Ladder, The Odyssey of Spirit* (Indianapolis, Hackett Publishers, 1997).

Haskins, C.H., *The Rise of the Universities* (Ithaca & London, Cornell University Press, 1957).

Hegel, G.W.F., *Aesthetics vol. 1*. trans. T.M. Knox (Oxford, Clarendon Press, 1998).

Hegel, G.W.F., *Aesthetics vol. 2*. trans. T.M. Knox (Oxford, Clarendon Press, 1998).

Hegel, G.W.F., Hegel's *Introduction to the Lectures on the History of Philosophy*, trans. T.M. Knox and A.V. Miller (Oxford, Clarendon Press, 1985).

Hegel, G.W.F., *Hegel's Logic* (Oxford, Oxford University Press, 1975).

Hegel, G.W.F., *History of Philosophy*, vol. II, trans. Haldane and Simson (New York, Humanities Press, 1974); Hegel, *Werke 19, Vorlesungen über die Geschichte der Philosophie II* (Frankfurt, Suhrkamp Verlag, 1970).

Hegel, G.W.F., *Phenomenology of Spirit* (Oxford, Oxford University Press, 1977).

Hegel, G.W.F., *The Philosophy of History*, trans. J. Sibree (New York, Dover Publications, 1956), p. 417; *Werke 12 Vorlesungen über die Philosophie der Geschichte* (Frankfurt, Suhrkamp Verlag, 1970).

Hegel, G.W.F. *Philosophy of Mind*, trans. W. Wallace & A.V. Miller (Oxford, Clarendon Press, 1990).

Hegel, G.W.F., *Philosophy of Right*, trans. T.M. Knox (Oxford University Press, 1967).

Heidegger, M., 'Letter on Humanism,' in *Basic Writings*, ed. D Krell (London, Routledge, 1993).

Heisenberg, W., *Physics and Philosophy* (London, Penguin, 1958).

Heisenberg, W., *Philosophie – la manuscript de 1942* (Seuil, Paris, 1998). German original edition: *Ordnung der Wirklichkeit* (Munich, R. Piper GmbH and Co KG, 1989). English version available at www.werner-heisenberg.unh.edu/ trans. M.B. Rumscheidt and N. Lukens.

Heisenberg, W., *The Physicist's Conception of Nature* (London, The Scientific Book Guild, 1962).

Herder, J.G., *Philosophical Writings* (Cambridge, Cambridge University Press, 2002).

Hesiod, *Works and Days* (Oxford, Oxford University Press, 2008).

Horlacher, R., '*Bildung* – a Construction of a History of Philosophy of Education,' *Studies in Philosophy and Education*, vol. 23 (2004).

Hugh of St Victor, *The Didascalion of Hugh of Saint Victor*, trans. J. Taylor (New York, Columbia Press, 1991).

Hutchins, R.M., *Education for Freedom* (Louisiana, Louisiana State University Press, 1943).

Hutchins, R.M., *The Great Conversation*, http://www.britannica.com/blogs/2008/12/the-great-conversation-robert-hutchinss-essay-for-the-great-books/

Hutchins, R.M., *The Higher Education in America* (New Haven, Yale University Press, 1967).

Isidore, *Etymologies*, trans. Priscilla Throop (Charlotte, Vermont, Medieval MS, 2005).

Isocrates, *Works Volume I*, ed. G. Norlin (Loeb Classical Library No. 209, 1928).

Isocrates, *Against the Sophists*, trans. G. Norlin (London, Heinemann, 1929).

Isocrates, *Antidosis*, trans. G Norlin (London, Heinemann, 1929).

Jaeger, W., *Aristotle* (Oxford, Oxford University Press, 1962).

Jaeger, W., *Paideia, The Ideals of Greek Culture vol. 1* (New York, Oxford University Press, 1965).

Jaeger, W., *Paideia, The Ideals of Greek Culture vol. 2* (New York, Oxford University Press, 1986).

Jaeger, W., *Paideia, The Ideals of Greek Culture vol. 3* (New York, Oxford University Press, 1986).

Jammer, M., *Einstein and Religion* (Princeton, Princeton University Press, 2002).

Kant, I., *Critique of Pure Reason* (London, Macmillan, 1968).

Kant, I., 'Determination of the Concept of a Human Race,' in *Anthropology, History, and Education*, trans. H. Wilson & G. Zoller, G. Zoller and R.B. Louden (eds.) (Cambridge, Cambridge University Press, 2007).

Kant, I., *Foundations of the Metaphysics of Morals*, 2nd edition, trans. L.W. Beck (New York, Macmillan, 1990).

Kant, I., 'Idea for a Universal History with a Cosmopolitan Intent,' in *Perpetual Peace and Other Essays* (Indianapolis, Hackett Publishing, 1983).

Kant, I., 'Lectures on Pedagogy,' *Anthropology, History, and Education*, trans. R.B. Lowden, G. Zoller and R.B. Louden (eds.) (Cambridge, Cambridge University Press, 2007).

Kaufmann, W., *The Future of the Humanities* (New Brunswick, Transaction Publishers, 1995).

Kierkegaard, S., *Philosophical Fragments/Johannes Climacus* (Princeton, Princeton University Press, 1985).

Kierkegaard, S., *The Concept of Irony* (Princeton, Princeton University Press, 1989).

Kimball, B., *Orators and Philosophers* (New York & London, Teachers College Press, 1986).

Koziak, B., *Retrieving Political Emotion: Thumos, Aristotle and Gender* (Pennsylvania, Pennsylvania State University Press, 1999).

Kristeller, P.O., *Renaissance Thought, The Classic, Scholastic, and Humanist Strains* (New York, Harper Torchbooks, 1961).

Kristeller, P.O., *Renaissance Thought and the Arts* (Princeton, Princeton University Press, 1990).

Lansing, R. (1998) *Convivio*, http://dante.ilt.columbia.edu/books/convivi/convivio.html.

Leff, G., 'The Trivium and the Three Philosophies,' in ed. W. Ruegg, *A History of the University in Europe* vol. 1 (Cambridge, Cambridge University Press, 2003).

Levinas, E., *Difficult Freedom* (London, Athlone Press, 1990).

Levine, P., *Nietzsche and the Modern Crisis of the Humanities* (Albany, SUNY, 1995).

Longe, A.A., *Stoic Studies* (Cambridge, Cambridge University Press, 1996).

Martianus Capella, *The Marriage of Philology and Mercury*, eds. W.H. Stahl and E.L. Burge (New York, Columbia University Press, 1977).

Masi, M., *Boethian Number Theory, A Translation of De institutione arithmetica* (New York, Rodopi, 2006).

McKeon, R., 'The Transformation of the Liberal Arts in the Renaissance,' in ed. B.S. Levy, *Developments in the Early Renaissance* (Albany, SUNY, 1972).

Melanchthon, P., *Orations on Philosophy and Education*, ed. Sachiko Kusukawa (Cambridge, Cambridge University Press, 1999).

Mirandola, P.d., *On The Dignity Of Man*, trans. C.G. Wallis, P.J.W. Miller & D. Carmichael (Indianapolis, Hackett, 1998).

Mommsen, T., 'Petrarch's Conception of the "Dark Ages," ' *Speculum*, vol. 17, no. 2 (April 1942).

Nauert, C.G., *Humanism and the Culture of Renaissance Europe* (Cambridge University Press, 2006).

Newman, J.H., *The Idea of a University* (London, Longmans, Green and Co., 1931).

Newton, I., *The Principia*, trans. A. Motte (New York, Prometheus Books, 1995).

Newton, I., *Newton's Philosophy of Nature* (Mineola, NY, Dover publications, 2005).

Nietzsche, F., *Genealogy of Morals*, in *Basic Writings* ed. W. Kaufmann (New York, The Modern Library, 1968).

Nietzsche, F., *Twilight of the Idols/The Anti-Christ*, trans. R.J. Hollingdale (London, Penguin, 1968).

Nietzsche, F., *The Will To Power*, ed. W. Kaufmann (New York, Vintage Books, 1968).

Nietzsche, F., *Thus Spoke Zarathustra* in *The Portable Nietzsche* trans. W. Kaufmann (New York, Penguin, 1982).

Nordenko, S.E., '*Bildung* and the thinking of *Bildung*,' *Educating Humanity*, Lovlie, Mortensen & Nordenko (eds.) (Oxford, Blackwell, 2003).

Oakley, F., *Community of Learning* (New York, Oxford University Press, 1992).

O'Donnell, J., *Cassiodorus*, at http://www9.georgetown.edu/faculty/jod/texts/cassbook/chap5.html.

O'Hear, A. and Sidwell, M., *The School of Freedom* (Exeter, Imprint Academic, 2009).

Parker, H., 'The Seven Liberal Arts,' *The English Historical Review*, no. XIX (July, 1890).

Paulsen, F. and Perry, E.D., *The German Universities: Their Character and Historical Development* (London, Macmillan and Co., 1895).

Petrarch, F., *Books on Matters to be Remembered*, in J.H. Robinson, *Petrarch* (New York, Haskell House Publishers, 1970).

Petrarch, F., *Letters on Familiar Matters* IX–XVI (New York, Italica Press, 2005).

Plato, *The Complete Works*, ed. John M. Cooper (Indianapolis, Hackett Publishing Co., 1997).

Plato, *The Laws* (London, Penguin, 1975).

Proctor, R., *Defining the Humanities*, 2nd edition (Bloomington, Indiana University Press, 1998).

Rait, R.S., *Life in the Medieval University* (Charleston Carolina, Bibliobazaar, 2007).

Rose, G., *Mourning Becomes the Law* (Cambridge, Cambridge University Press, 1996).

Ross, J.B. and McLaughlin, M.M. (eds.) *The Portable Medieval Reader* (London, Penguin, 1977).

Rothblatt, S., *Tradition and Change in English Liberal Education* (London, Faber and Faber, 1976).

Rousseau, J.J., *Emile* (London, Everyman, 1974/1993).

Rudolph, F., *Curriculum* (San Francisco, Jossey-Bass, 1977).

Ruegg, W. (ed.) *A History of the University in Europe vol. 2* (Cambridge, Cambridge University Press, 1996).

Ruegg, W., 'The Rise of Humanism,' in ed. Ruegg, *A History of the University in Europe, vol. 1* (Cambridge, Cambridge University Press, 2003).

Ryan, C., 'The Theology of Dante,' in *The Cambridge Dante* (Cambridge, Cambridge University Press, 1993).

Sartre, J.P., *Existentialism and Humanism* (London, Methuen, 2007).

Sayers, D.L., *The Divine Comedy: Hell* (London, Penguin, 1949).

Sayers, D.L., *Introductory Papers on Dante* (Eugene, Oregon, Wipf & Stock, 1954).

Schmidt-Biggemann, W., 'New Structures of Knowledge,' in ed. W. Ruegg *A History of the University in Europe*, vol. 2 (Cambridge, Cambridge University Press, 1996).

Schön, D., *Educating the Reflective Practitioner* (San Francisco, Jossey-Bass, 1987).

Seneca, *Letters from a Stoic* (London, Penguin, 2004).

Seneca, *Moral Epistles*, trans. R.M. Gummere (London, Heinemann, 1917).

Sorkin, D., 'Wilhelm von Humboldt: The Theory and Practice of Self-Formation (*Bildung*) 1791–1810,' *Journal of the History of Ideas*, vol. 44, no. 1 (Jan-March 1983).

Spitz, L.W., 'The Importance of the Reformation for Universities,' in eds. J. M. Kittleson and P. J. Transue, *Birth, Reform and Resilience* (Columbus, Ohio State University, 1984).

Stahl, W.H., *Macrobius: Commentary on the Dream of Scipio* (New York, Columbia Press, 1990).

Tubbs, N., 'Existentialism and Humanism: Humanity – Know Thyself,' *Studies in Philosophy and Education*, vol. 32, no. 5 (September 2013), pp. 477–490.

Tubbs, N., *History of Western Philosophy* (Basingstoke, Palgrave Macmillan, 2009).

Tubbs, N., *Philosophy's Higher Education* (Dordrecht, Kluwer, 2004).

Vasari, G., *The Lives of the Artists* (Oxford, Oxford University Press, 1998).

von Humboldt, W., *Ideen zu einem Versuch die Grenzen der Wirkamkeit des Staats zu bestimmen* (Brieslau, Verlag von E Trewendt, 1851).

von Humboldt, W., *Limits of State Action* (Indianapolis, Liberty Fund, 1993).

von Simson, O., *The Gothic Cathedral* (New York, Princeton University Press, 1988).

Weisheipl, J.A., 'Curriculum of the Faculty of Arts at Oxford in the Early Fourteenth Century,' *Medieval Studies*, vol. 26 (1964).

Weisheipl, J.A., *Nature and Motion in the Middle Ages* (Washington, the Catholic University of America Press, 1985).

West, A.F., *Alcuin and the Rise of the Christian Schools* (New York, Charles Scribner's Sons, 1903).

West, A.F., 'The Seven Liberal Arts' http://classicalsubjects.com/resources/TheSevenLiberalArts.com/ (accessed May 2013).

Westbury, I., Hopman, S. and Riquarts, K., *Teaching as Reflective Practice* (New Jersey, Lawrence Erlbaum, 2000).

Williams, R., 'Representing Reality' (1st Gifford Lecture, 4th November, 2013, University of Edinburgh), at http://www.youtube.com/watch?v=_ibHOy3vtA&list=SPEA9467E8E8D991AE.

Wright, M.R., in *Cosmology in Antiquity* (New York, Routledge, 1995).

Zammito, J.H., *Kant, Herder and the Birth of Anthropology* (Chicago, University of Chicago Press, 2002).

Index

Note: The letter 'n' following locators refers to notes.

Adorno, T.W., 157
Aesthetics, 153
agoraphobia, 19
Algerian liberation, 65
ambivalence of method, 38–40
American education, basic dogmas, 178n. 131
Anaxagoras, 104
anthropomorphism, 104, 106
Antidosis, 19
antiquity
  golden age of, 46–7
  Latin antiquity, 25–8, 38
  Western antiquity, 1
Aquinas, T., 24, 39, 40, 71, 88, 109, 186n. 29, 187n. 52
aristocratic paideia vs. rationalism, 15
Aristotelianism, 39, 44, 71
Aristotle (Aristotelian)
  culture, 22
  division of labour, 21
  harmony, 22
  hierarchy of intellectual virtues, 23
  intellectual virtues, 21
  knowledge, 24
  logic of necessity, 22, 30, 37, 41, 102
  logic of non-contradiction, 22
  metaphysics, 22
  natural philosophy, 170n. 18
  necessity, 138
  orthodoxy, 37
  philosophy, 21, 22
  relation of theory, 23
  resolution, 88
  scholasticism, 62
  social education, 112–14
  speculative knowledge, 24
  speculative philosophy, 21
  translations of logic and philosophy, 49

artes liberales, 7, 24, 37, 42–3, 58, 68–9, 72, 148
Astronomy, 30
atom, 104–6
  meaning, 104
  movement of motion, 105
St Augustine, 24, 26, 29, 32–6, 44

Ballard, E.G., 40, 170n. 29
Barad, K., 66, 106, 182n. 36
barbarian slave, 77
barbarism, 46, 66, 74, 76–9, 81, 127, 129, 133–4, 136–7, 139–41, 143–5, 148, 152
  of continual questioning, 78–9
  defined, 74
  of disturbance and unrest, 139
  element of, 136
  of error, 136
  of hell, 140
  illiberalism and, 141
  logic of necessity, 129
  pure, 76
  relativity and, 76
  repetition of, 148
  suppression of, 143
  virtue and, 76–7
Bataille, G., 98
Battle of the Arts, The, 39
battle of the books, 38–40
Bauman, R., 27, 119, 166n. 22
Bauman, Z., 119
Bernasconi, R., 67
Bevan, E., 183n. 17
Bildung
  civic humanism, 53
  defined, 50
  dualism, 50
  duality of inner and outer, 53
  efficacy, 53

etymology and various meanings of, 173n. 3
history of, 52
kinds of, 53
moral, 53, 56
moral citizen, 55
neohumanist, 50–1, 53
original use of, 57
philosophical descriptions, 56
political, 53
prudential formation, 56
role of, 51
Rousseauian, 53
Scholastic formation, 56
self-cultivation, 57
self-formation, 57, 66
specific form of, 53–4
stoical flavour, 53
Bloom, A., 3
Bodin, J., 47
Boethius, 26, 29–32, 137
Book named the Governor, The, 49
Booth, E., 164n. 72
Boter, T., 180n. 14
Bruford, W.H., 142, 143, 173n. 1, 186n. 39
Burckhardt, J., 45, 172n. 72

Campana, A., 41
Capella, M., 26, 29–30
Cassiodorus, 18, 26, 29, 31–2
cathedral schools, 37
character of error, 128–9
  ambivalence of self-moderation, 129
  error of contingency, 129
  logic of necessity, 128
  moderation and constancy, 128
On Christian Doctrine, 34
Christianity, 25, 28, 32, 34, 36, 49, 87, 142
Christian morality, genealogy of, 142
Church Fathers, 88
Church of the Holy Angels, 42
Cicero, 7, 24–6, 28, 32, 42–3, 49, 64, 115
Ciceronianism, 42
City of God, 35
civic discipline, 48
Classical Rome, 26

clemency, 28
comedy of errors, 129–32
Commedia, 40, 137
Confessions, 33, 40, 153
Convivio, 1, 41, 137, 139
Copenhagen interpretation, 108, 182n. 40
Copernican revolution, 89, 105
Copleston, F., 169n. 82, 185n. 26
core curriculum, 8, 61, 70
cosmological narrative, 99–101
  heavens, 99
  macrocosm, 99
  Platonic model, 99
cosmopolitanism, 66–7
critical skepticism, 62
Crystalline Heaven, 140
cultures of error, 87–9
curriculum, 156–9
  assessment, 156
  faculty-led generalist, 8
  pedagogy, 156
  post-foundational thinking, 158
  preparation, 158
  rationale, 156
  structure, 156
  substance of, 158
cynical nihilism, 147

d'Andeli, H., 38, 39
Dante, 1, 41–2, 110, 129–30, 137–41
  Aristotelian definition of a comedy, 130
  Convivio, 1, 41, 137, 139
  divine comedy, 137–41
  drama of salvation, 140
  humanity in, 42
  logic of necessity of life and death, 110
  notion of justice, 141
  pilgrim, 6, 111
  renaissance thinking, 41
Davidson, T., 165n. 5
da Vinci, L., 100
death rites, 61
Declaration of Human Rights, 118, 121
Deleuze, G., 66, 68
Democritus, 104

De oratore, 26
De ordine, 33
Descartes, R., 2, 88
De trinitate, 31
dialectical scholastic method, 8
discipline and freedom, 68–70
    dualism of, 50, 63
Discourses, 114
disharmony, universality of, 90
divine comedy
    ancient logic of necessity, 139–40
    comedic aspects, 141
    cultural ressentiment, 142
    Dante's, 137–41
    dialectical, 133
    disharmony, 134
    educational, 133, 143
    educational journey of
        philosophical reason, 139
    of facilitator, 155
    harmony, 133–4
    health and disease, 134
    humanitas, 147
    idea of virtue, 132
    justice to, 136
    literal action of, 140
    literal end of, 140
    master/slave relation, 142
    meaninglessness of education, 147
    metaphysical errors, 131
    nature of the, 138
    Nietzsche's divine comedy, 141–5
    Plato's, 133–7
    religious ressentiment, 142
    sublime experience of leadership, 6
    tranquillity of identity, 141
    truth of the identity, 141
    vice and virtue, 134
divine philosophy, 31
doctrinal philosophy, 31
On Duty, 28

economic slavery, 124
ecstasy, 95
educational comedy, 130
education as modern logic, 91–3
    European Enlightenment, 92
egalitarianism, 62

Einstein, A., 74, 89, 101, 103, 104,
    181n. 28
    absolute persistence of motion, 101
    cosmic religious feeling, 104
    logic of necessity, 101
    model of universe, 103
    natural relation of motion, 103
    notion of God and religion, 104
    theory of relativity, 103, 181n. 28
Eleatics, 104
empiricism, 8, 24, 40
encyclic arts, 26
enkuklios paideia, 26, 29
Enlightenment, 24, 54, 59, 77, 92–3,
    112, 116–17, 122
    dialectic of, 147
    ideals of, 66
    universality of, 92
Epictetus, 114–15, 128
error of culture, 87–8, 119, 131
error of infinite regression, 87, 92, 94,
    119–20, 129, 149, 155
ethic of individualism, 62
Etymologies, 32
Euclidean grid map, 74
European consciousness, 42
existentialism, 65
Exposito Psalorum, 31

falsities, 35
Fanon, F., 65, 66
Feynman, R., 105
Fichte, J.G., 51, 55, 56
Ficino, M., 45, 174n. 21
Flexner, A., 53
free man, dualism of, 2
French Revolution, 65
Friedrich, H., 58, 173n. 1

Gadamer, H.G., 51, 56, 57, 58, 161n. 1
Galileo, 4, 74, 100–1, 103
Gellius, A., 27
generalist education, 8
Gilson, E., 40, 42, 166n. 23, 185n. 38,
    186n. 26, 186n. 29, 186n. 31

God, 94–7
anthropocentric representation
of, 96
death of God (scepticism), 94
modern conception of, 96–7
notion of, 96
personal God (religion), 94
philanthropia of, 165n. 20
picture-thinking, 95
as subjective, 96
theoretical knowledge, 33
Gorgias, 18
grammatica speculativa, 38
Grant, E., 170n. 21
Gray, H.H., 61
Great Books tradition, 156
Greek curriculum, 25
Greek encyclical or general
education, 26

harmony
ancient logic of, 3, 11, 51, 69, 80,
98, 117–18, 121, 131
Aristotelian logic of necessity
of, 37
Athenian idea of harmony, 12
disharmony and, 134, 136
divine comedy, 133–4
first principle of, 12–13
form of, 3
of God's creation, 35
of *humanitas*, 42
inner harmony, 51
intellectual, 85
kinds of, 21
mathematical harmonies, 11
Plato's definition, 134
political, 133
proportions of the natural
universe, 11
re-defined, 90
rhythm and, 15
self-completing, 97
of self-determination, 90
of self-sufficient necessity, 45
struggle for, 17
virtue of, 11–12
Heauton Timorumenos, 28

Hegel, G.W.F., 4, 16, 51, 56, 74, 90,
152, 162n. 30, 176n. 77
alienation, 57
argument over atom, 105
art styles, 153
contradiction principles, 157
education process, 58–60
humanity, 66–7
ideal teacher, 153–4
immediacy of nature, 57
mediaeval cultures of error, 89
mediation, 93, 101, 104
modern educational comedy, 130
modern metaphysics, 84
return, 57
self-knowledge, 58
Heidegger, M., 64, 177n. 97
Heisenberg, W., 105, 106, 107, 108,
182n. 40–1
Herder, J.G.von, 51, 53, 54, 55, 57,
119, 177n. 119
Higher Learning in America, The, 72
History of the Florentine People, 47
humanism, 8–9, 14–16, 21, 28, 37,
40–4, 48–53, 56–8, 63–8, 106,
119, 143, 147
academic, 21
born as cultural education, 14
characteristic, 65
civic, 44, 48
classical rhetorical, 37
consciousness-centred, 64
creation of the Greeks, 14
creativity of, 56
existential, 65
history of, 21
quality of, 51–2
humanistic studies, 38
humanist interest, 19, 44
humanist movement, 42
humanitas, 8–9, 13, 26–8, 41, 52, 54–6,
58, 60, 62, 64–8, 70, 144,
147–8, 155
ambiguities of, 54
ambivalence, 27–8, 59, 129
common human understanding, 56
defence, 166n. 21
divine comedy of, 147
elements of, 55

humanitas – continued
  exhaustion of, 68
  harmony of, 42
  Herder's notion, 54
  meaning, 173n. 1
  principle of, 148
  rhetoric and, 26–8
  Roman, 27, 41, 64
  severity and cruelty, 28
  slavery, 52
  truth of, 155
  universalism of, 44–5, 47
  Western, 65
Hutchins, R.M., 11, 62, 70, 71, 72, 82,
  178n. 131–2, 178n. 35
Hymn to Hermias, 12

identity, ancient logic
  of, 118
imperialism, 3, 61, 70, 122, 124,
  146, 156
individualism, critical spirit
  of, 24
infinite regression
  absurdity of, 37, 102, 133
  chaos of, 2, 76, 122–4
  contingency within, 89
  contradiction of, 122
  error of, 92, 94, 109, 119–20, 129,
    149, 155
  fear of, 74
  illogical, 101
  irrationality of, 92
  madness of, 119
  mediation and, 88, 120
  modern metaphysics, 83
  negative logic of, 75
  nihilism of, 122
  path of, 99
  prejudiced against, 149
  pure, 2
  relations, 4
  relativity of, 104
  repeated errors of, 87
  resistance to, 75
  self-mediation, 118
  significance, 4
  threat of, 86
  truth of, 125

  unavoidable, 154
  unprincipled, 76
  vulnerability to, 74
  weapon of mass destructive, 75
Institutiones (*Introduction to Divine and
  Human Readings*), 31
intellectualism, 38–40
intellectual rationality, 62
intellectual superiority, 187n. 47
intellectual virtues, 86
*Introduction to Divine and Human
  Readings*, 31
Isidore, 29
Islam, 87
Isocratean version of liberal
  education, 38
Isocrates, 17–21, 24, 26, 49, 58, 64
  ambivalences, 18
  brevity of dialectic, 18
  compactness of dialectic, 18
  comprehension, 17
  father of "humanistic" culture, 21
  ideal of *paideia*, 20
  imaginative literary creation, 20
  notion of moral perfection, 20
  perception, 17
  rhetoric, 18
  tensions, 18

Jaeger, W., 13, 15, 20, 21, 27, 44, 57,
  85, 165n. 9, 167n. 50
Janus-face of enlightenment, 92
John of Salisbury, 38–9
Judaism, 87–8

Kant, I., 4, 51, 54–7, 74, 84, 87, 89–93,
  101, 104, 121, 124
  age of discipline, 56
  ambivalence, 107
  Copernican revolution, 89, 105
  cosmopolitanism, 67
  humanism, 57
  humanity, 66–7
  racism, 67
  support of *humanitas*, 66
  slave trade, 67
  wars and revolutions, 66
Kierkegaard, S., 135

Kimball, B., 7, 8, 21, 26, 32, 37, 39, 72
    160n. 1, 165n. 3, 165n. 8, 166n.
    32, 167n. 50, 168n. 74, 176n. 94,
    183n. 9
    ambivalence, 37
    ancient logic of harmony, 69
    artes liberales, 68–9, 148
    dialectical tension, 69
    Enlightenment, 24
    Homeric poetry, 18
    imaginative nation-building, 26
    liberal arts, 18, 20, 49, 62
    liberal education, 20, 38
    oratorical tradition, 18, 61
    paradox of grammar, 38
    rehetorical tradition, 20
    Renaissance humanism, 43
Kristeller, P.O., 33, 42, 44, 45, 64,
    160n. 1, 172n. 75

Lady Philosophy, 137–8
Laertius, D., 18, 27
learning subjectivity, 5
leisure, 2–3, 113–14, 146, 183n. 9
Leucippus, 104–5
Levinas, E., 66
Levine, P., 143
liberal-free ideal of freedom, 62
liberalia studia grammar, 26
life and death, 108–11
    death is absence of self-movement,
        108–9
    fear and anxiety of death, 109
    life is posited as self-animation, 108
    life is truth and death is
        error, 109
Limits of State Action, 51
Lives of the Artists, 47
Locke, rationalism of, 88

Machiavelli, 46
MacIntyre, A., 128
macrocosm, 80, 99, 111–12
Magnus, A., 39
mankind, 41
Marriage of Philology and Mercury,
    The, 29
Masi, M., 167n. 50
mass destructive relativity, 75

mathematica, 14
mathematical cosmology, 13
McKeon, R., 40, 47, 168n. 74
mediaeval culture, 60
mediation, 4, 48, 75, 77–9, 82, 86–8,
    90, 93–4, 101, 104–8, 117–21,
    123–4, 129, 131, 133, 141,
    147–50, 152, 157
    chaos of, 79
    contradiction of, 120
    educative experience, 90
    error of, 77–8, 117, 147
    finite, 147
    non-identity of, 93
    of observation, 107
    power of, 117
    regression of, 4, 94, 131
    of senses, 48
    subjective, 147
    temporal, 147
    threat of, 88
    trubulence of, 147
    universality of, 117
Meditations, 128
Melanchthon, P., 48, 49, 172n. 85,
    173n. 87
metaphysical education, 89–91
metaphysical humanism, ambivalence
    of, 64
Metaphysics, 23, 85, 108
metaphysics, 4, 11, 13, 22–4, 39, 47,
    60, 63–4, 67–8, 70–5, 79, 81–5,
    87–97, 102, 104, 107, 117, 125,
    128, 131–3, 137–41, 147, 151, 158
    ambivalences of, 67
    ancient, 85–7, 90, 112, 140
    Aristotelian, 39, 89, 91–2, 170n. 18
    Copernican revolution, 89
    death of, 63, 131–2
    demise of truth, 75
    descriptive, 151
    elemental divison, 83
    end of, 64, 81, 95
    ethics and, 39
    explanatory logic of necessity, 151
    fundamental observations, 84
    of identity, 92

metaphysics – *continued*
  logic of, 87
  modern, 5, 69, 73–4, 82–4, 89–96,
    101–2, 106–11, 120, 128,
    130–1, 143, 145–6,
    150–1, 159
  of modern comedy, 131
  of non-contradiction and
    identity, 92
  philosophical relation, 84
  Platonic, 38, 88
  rational, 60
  realms of, 24
  relation with dialectics, 162n. 29
  science and social theory, 74
  traditional, 102, 104
  versions of, 85
  Western, 91
microcosm, 80, 99, 111–12
Middle Ages, 29–30, 38, 139
Mirandola, Pico della, 45
modern logic of education, 117, 131,
  146, 156
modern quantum relation, 106–8
Mommsen, T., 46, 172n. 77
Monarchy, 41
monastic schools, 37
moral philosophy, 35

nation-building, imaginative, 26
natural philosophy, 31, 35, 40, 48, 73,
  79, 100
natural universe, principle of, 8
Nauert, C.G., 172n. 72
necessity and freedom, dualism of, 67
necessity of pure reason, 121
Nelli, F., 42
Neoplatonic Christianity, 109
Newton, 4, 55, 74, 101–4
  absolute persistence of motion, 101
  conception of gravity, 102
  laws of motion, 101–2
  logic of necessity, 101
  natural relation of motion, 103
  Newtonian physics, 106
  relativity of position, 102
Nicomachean Ethics, 23, 85
Nietzsche, F., 54, 129, 131, 132, 141,
  142, 143, 144, 186n. 38

nihilism, 4, 118, 122, 143
Noctes atticae, 27
Nussbaum, M., 3

Oakley, F., 176n. 92
O'Donnell, J., 31
On His Own Ignorance, 100
open palm of freedom, 8, 25
orators, 17–21
Orators and Philosophers, 7

paganism, 29
pansophy, 167n. 44
Parker, H., 25, 26, 29, 164n. 1
pedagogy, 152–4, 156
Petrarch, F., 42, 44, 46, 47, 49, 100,
  167n. 50, 172n. 77, 173n. 1
Phenomenology of Spirit, 59
philanthropy, 27
philosophers, 16–17
philosophical educational
  relations, 74
philosophical mysteries, 35
philosophical speculation,
  model, 30
Philosophie, 107
*Philosophy and Modern Liberal
  Arts*, 72
Philosophy of History, 54, 59
Philosophy of Right, 58
phronesis
  first principle of, 22
  flexibility and creativity, 22
Physics and Philosophy, 108
picture-thinking, 95
Plato, 6, 13, 16–18, 21–2, 24, 27, 30–2,
  35, 44, 58, 64, 80, 85–7, 89, 98–9,
  109, 129, 132–6, 139, 144
  appetite, 17
  -Aristotle relation, 80
  divine comedy, 133–7
  early education, 17
  higher education, 17
  logical philosophy, 16
  mental philosophy, 16
  Parmenides, 16
  Phaedrus, 17
  philosophical education, 16
  Platonic love, 45

Platonic metaphysics, 38
Platonic philosophy, 19, 35
Platonic speculation, 39
polemic against the Sophists,
   160n. 1
Republic, 16–17, 153
Timaeus, 16, 30
Platonic philosophy, 32
Platonism, revival of, 45
political vocation, 19
Politics, 16, 113
post-foundational thinking, 95
post-metaphysical theory, 68
potentiality, totality of, 108
Prime Mover, 1, 8, 11, 75, 77, 85,
   99–101, 103–4, 109, 122,
   140, 151
Principia, 103
Proctor, R., 45
property relation, 75–8
Protrepticus, 23, 85
Purpose of Higher Education, 56
Pythagoras, 12–13

quadrivium, mediaeval, 17
quantum mechanics, peculiarities
   of, 105
quantum physics, 98, 106
quantum probability, 105
quantum theory, 107

racist text, 155
Rait, R.S., 170n. 21
Reformation, 49, 116
relativism, 3, 64, 70, 100, 103,
   105, 143
religious prejudice, 77
Renaissance, 24, 28, 37, 40–6, 49, 62,
   64, 100–1, 148
dualism, 40
history, 44–9
humanism, 28, 42–4, 46
influx of new translations, 42
intellectualism, 40
liberal arts, 28, 40
subjectivity, 44–9
universalism, 44–9
Republic, 16–17, 21, 27–8, 31, 46, 85,
   133–6, 153

Retractions, 33–4
Roman curriculum, 25
Roman liberal education, 38
Rose, G., 184n. 12
Rothblatt, S., 176n. 94
Rousseau, J.J., 53, 174n. 21,
   183n. 12
Rudolph, F., 61, 178n. 128
Ruegg, W., 172n. 76
Ryan, C., 185n. 25

Sartre, J.P., 65, 66
Satyricon, 167n. 40
Sayers, D.L., 140, 141
scholastic culture, 60
scholasticism, 37, 40, 48–9, 63
culture of, 42
dialectic of, 8
self-animation, 1, 33, 107–8, 110,
   117–18, 121, 123
principle, 2, 104, 110
self-consciousness, universal, 59
self-mediation
identity and subjectivity, 117
implications of, 119
Seneca, 26
slavery, 1, 41, 52, 55, 67, 82, 109, 113,
   115, 118, 124, 144
abolition of, 124
colonialism, 124
forced, 113
imperialism, 124
legacy of, 124
   master/slave relation, 41,
      125, 142
natural slavery, 113
science of life, 115
wage slave, 124
social education
abolition of slavery, 124
Aristotle, 112–14
education in otherness, 121–3
freedom is to learn, 119–21
freedom is to think, 114–17
freedom is to think for itself,
   117–19
mutual recognition, 120

social education – *continued*
  otherness, 123–5
  pseudo-universalistic, 122
  roots of the politics, 113
  slave, 123–5
social theory, 4, 74–5
Socrates, 7, 26, 34–5, 68, 80,
    87, 135
  of Athens, 55
  ethics, 32
  of humanity, 55
  liberal education, 7
  modern Socrates, 55
  of modernity, 55
  morality, 35
  philosophical tradition, 24
  phronesis, 85
  relation of truth and non-truth, 109
  truth-in-itself, 91
solipsism, 94
Solon, 12
Sophists, 13–16
  aim of, 14
  humanism, 15
  nobility of bloodlines, 14
  political *areté*, 15
  political awareness, 13
  political leadership, 16
  political self-consciousness, 15
  techne, 14
  trivium, 15
Sorkin, D., 53
sovereignty, 49, 78, 80, 82, 84, 88, 91,
    93, 107, 119, 121
speculative philosophy, 31, 35, 61
speculative sciences, classification of
    the, 164n. 85
stoicism, 51, 80–1, 88, 112,
    114–15, 119
  freedom, 114
  shape of subjectivity, 115
Stoic philosophy, 32
student voice, 150–2
  aim for, 150
  ambiguity, 150
  cleansing of contradiction, 150
  programmes, 150
studia humanitatis, 9, 24, 41–3, 49
subjectivism, 50, 53

subjectivity, 5, 93–4
  shapes of, 5, 112
superstitions, 35

teacher, 152–6
  disillusionment of, 154
  humanity of, 155–6
  ideal, 154
  ironic, 154
  kinds of, 152
  neutrality of, 154
  pleasing, 153
techne, 14, 21, 87, 113–14
tenebrae (darkness) era, 46
Theaetetus, 68
theological orthodoxy, 37
theory of the forms, 85
Timaeus, 16, 30, 85, 133, 136
Topics, 21
tragedy, 5
true liberty, 169n. 76
Truth and Method, 56

urban schools, 37

Varro, 18, 25, 29, 43
  secret path, 25
  seven liberal arts, 28–32
Vasari, G., 47
Vinci, Leonardo da, 100
Vita Nuova, 140
von Humboldt, W., 51, 173n. 4

Weber, M., 122
Weisheipl, J.A., 29, 31, 167n. 40,
    167n. 48
West, A.F., 3, 4, 12, 15, 29, 66,
    167n. 50
Western social relations, 118
Western subjectivity, conception
    of, 114
Williams, R., 150, 151, 155, 188n. 2
  Representing Reality, 188n. 2
Wretched of the Earth, The, 65
Wright, M.R., 180n. 6

Xenophanes, 99

Zarathustra, 142–3
Zeno, 7, 17

Lightning Source UK Ltd.
Milton Keynes UK
UKOW07n1636100215

246024UK00004B/42/P